NEW STAR PAPERS.

NEW STAR PAPERS;

OR,

VIEWS AND EXPERIENCES

OF

RELIGIOUS SUBJECTS.

BY

HENRY WARD BEECHER.

NEW YORK:
DERBY & JACKSON, 119 NASSAU STREET.
1859.

W. H. TINSON, Stereotyper

GEO. RUSSELL & CO., Printers.

SOMERVILLE & BROTHER, Binders.

PREFACE.

THESE papers are, for the most part, taken from the columns of the New York Independent. If unworthy of a book form, the Public has itself to blame, in part, for encouraging a like collection of Star Papers, some years ago.

A few things have been added, from other sources. But little revision has been attempted, except in the case of those several articles which were not originally written, but reported or condensed for print, from sermons or lectures. Many persons may be tempted to read a short religious article, who would never attempt a profound book.

HENRY WARD BEECHER.

BROOKLYN, *June* 1, 1859.

CONTENTS.

	Page
Christ Knocking at the Door of the Soul,	9
Church Music,	17
Trust,	24
Abide with Us,	28
Thoughts for the Close of the Year,	32
God's Pity,	38
The Mountain and the Closet,	47
The Liberty of Prayer,	54
Faults in Prayer,	60
Aids to Prayer,	66
Forsaking God,	70
A Rhapsody of the Pen upon the Tongue,	76
An Aged Pastor's Return,	80
Lessons from the Times,	86
Christian Consolation,	103
Troubles,	109
Phases of the Times,	116
Fullness of God,	124
Christ in you, the Hope of Glory,	135
Prayer-meetings,	141
One Cause of Dull Meetings,	146
Working out Our Own Salvation,	151

Page
Trust in God, ... 156
We Spend our Years as a Tale that is Told, . . 165
Sudden Conversion, ... 174
"Total Depravity," 178
Working with Errorists, ... 187
Mischievous Self-Examination, ... 201
Where Christians Meet, ... 204
The Day and the Desk, ... 209
Is Conversion Instantaneous? 213
Natural Laws and Special Providences, . . . 218
The Dead Christ, ... 232
An Exposition, ... 236
The Episcopal Service, ... 242
Congregational Liturgy, ... 247
Churches and Organs, ... 260
Patriotism and Liberty, ... 264
Purity of Character, ... 276
How to bear little Troubles, ... 278
"Sin Revived and I Died," 281
Humility before God, ... 283
Who shall Help the Unfortunate? . . . 286
Plymouth Church, ... 291
Organ Playing, ... 298
How to become a Christian, ... 304
God's Witness to Christian Fidelity, . . . 322
The Progress of Christianity, ... 341
Duties of Religious Publishing Societies, . . 351

VIEWS AND EXPERIENCES

OF

RELIGIOUS SUBJECTS.

CHRIST KNOCKING AT THE DOOR OF THE SOUL.

"Behold, I stand at the door, and knock; if any man hear my voice, and open the door, I will come in to him, and will sup with him, and he with me."—Rev. iii. 20.

This, in the highly figurative language of the Apocalypse, is a representation of the Human Soul and of Christ's endeavor in its behalf. It is a favorite method of Scripture to represent man by the figure of a mansion, or building. Sometimes it is a temple. "Know ye not that ye are the temple of God?" As nothing was more criminal than to desecrate temples by bringing into them evil things, so it is criminal in the sight of God to desecrate that temple which he has made of man, by bringing into the mind thoughts and feelings that are corrupt and depraved. Sometimes the human soul is a tabernacle, or a tent. Man is represented as a tenant, or a dweller in a tabernacle; and death is the striking of the tent—the taking down of the tabernacle that the occupant may go free. Christ employed the same representation when he said: "If a man love me, he will keep my words, and my father will love him, and we will come unto him, *and make our abode with him:*" This is as if one were to offer to take rooms in the soul, and to become a dweller therein, as people take rooms in a house and abide in it. All those passages of Scripture which speak of *indwelling*, represent the same idea. A modification of it is found in the apostle's figure of building, and of the master-builder. This manner of speaking pervades the Bible, and the figure is appropriate and instructive.

The soul is a dwelling of many apartments. Each sense, affection, sentiment, faculty, may be regarded as a separate room. And in one regard all men are alike; they have the same number of rooms. No one has a single room less or more than another. In a material building, one man may have one room, another two, and another a score; but, in the soul-house, all men have just exactly the same number of apartments. Yet there is a great difference between one man and another, in the size and furnishing, or in other words, in the contents, of these apartments. Some men are built like pyramids, exceeding broad at the base—or on the earthy side, and narrow and tapering as they go up—or heavenward. Their rooms are very large at the bottom of the house, but very small at the top. Other men are built substantially alike, from bottom to top, like a tower which is just as broad at its summit as at its foundation.

But there is, in general, a great part of the structure of every man that is not used, and remains locked up. And usually the best apartments are the ones neglected. Those that have a glorious outlook, that stand up to sun and air, from whose windows one may look clear across Jordan, and see the fields and hills of the Promised Land—into these men seldom go. They choose rather to live in that part of the soul-house that looks into the back-yard, where nothing but rubbish is gathered and kept. Many men live in one or two rooms, out of thirty or forty in the soul.

If you should take a candle—that is, God's Word, which is as a lighted candle—and go into these soul-houses, and explore them, you would find them, generally, very dark. The halls and passage-ways, the stairs of ascent, the vast and noble ranges of apartments—all are stumbling dark. There, for example, is the apartment, or faculty, called Benevolence. You can tell by the way the door grates, that it is seldom opened. But if you were to thrust in a light, you would see that the room is a most stately place. The ceilings are frescoed with angels. The sides and panels are filled with the most exquisite adornments. The whole saloon is most inviting to every sense. Seats there are, delightful to press; and the niches are filled with things enticing to the eye. But spiders cover over with their webs the angels of the ceiling. Dust blackens the ornaments. The hall is silent, the chambers are neglected. The man of the house does not live in this room!

Turn to another; it is called Conscience. It is an apartment wonderfully constructed. It seems to be central. It is connected with every other apartment in the dwelling. On examination, however, it will be found that, for the most part, the doors are all locked. The floor is thick with dust. The dust is its carpet. The room is very dark. The windows are glazed over with webbed dirt. The light is shut out, and the whole apartment is dismal. The man who owns the house does not frequent this room!

There is another chamber called Hope—if haply you can see the inscription over the door. It has two sides, and two windows. From one of these you may see the stars, the heaven beyond, the Holy City, the Angels of God, the General Assembly and Church of the First-born. This is shut! The other window looks out into the World's Highway, and sees men, caravans, artificers, miners, artisans, engineers, builders, bankers, brokers, pleasure-mongers. That window stands wide open, and is much used!

The room called Faith is shut, and the lock rusted. It is lifted up above all others, and rests, like a crystal-dome observatory, upon the top of the dwelling. But its telescope is unmounted—its implements all gone to waste! The chamber of Worship is silent, unused, unvisited, dark and cheerless.

Indeed, in those upper and nobler apartments, on which the sun rests all the day long, from which all sweet and pleasant prospects rise, to which are wafted the sweetest sounds that ever charm the ear, and the sweetest odors that ever fall from celestial gardens, around about which angels are hovering—these are, in most soul-houses, all shut and desolate!

But if you go into the lower ranges, you shall find occupancy there, yet with various degrees of inconvenience and misery. If you listen, you shall hear in some rioting and wassail. The passions never hold Lent; they always celebrate carnival! In others, you shall hear sighs and murmurs. The dwellers therein are disappointed, restless desires, crippled and suffering wishes, bed-ridden ambitions! In others you shall hear weepings and repinings; in others, storms and scoldings; in others, there are sleep and stupidity; in others, toil and trouble; in others, weariness and disgust of life.

You would be apt, from these sights and sounds, to think that you were in an ill-kept hospital. The wards are filled with sad cases. Here and there, if you enter unadvisedly, you shall find awful filth. You shall even come upon stark corpses—for there is not a soul that does not number, among its many chambers, at least one for a charnel-house in which Darkness and Death abide! It is a dreadful thing for a man to be enlightened so as to see his feelings, passions, sins, crimes, thoughts and desires, motives and imaginations, as God sees them! It is a dreadful thing to go about from room to room, and see what a place the soul is! How unlighted and gloomy! How waste and unused! How shut and locked! And where it is open and used, how desecrated and filthy!

Now, it is to the door of such a house—to the human soul with such passages and chambers—*that Christ comes!* To such a dwelling, he comes and knocks for entrance! We can imagine the steps of a good man coming to houses that are nothing but habitations of wretchedness, to places of misery and infamy, to jails and houses of correction. But none of these can convey a lively impression of the grace and condescension of God, in coming to the doors of the soul-houses of men, and knocking to be admitted into their darkness, squalidness and misery! For it is not because they are beautiful that God comes, or because he is mistaken about their condition, or thinks them better than they are. It is because He knows the darkness and the emptiness of some; the abuses and misery in others; the rioting and desecration in others. And to all he comes to bring light for darkness, cleansing for foulness, furniture for emptiness, and order for confusion! He comes to turn the rusted locks, and to open the closed doors of every chamber—to let men up into every part of themselves—and to fill the whole dwelling of the soul, from foundation to dome, with light and gladness, with music and singing, with joy and rejoicing!

"*Behold I stand at the door and knock.*" Christ comes to the soul-house, and stands there and knocks. On getting no answer, he goes away only to come and knock again. He waits at the door, and listens for a voice within, and goes away. He comes again, and waits, and goes away! He knocks, not at one door, but goes round to every door, and waits for an answer. As one who returns to his dwelling in the night, after a journey, and finding it locked, knocks at the accustomed door of entrance in the front, and getting no answer goes to the door in the rear, then to the side door—if there be one—and then to every other door, in order, if possible, to get into his house; so Christ, who longs to enter into the soul, goes to every door in succession, and knocks, and listens for an invitation to come in, and leaves not one chamber in the soul-house unsought, or one door untried! He knocks at the door of Reason; at the door of Fear; at the door of Hope; at the door of Imagination and Taste, of Benevolence and Love, of Conscience, of Memory and Gratitude! He does not neglect a single one!

Beginning at the upper and the noblest, where he ought to come in as a King of Glory, through gates of triumph, he comes round and down to the last and lowest, and retreats wistfully and reluctantly, returning often—morning, noon, and night—continually seeking entrance, with marvelous patience, accepting no refusal, repulsed by no indifference to his presence, and no neglect of his message!

If he be admitted, joy unspeakable is in the house, and shall be henceforth. The dreary dwelling is filled with light from the brightness of his countenance, and every chamber is perfumed from the fragrance of his garments. Peace and hope, love and joy, abide together in the house—for Christ himself takes up his abode therein. But if, after his long knocking at the door and patient waiting for entrance, his solicitation be refused or neglected, by and by there shall come a time when you who have denied him, shall be denied of him. For when you shall knock at the gate of heaven for admittance into the mansions which he has prepared from the foundation of the world, he will say unto you, as you said unto him, Depart! But that dreadful day has not yet come, and he still stands at the door—his locks wet with the dews of the morning—and waits to be invited into the chamber of your soul. Hear his voice once more, and yield to its gentle persuasion: "*Behold, I stand at the door and knock; if any man hear my voice, and open the door, I will come into him, and will sup with him, and he with me!*"

CHURCH MUSIC.

It is probable that music, since the world began, has been employed to express religious feeling. It has great power to excite that feeling. It may be questioned whether hymns and music do not divide power with preaching. If the sources of popular religious doctrinal knowledge could be examined, it is suspected that the hymn and psalm would be found to be the real sermon, and singing the most effectual preaching.

It is very certain that strong religious feelings incline men to the use of singing. And the apostle prescribes psalms, hymns and spiritual songs as a means both of gaining and of expressing religious feeling.

Religious reformations seem always to have developed singing. Under Luther's administration, and Calvin's government, singing became so general and characteristic that psalm-singing and the Protestant heresy were synonymous terms. The great reformation under the Wesleys was marked by the outburst of religious music. In the revivals of New England, not far from the same period, there was as marked a revival in singing as in religion. Indeed, so full were the young converts of song, that they went to and returned from church with the voice of psalms and hymns; and President Edwards devotes a special chapter, in his account of the religious history of that period, to a justification of this practice, against those who unduly censured it.

Whenever revivals of religion visit communities, their presence is attested by new zeal in singing. And it is to be noticed, also, that not only is the spirit of singing revived, but, as with a common instinct, all exhibitory music is dropped as dead or sapless, and the heart feels after hymns of deep emotion, and after tunes which are born of the heart, and not of the head. Revival melodies are but another name for tunes that express strong feeling. It is quite remarkable how a congregation, in times of spiritual coldness and musical propriety, will tolerate only classical music, or those tunes which the reigning musical pedants of the day favor. The choir sings as clocks strike, with mechanical accuracy, and with the warmth and enthusiasm of a clock. But as soon as a congregation are really brought together under the power of a common earnest religious feeling, away go the cold and formal tunes; and wild airs, plaintive melodies, or passionate and imploring tunes, take their place without regret or a thought of musical dignity and propriety.

But though music holds so high a place of power, and is susceptible of such beneficent effects, it is doubtful whether it is not the most troublesome thing in the whole administration of public worship. It would seem as if the history of music were but the history of continual expedients. Churches are undergoing perpetual musical revolutions. There do not seem to be any principles which are known and recognized, and which underlie musical administrations in our churches, and give them unity and efficiency. The Roman and the Episcopal services incorporate music with their service, congruously and harmoniously with the whole system of worship. The skill or efficiency of musical execution may vary; but this never affects the basis upon which music stands.

But with our other churches there does not seem to be any musical stability whatever. There is hardly anywhere a deep and controlling feeling that music is at all a religious act. It is but a religious embellishment at the best. Churches that have choirs wish they had none. They that have none wish they ha l a choir—until they get it. A large choir falls into confusion very easily. It is too unwieldy to be kept up without great labor, time, and expense; and thus it is an open magazine, subject to explosion at any moment. If the clumsiness of a large choir is got rid of by substituting a quartette, the church usually rids itself of discord and of religious feeling at the same time. The quartette is professional. Skill is the criterion. Music exhibits itself; but it never exhibits religious truth. Four singers in the gallery forbid anybody to sing in the pew. One might as well talk in sermon-time as to sing in singing-time, when a quartette is performing. I do not say that four persons *could* not be deeply religious, and sing so as to edify the Christian congregation. But I do say, that four persons who are musically gifted to a degree that fits them to perform the singing, are not easily found, and when found, are seldom under the control of deep religious feeling. Experience shows that trained singers, worldly, and religiously indifferent, constitute the greatest number of quartette choirs.

As music grows less robust, and more and more cold, as it becomes more and more "classical," a revolution takes place. It is determined to have congregational singing. It is not asked whether there is any congregational feeling, or whether the church is only a caravansary of one hundred and fifty separate pews, with separate families, in separate circles of life, anxiously keeping themselves clear of improper social connection with each other. It is not asked whether there is any common religious feeling that demands a common channel of expression. It is not considered whether or not the church has been trained to feel, act, or work together, or whether the members hang like icicles upon the eaves, united only by being frozen together.

Congregational singing *must either spring from a common religious life in the church, or it must lead to it;* or else it will not long live at all.

But, in multitudes of cases, congregational music flourishes only while it is a novelty. A leader is appointed. The choir is got rid of with unnecessary dispatch, and the best voices, perhaps, in the congregation are mortified and offended. Good tunes are to be sung. Slow tunes are supposed to be very pious. Very slow and very solemn tunes are used. For a few

Sundays all goes well. But first the young people are dissatisfied. It is very dull and most unmusical to them. But it is the voices of the young that always must give power to congregational singing. As they fall off, the sound grows thin and meager. A wet day, or the leader sick, leaves the decorous congregation to a mortifying experience of ludicrous failure. In a year, at most, the experiment ends. It was begun without knowledge, and ended as it begun. It was a caprice, an expedient, a reaction of disgust from choir-singing.

A new choir is inaugurated, a new leader, a new dispensation of ambitious display, of musical sensitiveness, of quarrelling and disgust, of revolution and quartette, until at length, in some congregations, all that any one hopes or dreams of is, singing that shall *not* damage all the rest of worship. In other churches, having lost every vestige of sanctity, music is regarded outright as one of those forms of moral amusement in which men may indulge without sin, in the church, and on the Sabbath; and they plunge their hands into their pockets and pay for professional singing. Then King David finds himself in the hands of the Philistines. The unwashed lips that all the week sang the disgustful words of glorious music in operas, now sing the rapture of the old Hebrew bard, or the passion of the suffering Redeemer, with all the inspiration of vanity and brandy. When the exquisite mockery is done, and the opera-glasses are all closed, the audience close their eyes too, and the sermon proceeds. Thus, music, apostatizing from piety, is no longer a heavenly bird, but a peacock, that struts and flares her gaudy plumes for admiration!

The loss of positive good is not the whole mischief of this state of things. This false singing desecrates whatever it touches. The hymns which are used are killed. They become suggestive of drawling discords, or of pedantic accuracy and dullness, or of ostentatious trill and shake, or of quarrels and troubles. The divine flavor goes out of them, and they lie sapless and dry. And thus music, that should nurse hymns upon its bosom, abuses them, like a cruel step-mother, and thrusts them away. Hundreds of hymns have been served worse than Herod served the innocents—for he killed *them* outright; but a hymn cursed by musical associations, cannot die, but creeps aside like a crippled bird, to hide its wounds in a songless covert, until time healing them, gives them wing and song again!

Meanwhile, only those who are unblessed with musical taste are happy. The most gifted are the greatest sufferers. The pastor sees constantly recurring quarrels in the congregation. One by one good men attempt to do something; but being caught in a passionate musical eddy, and whirled about for a time, disgusted and irritated, they get upon the shore, with a solemn vow never to meddle with music again.

So deeply are some good men impressed with the mischief of music, that not a few, and those who aforetime have been leaders in musical matters, seriously ponder whether religion would not gain by the utter exclusion of music from the church!

Are trouble and music twin brothers? Is there no way of edification through music, or must we regard and endure it as a necessary evil?

TRUST.

A CHILD has an exalted idea of the knowledge and power of its parent. A father stands in a child's mind as the type of courage and capacity; and a mother, of love and goodness. The feeling of trust is perfect. Children do not think about their own support, or their own manifold wants. There is an inexhaustible certainty that everything will be thought of, sought, and procured by their parents for to-day, to-morrow, next week, the month, and the whole year. Nor does sickness or trouble diminish this feeling. It then grows even stronger. Trouble sends the child right home to the parental bosom.

It is this experience that God employs to designate the relations of confidence and implicit trust that should exist between every human heart and Christ. The earthly parent succeeds very poorly in reproducing love, care, kindness, foresight, providence. He is trying to do, on a small scale, in a narrow nature, in a sinful world, what God does gloriously, in an infinite sphere, with a perfect nature, and with transcendent excellence. God is unlike an earthly father, but it is on the side of excess, abundance, profusion. He cares not less, but infinitely more, for every child, than any earthly parent ever can. He watches more willingly, provides more surely, gladly, and abundantly.

But few Christians, however, reproduce the feeling of children towards a parent in respect to trust. They believe in God upon visible evidence. Prosperity makes them trustful. Trouble leaves them without a ray of quiet light. Men trust in God when they are in health, in strength, when successful in their affairs, or when surrounded by all that heart can wish. When sick, alone, baffled in their business, vexed and troubled, hemmed in and shut up, they fall away from confidence, and go into despair.

You can leave your affairs to God when they go well; can you when they go ill? You can rest quietly in God's hands when you are in health; can you when sick? You can trust your family with God when you are comfortable and happy; can you when you are perplexed how to get along, and your children are sick, and long sick?

But what is a trust in God good for that departs when you need it, and comes again only when you can get along without it? What is a ship good for that is safe in a harbor but unsafe on the ocean? What is a sail good for that is sound in a calm, but splits in the first wind? What patience is that which only lasts when there is nothing to bear? Courage, when there is no danger; firmness, where is no pressure; hope when everything is before the eyes; what are all these worth? But such is the trust which most Christians have in God. It has no virtue in it. It is like a lighthouse that burns only in daylight, and is extinguished at sundown.

We need a trust that shall take hold upon God

with such a large belief of his love and constancy, as shall carry us right on over rough as well as over smooth ground; right on through light and darkness; right on through sickness, bereavement, loss, trouble, and long-pressing afflictions. At noon one does not need a torch. It is in darkness that one should carry a light. Sometimes God communicates his goodness to us through our worldly conditions. Every day and every hour seem mails from heaven bringing letters of divine remembrance and tokens of love. But, at other times, God prefers other channels. He chooses to approach us by other instruments. A Christian should understand that every experience contains the love and presence of Christ. God wears many robes. He comes in new apparel. Whatever change takes place, it is only God in another dress. A Christian should learn to look at the face and not at the dress. If your father or your mother came to you, you would know them by the eye, by the mouth, by the expression, no matter how strangely they were dressed. We should feel mortified to find that a dear friend did not enough know us to carry the firm trust of friendship through all our moods and changes of appearance.

It will be a help towards this state, if every Christian will reckon with himself in a manner exactly the reverse of that usually practised.

Count for nothing that which you feel in hours of glee or prosperity. Consider that only to be genuine trust in God which you have in hours of darkness. Begin there. Put your criterion and standard there. If you have none there, you have none at any time.

"*Although the figtree shall not blossom, neither shall fruit be in the vines; the labor of the olive shall fail, and the fields shall yield no meat; the flock shall be cut off from the fold, and there shall be no herd in the stalls;* YET, *will I rejoice in the Lord, I will joy in the God of my salvation.*"

ABIDE WITH US.

Even a glance of the sun is cheering, in a day of storms, or of clouds, which, without storming, fill the air with sullenness, and make twilight even at noonday. But what is this compared with the brightness of the unobstructed sun all the day long, filling the air above, overlaying the earth, and pouring gold upon every tree, stone, or house, until the eye shrinks for very brightness!

But the sunlight of a single day brings forth nothing. Such days come in December, in January, and amid the boisterous weeks of February, and the tumult of March. But nothing springs up. The tree makes no growth. The light does not enter in. It lies wide abroad, indeed most beautiful, but nothing is created by it; for burnished icicles and frost-drops are the only stems and flowers which come from the slant and cold brightness of the winter's sun.

It is only when, at length, the sun returns from its equatorial pilgrimage, and enters into the earth, and abides within it, that life is awakened. The earth knows his coming. In winter, nature lies as if dead. The sun stretches itself upon it, as did the prophet upon the woman's son, and from every part there is resurrection of root, stem, bud, and flower. But none of these things happen to casual and infrequent shining. They are the fruit of indwelling heat. Not till the sun enters in, and abides in the soil, not till days and nights are struck through with warmth, is there life and glory.

If this be so of the lower physical nature, how much more eminently it is true of the human soul, and of its Sun of Righteousness! It is a gladsome thing in toil and trouble, to have a single bright flash from the face of God. A prisoner in a dungeon may have but one small window, and that far up, and out of the way of the sun, while for months and months not one single day does the yellow sun send one single and solitary ray through the poor little window. But at length, in changing its place in the heavens, there comes a day in which, to his surprise and joy, a flash of light springs through and quivers on the wall. It vibrates upon his heart still more tremulously than on the wall. Even thus much gives joy. It warms nothing, and lights but little; but it brings back summer to his soul. It tells him that the sun is not dead, but walks the heavens yet. That single ray speaks of fields, of trees, of birds, and of the whole blue heavens! So is it, often, in life. It is in the power of one blessed thought, in a truly Christian heart, to send light and joy for hours and days. But that is not enough. It is not enough for Christian growth, or Christian nourishment, that despondency sometimes hopes, and darkness sometimes smiles into light. A Christian is to be a child of light, and to *dwell* in the light. The whiteness of heavenly robes is the light which they reflect from the face of God. A Christian is to bear *much* fruit. This he cannot, unless he abides in summer. For mere relief, even a casual visit of God's grace is potential. But for fruit—much fruit, and ripened fruit—nothing will suffice but the whole summer's sun.

Now this steadfastness of God's presence is both to be prayed for, and to be possessed. There is provision in the Gospel for this very blessing. It is the promise of the Father, and the pledge of the Son. It is made to be a Christian's duty to pray for it and to expect it. For, in very deed, there can be no true and full Christian ripeness without it. The soul forms no habits, and comes to no spiritual conformity to God, by the jets and flashes of excitement. These have their use, and are to be gladly accepted. But the soul must lie long in the light; it must abide in divine warmth. There must be spiritual summer where there is to be much fruit. Our thoughts are like our bodies; men cannot come to good breeding by an occasional entrance into good society. It is habitual commerce with grace and amenity that fashions a man to politeness. It is living in studious habits that makes a man learned. And even more, it is abiding in God, and having the indwelling of God with us, that bring the soul to good manners and in divine things.

It seems an impossible thing, to many, to carry the presence and influence of the Spirit of God through all the whirl and occupation of life. Is it impossible for a young soldier to carry the spirit of love with him, through camp, march, and battle? Is it difficult for the parent to carry his soul full of domestic affections through the business of the day? Is it impossible, or even difficult for us to carry within us any feeling which is deep and strong, and which we love, in spite of exterior disturbance?

Nay, do we not see every day that the heart, by such enthusiasms or deep emotions, not only goes unchanged through burdensome life, but casts out of itself a flood of radiance, and makes its path light by its own cheerfulness or joy? Love in the soul is like perfume in the garments. Heat cannot melt it, nor cold freeze it, nor the winds blow it away. Going forth or coming home, it scatters itself but is not wasted; it is forever going but never gone. And the love of God shed abroad in the soul surpasses all fragrance, in inexhaustible diffusiveness. If men have only a little love, an occasional spark, it may be troublesome to nourish it when the world casts down on it green fuel. A large fire waxes larger by that very wind which blows out a small flame. It is even as St. Peter saith: "If these things be in you, *and abound*, they make you that ye shall neither be barren nor unfruitful in the knowledge of our Lord Jesus Christ."

THOUGHTS FOR THE CLOSE OF THE YEAR.

As there is something piquant and memorable in the novelty of first experience, so there is something sad, and even solemn, in the view of last times. And yet, the two antitheses in a man's own life, his birth and his death, are usually without experience or consciousness. Birth and death are alike blind and insensible. The first two years leave almost nothing to memory. Then come only a few clusters for the memory. We are five or six years in the world before we have brain enough and nerve enough to receive durable impressions. And, looking the other way, by far the greatest number of people die without apparent pain, without mental sensibility—apparently as little conscious of failing life as flowers are of the loss of their petals, when ripeness plucks them one by one.

But it is a very different experience that we have, when in full manhood—in strength, vigor, nerve, we take record, day by day, of change; passing from some things forever, entering upon some, and palpitating with various emotions—sadness for the past or hope for the future!

But, as one may carelessly read a book and fail of half its meaning; as one may but glance at a picture and perceive not half its beauty; as one may part from a traveling acquaintance almost without any insight; so the periods and events of our life are irregularly dealt with. We glance off from events before we see even a tithe of their meaning; we hasten on to new things without reading yet more valuable lessons in the old. Should such things be put in a book as are happening to each of us every day, we should hang over the chapters as if a strange enchantment possessed us.

Let us redeem some thoughts from the past. Let us call up its shadows. Let us pass the events again before us, and pour upon them the light of sober reflection.

When speaking of the end of time, we do not reflect that it is ending every day, every hour. While we are looking forward to the close of our history, we neglect to look back and perceive that our history has been a series of closings; that the past is heaped up and crowded full of things—left, ended, finished forever.

All the periods of time which have appeared days and years to us, are as effectually ended as they will be at God's last day, when the angel shall lift up his hand and swear before him that liveth forever and ever that time shall be no more.

Tell me, what can you remember, and what recite, of your *first five years?* They are gone without a trace. To you the time is not only gone, but it left you almost without a remembrance.

Of the next five years, how much can you recount? A glancing thing, here and there, is reproducible in your thought. But the years—the years—they are rolled away, died out, and gone as have the clouds of last summer!

Then, year followed year. They came, grew, orbed to the full, waned, died, and went like shadows! Years that wrought upon you like eternity—whose marks you will carry forever, dissolved and passed like drops of dew. One by one, years are dead—twenty—thirty—forty—fifty—eighty! Go to the shore and call them. They shall not hear you, nor obey! Were they good, were they evil—were they misspent and poorly used? Nothing can retouch their period, nor add to their record. Is it a solemn consideration to look forward to that time when you shall stand on the brink of life, and look back on all your years? It is a great deal more affecting to you to stand in the freshness of youth, or mid-life, and look back upon what years are gone! They are registered and judged! Not when God's judgment-day dawns will they be more fixed and judged, than they are already!

Not only is there room for solemn thought in the larger periods of time, but there is something affecting in the subdivisions of time. Every Saturday evening has, to my ear, a gentle knell. The week tolls itself away—one, two, three, four, five, six, and the perfect seven—and I can almost hear the sound dying away as if days had slipped their cables, and were drifting down the stream, but beating faint measures as they recede! And of every one, I may say—ended! gone! I shall see thee no more!

Days likewise have some voice in dying. They scowl and shut down drearily sometimes, but oftener die in gorgeous apparel. As the sun stoops in the west, passes the horizon and is gone, I hear no audible voice. The scene speaks to the soul, as no voice may to the ear—"The day is gone—forever." No temple was ever builded as some days are—of wondrous deeds, of strange thoughts, of marvelous fancies, of deep feelings, of strange experiences. All the frescoes upon the Vatican are not so wonderful as those which our experience paints upon single days—that move on to the horizon, sink and go to the bottom, with all that they have!

In like manner it is with seasons—the promise of spring—the flush of summer—the fulfillment of autumn, and the year's long sleep—winter! Each of them goes, with a gradual and lingering step—so that we cannot remark their exit; and we only know their departure after they have gone. Memory may glean them, but never renew. Upon the future we cast hopes—but none upon the past! Upon the future we throw good resolutions of amendment—but none upon the past. Upon the future we cast a fertile fancy, and fill it with thick deeds; but the past—upon that we cast only sighs or tears, or faint joys—faint as dried flowers are fragrant of the summer that is gone!

But how much more marked are the completions of *experiences*—the era of early youth, the beginnings of things whose endings are with us yet; the seeds whose stalks are yet growing; the foundations upon whose walls we are still building! We can look back to days of sorrow that gathered as clouds for storms—that rained and drenched us; that threatened to overwhelm us; that passed and forever left us, and now lie in memory, rounded out and completed things.

How many hopes, born, ripened, perished? How many fears that quivered, struck—like harmless lightnings in summer evenings—and ended! How many aspirations that flew, soaring high, till the head was dizzy with height! How many loves lighted the path of those who are gone, while the love shines on, like sepulchral lamps, fed by the living to cast their faithful light upon the ashes of those that are for earth no more.

How, when the whole reality comes back to us, do we stand struck with wonder at the deeds done—the events accomplished, the experiences ripened, the transitions completed? Of our youthful companions how many are with us yet? What part of old companionship is left? If the schoolroom, where we used to sit, should be again filled with the former scholars, how many would sit there as spirits, and how many in body? Of our childhood home, how many would come to our summons in shadow, and how many in substance? How, as we advance in life—the *past* gathers treasures. What a magazine of things ended, laid up, perfected!

In the softened mood of such thoughts, how well it is for us to employ the last days of the year in solemn reflections. How wise it is to make an estimate of our own place, our character, our prospects!

Another year is gone. Before we enter the next, let us reckon with ourselves earnestly and honestly, what the old year has done for us and with us. And should it be our last year, let us make such timely preparation, that at whatever hour the summons comes, we may depart gladly, rise with triumph, and take hold of immortality in Heaven.

GOD'S PITY.

"Like as a father pitieth his children, so the Lord pitieth them that fear him."—Ps. ciii. 13.

How strange it seems, to fall upon such a wonderful lyric as is this psalm of David, singing to us out of the rude ages of the past, where we naturally expect harshness and severity! How wonderful that Our Age should go back to this old warrior to learn tenderness!—that the most exquisite views of divine compassion should spring forth from the world's untrained periods, from Moses, the shepherd and legislator of the Desert, and from David, the sweet singer of Israel, whose hand was mightiest among the mighty, whether laid upon the strings of the bow or of the harp!

Noble old warrior! Thou didst send dismay to thine enemies, and breathe joy among thy friends. Thy bow abode in strength, and thine arrows were terrible in the day of battle. But those silver shafts of song, from a lyre surpassing the fabled sweetness of Apollo's have sped through the dusky years, through thousands of them, and are flying yet; not for wounding, but for life and healing.

If we remember the times of David, we shall be no less surprised at the ripeness of the views of God, which he gives, their symmetry and all-sidedness, gentle without moral weakness, and strong without harshness; building up the divine glory in justice and truth, and walling it about with majesty and stability. But then, as in a garden inclosed with mighty walls, oh Psalmist, thou didst cover the bosom of God with flowers and fruits, and make the thought of Him sweeter to the fainting soul than all the breath of flowers, or sound of cooling waters!

As but a few years intervened between the era of David and of Homer, not the measure of a man's lifetime, it is interesting to observe the views which they held, synchronously, of the character of God. While David was filling Jerusalem with these matchless lyrics, Homer, the blind wanderer of Greece, whom the world has since made a universal citizen, was singing of the Grecian gods. If any one would know the glory of the Hebrew bard, let him contrast the psalms of David with Homeric representations of God. How could Greece be so dark when such a star shone over Mount Zion? How could Olympus be so mean while Sinai flamed with such grandeur? Living in the same day, a thousand years of religion divided them. Our hearts decide in a moment which was the true prophet, and the teacher of the true God!

Let us select from David's chants but the single strain—*God's Pity.*

Pity is a mode or particular development of benevolence. It is sympathy for persons on account of weakness or suffering. It is not mere compassion, but is mingled with a desire to aid and relieve.

Pity and compassion are the antitheses of those affections by which we take hold of men who are good, lovely, desirable for their grace of nobleness and purity; or of those who are prosperous, strong, and happy. For such, to be sure, we have a lively sympathy, but it is of a different sort. God has gladness for those who are glad, and pity for those who are sad.

The pity of God, as disclosed in this psalm, is the working out of the whole divine nature of goodness toward the human family, in their unformed, immature, sinful, struggling existence. The race was not born perfect—men were sown as seeds are. They come of germs, turn to leaves, shoot forth a slender stem, grow little by little to branches, and find firmness and solidity only after a long probation of weakness, temptation, sin, and all its sorrows. This is true of individual men. It is true historically of mankind. The need of compassion for the race has been just as great as is the need in every household of compassion towards babes and young children. It is still the need of each man and of the whole world.

As much crime as there is, calling for punishment; as much deliberate wrong, to be met by deliberate justice; as much license as there is, and overflowing passion and desolating lust—there is even more ignorance, mistake, sorrowful weakness, and unwitting evil! The world wanders like a half-grown orphan, calling for aid without answer, and weeps for trouble and wanders still, stumbling through ages! And though it needs reproof and correction, it needs kindness more. Though it needs the grasp of the strong hand, it needs, too, the open palm of love and tenderness. It requires punishment; but it needs pity even more than avenging justice.

While, therefore, the divine character drawn in the Bible hath great depth of shadow in justice, all its salient points stand forth in the high lights of love and mercy! God is full of near, real, overflowing, and inexhaustible compassion for man!

But, it is declared that God's pity is not simply pity—*it is a father's pity.*

If a man be found weltering by the road, wounded, and a stranger comes who never before had even seen him, he will pity him. No matter if born under a different heaven, or speaking a different tongue, or worshipping at a different altar, he pities him; for the heart of man speaks one language the world over, and suffering wakes compassion.

But if, instead of being a stranger it were a near neighbor, how much more and more tender the pity, as he ran to his help. But if, instead of one who stood only in the offices of general and neighborhood kindness, it were a strong personal friend—yea, a brother—how much more intense would be the throbbing emotion of tenderness and pity!

But all these fade away before the wild outcry of the man's own father, who would give his life for his son, and who gives pity, now, not by measure, but with such a volume that it is as if a soul were gushing out in all its life!

But the noblest heart on earth is but a trickling

stream from a faint and wasting fountain, compared with the ineffable soul and heart of God, the everlasting father! The pity of God is like a father's, in all that is tender, strong, and full, but not in scope and power. For every one of God's feelings moves in the sphere of the infinite. His pity has all the scope and divinity which belong to power, wisdom, justice! Yea, power, wisdom, and justice are God's lesser ways, and come towards that side of his being where there would be restriction, if anywhere; while love and mercy are God's peculiar glory. In these he finds the most glorious liberty of the divine nature.

Nothing so soon wears out and exhausts men as deep feelings and strong sympathies, especially those which have in them an element of pain, as pity hath. Our life requires to be broken in two each day and replanted, that it may spring up again from sleep, as new blossoms out of soil. We are buried every night for a resurrection of each morning; and thus our life is not a continuous line, unbroken, but a series of lives and deaths, of deaths and births.

But God, in his almightiness, asks no rest and requires no slumber, but holds straight on without weariness, wearing out the ages, himself unworn; changing all things, himself without variableness or shadow of turning! God is like the sun at noon, that casts down straight rays, and so throws down the shadows upon the ground underneath each tree; but he never, like the sun, goes westward towards his setting, turning all shadows from under the trees, and slanting them upon the ground. God stands in eternal fullness, like a sun that knows neither morning nor evening, nor night, but only noon, and noon always!

God's pity abides, even as he abides, and partakes of the divine grandeur and omnipotence. There is a whole eternity in it, for substance and duration. As God himself cannot be measured with lines of latitude and longitude, but is boundless, so is his every attribute. His pity is infinite, moving with equal step to all the other attributes of God, and holding its course and path as far forth as omniscience doth; it paces with omnipresence along the circuits of infinity! For as heaven is high above the earth, so great is his mercy towards them that fear him. As far as the east is from the west, so far hath he removed our transgressions from us!

God's pity is not as some sweet cordial, poured in dainty drops from a golden phial. It is not like the musical water-drops of some slender rill, murmuring down the dark sides of Mount Sinai. It is wide as the whole cope of heaven. It is abundant as all the air. If one had art to gather up all the golden sunlight that to-day falls wide over all this continent—falling through every silent hour; and all that is dispersed over the whole ocean, flashing from every wave; and all that is poured refulgent over the northern wastes of ice, and along the whole continent of Europe, and the vast outlying Asia and torrid Africa; if one could in anywise gather up this immense and incalculable outflow and treasure of sunlight that falls down through the bright hours, and runs in liquid ether about the mountains, and fills all the plains, and sends innumerable rays through every secret place, pouring over and filling every flower, shining down the sides of every blade of grass, resting in glorious humility upon the humblest things—on stick, and stone, and pebble;—on the spider's web, the sparrow's nest, the threshold of the young foxes' hole, where they play and warm themselves;—that rests on the prisoner's window, that strikes radiant beams through the slave's tear, that puts gold upon the widow's weeds, that plates and roofs the city with burnished gold, and goes on in its wild abundance up and down the earth, shining everywhere and always, since the day of primal creation, without faltering, without stint, without waste or diminution; as full, as fresh, as overflowing to-day as if it were the very first day of its outplay!—if one might gather up this boundless, endless, infinite treasure, to measure it, then might he tell the height and depth, and unending glory of the pity of God! The Light, and the Sun its source, are God's own figures of the immensity and copiousness of his mercy and compassion. (Ps. lxxxiv. 11–12; Is. lv. 6–13.)

This divine pity applies to us on account of our weakness. God looks upon our littleness, as compared with his angels that excel in strength, much, it may be supposed, as we look upon little children as compared with grown-up men.

Divine pity is, also, exercised in view of our sufferings, both of body and of mind. We sometimes fear to bring our troubles to God, because they must seem so small to Him who sitteth on the circle of the earth. But if they are large enough to vex and endanger our welfare, they are large enough to touch his heart of love. For love does not measure by a merchant's scales, nor with a surveyor's chain. It hath a delicacy which is unknown in any handling of material substances.

It sometimes seems as if God cared for nothing. The wicked are at ease. The good are vexed incessantly. The world is full of misrule and confusion. The darling of the flock is always made the sacrifice. Some child in the very midst of its glee becomes suddenly silent—as a music-box, its spring giving way, stops in the midst of its strain, and never plays out the melody. The mother staggers, and wanders blindly as though day and night were mingled into one, and struck through with preternatural influence of woe. But think not that God's silence is coldness or indifference! When Christ stood by the dead, the silence of tears interpreted his sympathy more wonderfully than even that voice which afterwards called back the footsteps of the brother from the grave, and planted them in life again! When birds are on the nest, preparing to bring forth life, they never sing. God's stillness is full of brooding. Not one tear shall be shed by you that does not hang heavier at his heart than any world upon his hand!

Be not impatient of God. Your sorrow is a seed sown. Shall a seed come up in a day, or come up all in blossom when it does spring? Let God plant your sorrows, and water and till them according to his own husbandry. By and by, when you gather their fruit, it will be time to judge his mercy. Now no affliction "for the present seemeth to be joyous but grievous; nevertheless, afterwards it yieldeth the peaceable fruit of righteousness unto them which are exercised thereby." Trouble is like any other crop. It needs time for growing, for blossoming, and for fruiting.

THE MOUNTAIN AND THE CLOSET.

"And when he had sent the multitudes away he went up into a mountain apart to pray; and when the evening was come, he was there alone."—MATT. xiv. 23.

HE left the crowded shore, the thronged highway, and crossing the turfy fields, Christ came to the edges of the mountains. His pulse throbbed, and his breath quickened, as he clomb, as ours does when we climb. The sparrow, not knowing its creator and protector, flew away from his coming. His form cast its shadow, as he passed, over bush, and flower, and grass, and they knew not that their Maker overshadowed them. Sounds grew fainter behind him. Those who had followed him, one by one, dropped off, and the last eye that looked after him had lost his form amid the wavering leaves, and was withdrawn. He was in the mountain, and alone. The day was passing. The last red light followed him, and stained the air of the forest with ruddy hues. At length the sun went down, and it was twilight in the mountains, though bright yet in the open field. But when it was twilight in the field, it was already dark in the mountain. The stars were coming forward and filling the heavens.

No longer drawn outward by the wants of the crowd, what were the thoughts of such a soul? And what were the prayers? Even if Christ were but a man, such an errand and of such a man, would be sublime! But how foolish are all words which would approach the grandeur of Christ's solitude upon the mountain, if we regard him as very God, though incarnated, communing with his coequal Father!

What was the varied prayer? What tears were shed, what groans were breathed, what silent yearnings, what voiceless utterances of desire, no man may know. Walking to and fro, or sitting upon some fallen rock, or prostrate in overpowering emotion, the hours passed on until morning dawned. When he went down to his disciples, they neither inquired nor did he speak of his mountain watch.

If prayer be the communion of the soul with God, it is but a little part of it that can be uttered in words; and still less of it that will take form of words in the presence of others. Of outward wants, of outward things, of one's purely earthly estate, we can speak freely. But of the soul's inward life—of its struggles with itself, its hopes, yearnings, griefs, loves, joys, of its very personality, it is reserved, and to such a degree, that there can be no prayer expressive of the inward life, until we have entered into the closet, and shut to the door. Every Christian whose life has developed itself into great experience of secret prayer, knows that the hidden things of the closet transcend all uttered prayer as much in depth, richness, and power, as they do in volume and space.

Sometimes we mourn the loss of old books in ancient libraries; we marvel what more the world would have had if the Alexandrian library had not perished; we regret the decay of parchments, the rude waste of monks with their stupid palimpsests. We sorrow for the lost arts, and grieve that the fairest portions of Grecian art lie buried from research; that the Parthenon should come down within two hundred years of our time, with its wealth of magnificence, a voice in stone from the old world to the new, and yet perish almost before our eyes!

But when one reflects upon the secret history which has transpired in men's thoughts, and that the noblest natures have been they whose richest experiences could never have been drawn forth through the pen, or recorded in books; but have found utterance through prayer, and before the conscious glory of the Invisible Presence; I am persuaded that the silent literature of the Closet is infinitely more wonderful in every attribute of excellence, than all that has been sung in song, or recorded in literature, or lost in all the concussions of time. If rarest classical fragments, the perished histories and poets of every people, could be revived, they would be as nothing in comparison with the effusions of the Closet, could they be gathered and recorded.

The noblest natures, it is, that resort to this study. The rarest inspiration rests upon them. Flying between the heavens and the earth, with winged faith, they reach out into glories which do not descend to the lower spheres of thought.

How many souls, so large and noble, that they rose up in those days of persecution, and left home and love for the faith of Christ, and went to the wilderness and dwelt therein, gave forth in prayer their whole life! Doubtless their daily prayers were rich and deep in spiritual life. But there are peculiar days to all—days of vision—days when we see all human life as in a picture, and all future life as in a vision; and when the reason, the imagination, the affections, and the experiences of life, are so tempered together, that we consciously live more in an hour than at other times in months. Every man has his mountains of transfiguration, and sees and talks with the revealed and radiant dead. In such experiences, what must have been the wonders of prayer, when the noblest natures—rich in all goodness, deeply cultured in knowledge, refined in all taste, and enriched in pure lives, but driven out among the wild shaking leaves of the wilderness for their faith's sake, poured out their whole soul before God; their conscious weakness and sinfulness, their yearnings and trials, their hopes and strivings, their sense of this life, and their view of the other, their longing for God's church on earth, and their prospect of the glorified church in heaven! What if some listener had made haste to put down the prayers of Luther, with all his strong crying and tears, if that had been possible! How many noble natures gave up to celibacy and virginity the wondrous treasures of multitudinous affections. And when at periods of heart-swellings, in hours when the secret tide set in upon men from the eternal ocean, and carried them upon mighty longings and yearnings towards God, before whom they poured forth in mingled sobs and words those affections which were meant to be eased in the love-relations of life, but which, hindered and choked, found tumultuous vent in mighty prayer to God!

Consider what mothers' hearts have always been. How many thousand thousands of them have watched day and night over the cradle till the body failed, but the spirit waxed even keener ; and, with what wondrous gushes of words, such as would disdain to be called eloquence, have they besought God, with every persuasion, for the life of the child! We judge these things by our own experience. All the words that were ever spoken, and all the thoughts that we have conceived, are unfit to bear up the skirt of those prayers, which burst, without words, right out of our hearts, for the life of dying children!

Consider what a heavenly wonder must be the Book of Prayer that lies before God! For groans are interpreted there. Mute joys gain tongue before God. Unutterable desires, that go silently up from the heart, burst forth into divine pleadings when, touched by the Spirit, their imprisoned nature comes forth! Could thoughts or aspirations be made visible, could they assume a form that befitted their nature, what an endless procession would be seen going towards the throne of God, day and night! Consider the wrestlings of all the wretched, the cry of orphans, the ceaseless pleadings of the bereaved, and of those fearing bereavement; the prayer of trust betrayed, of hope darkened, of home deserted, of joy quenched; the prayers of faithful men from dungeons and prison-houses; the prayers of slaves, who found man, law, and the church twined around and set against them, and had no way left to look but upward towards God! The hearts of men by myriads have been pressed by the world as grapes are trodden in a wine-press, and have given forth a heavenly wine. Beds of long lingering sickness have learned such thoughts of resignation, and such patient trust and joy, that the heavenly book is bright with the footprints of their prayers! The very silence of sickness is often more full of richest thoughts than all the books of earth have ever been!

"And when he had taken the book, the four beasts and the four and twenty elders fell down before the Lamb, having every one of them harps and golden vials full of odors, *which are the prayers of the saints.*" And the other magnificence of the scene one may read in the fifth chapter of that gorgeous book of divine pictures, the Revelations of St. John! How remarkable would it seem, if it were revealed to us that there dwelt in the air a race of fine and fairy spirits, whose work it was to watch all flowers of the earth, and catch their perfumed breath and preserve it in golden vials for heavenly use! But how much more grand is the thought that all over the earth, God's angels have caught the heart's breath, its prayers and love, and that in heaven they are before God like precious odors poured from golden vases by saintly hands! Again the divine head is anointed with precious ointment, not now from the broken alabaster, a woman's gift, but by heavenly hands poured sweeter still from broken hearts on earth.

The influences which brood upon the soul in such a covert as the closet, are not like the coarse stimulants of earthly thought. It is no fierce rivalry, no conflict for victory, no hope of praise or hunger of fame, that throw lurid light upon the mind. The soul rises to its highest nature, and meets the influence that rests upon it from above. What is the depth of calmness, what is the vision of faith, what is the rapture, the ecstasy of love, the closet knows more grandly than any other place of human experience!

THE LIBERTY OF PRAYER.

One may perceive at a glance how exceedingly wide is the scope of prayer

It will begin with a supplication for our temporal wants. These are first felt, and felt longest; and, by greatest number of the world, felt chiefly. Next higher, will come petitions for relief from trouble, for remedy, for shelter in danger. In this, too, the soul may exercise its own liberty; there are no metes nor bounds. Then, next, prayer is drawn forth by heart-sorrow. A wounded spirit, a bruised heart, naturally turns for confidence and soothing towards God. Its prayer may be supplication for help, or it may be only recitation for the sake of peace. Next, and far higher, prayer becomes the resource of a heart exercised for its own religious growth. It is the cry for help against temptation. It is the voice of confession. It is a recital of sins committed, and a plaint of sorrow for them. It is the soul's liberty to go to its father with all its growing pains, its labor and travail in spiritual things. Prayer, also, to one who lives in daily service of God, oftentimes takes the form of simple communion, the spreading out of our life to one who is worthy, whom we love and trust, not for sake of any special advice, nor for sake of special help, but for the heart-rest which there is in the thing itself. For none love confidences so much as they who rarely have them. None love to speak so much, when the mood of speaking comes, as they who are naturally taciturn. None love to lean and recline entirely upon another so much, as strong natures that ordinarily do not lean at all. And so the heart that goes shaded and shut, that hides its thoughts and dreads the knowledge of men's eyes, flings itself wide open to the eye of God.

Thus, I have sat down within the forest, and while men were passing, feet tramping, and voices shouting, everything in the boughs and among the leaves hid itself. But after the noise had died out, sitting still and motionless as the tree I leaned against, I have heard a sweet note sounded near me; then a brief response from yonder bush; a bird had hopped down upon the leaves, squirrels had come forth lithe and merry; and in a few moments all the secrets and confidences of sylvan shades were revealed to me. And thus it is in the soul that shuts itself and holds its peace while the world is near, but grows securer in silence of contemplation, and lets out its gentle thoughts and whispering joys, its hopes or sad fears, unto the listening ear and before the kindly eye of God!

But in souls which have caught something of the beauty of the divine life, prayer in many of its moods becomes more than this. There are times of yearning and longing, far beyond the help of the most hopeful. There is a prayer which is the voice of the soul pleading its birthright, crying out for its immortality; it is heavenly home-sickness!

There are times, too, of great joys and gratitudes—times in which nothing is so congenial as to exprsss the soul's thoughts of gladness, its spiritual gaiety. In some lovely morning of spring, after days of storm have made nature mute, when the bright, warm dawning comes, can any man tell what it is or why it is that birds are wild with ecstatic song, and sit singing with perpetual warbling? Can any man tell why it is that they fly singing, turn and wheel in the air with every fantastic gyration, or briskly leap from bough to bough, and twig to twig, or sportively whirl in a feathery fury of mingled delight, a hundred voices crossing and mingling, with strange melody of dissonance? And can any man, then, give a square and solid reason for those experiences that sometimes come to all—and that come often to some, when thoughts are high and imaginations divinely radiant, and the affections full of vibrations of joy, and the whole soul is full of rising gladness, gratitude, happiness, and at times ecstasies? Have you never felt this? I am sorry for the man that has not! One day, one hour, of such peaceful joy, were worth a year of common pleasure!

But the soul does not always live willingly itself with itself. There is a privilege of sympathy with God which shall bring us hours of most serene delight. It is the privilege of God's people to come into such spiritual relationship with him that they shall have meditations, almost visions, of the divine goodness and glory, which will take away from them all thought of self-worth or demerit, of joy or sorrow, of thrift or adversity; and will fill them with overpowering gladness for the greatness and the glory of God! As one who stands before some magnificence of nature, or in the presence of some stupendous marvel, or before an outspread and glorious work of art or in a cathedral full of dreamy beauty, or within a gallery of paintings, where there is a perfect wilderness of colors and forms, as if there were as many as there are flowers in the wilderness;—as persons, amid such surroundings, are utterly unconscious of self, and forgetful whether they are in the body or out of it, whether rich or poor, whether in trouble or in joy, but are carried quite out of themselves, and made to dwell in the realm and glory of the scene before them; so, and much more, is it in the power of God to open such views of himself to the soul, as to fill and overflow its capacity and to make its life, for the time, a life beyond the body—a life that goes forth, as it were, out of doors, and mounts up to the very heavens, and stands before the eternal glory of Love, and among the radiant multitudes in the endless processions of heavenly hosts that are for ever praising God!

Who shall lay tax upon the tongue, or upon the thoughts, in such glorious visions as these? Who shall criticise or regulate the prayer that springs from such experiences as these? Let a man arrogantly teach rain how to fall, or clouds how to shape themselves, and with what paces to march their airy rounds, or the season how to plant, and tend and garner; but let him not teach a soul how to pray, upon whom the Holy Ghost thus broods and breathes!

They to whom is given such communion cannot but bear the burden of the Lord in earthly things. Christ's cause, and glory in the salvation of souls, will oftentimes move their prayers with deep and inexhaustible desires. They may not seek such experiences. They do not come by common asking. They are given to them who are one with Christ; who have entered into such sympathy with God, that they must needs bear his cross and, as it were, be crucified for sinners.

And, in like manner, God makes his servants to bear the burden of God's cause on earth at large; so that, at times, the desires, the yearnings and prayers for the prosperity of Zion, will be almost more than flesh can bear; so that in the expressive language of Scripture, they *travail in birth* for God's work on earth!

There are yet other modes of prayer; but who shall frame words to express what that communion is which the soul holds when, in the fullness of its own feeling, it overflows with praises. It is apparent how great is the folly of those who decry prayer as being useless, inasmuch as God knows what we need—as if asking for enjoyable things is all that a soul does in prayer. What if a man should have an idea as ignoble as this of sounds and space, and should say that no words or sounds are sensible, or of any value and desirableness, except such as articulate well-defined wants; as if they were of no use in exclamations of gladness, in tones and words of joy, in the mazes and tropical exuberance of love, in the sweet endearments of friendship; as if they were of no use in music, in shouts of gladness, and, in short, in any utterance except those for servile uses!

With regard to forms of prayer, these are of use, and are proper to be used by all who need them; but they can never include the whole of that utterance which the soul *should* express to God in prayer!

Some persons are often troubled respecting familiarity and irreverence in prayer. But it should be remembered by such that the confidence of love is not irreverence. God permits his people to plead with him, and to pour out their confidence freely. The exhortation is explicit, "Let us come *boldly* to the throne of grace!"

Some are discouraged, when after continued communion with God, they do not find any such range and progression in prayer. To pray is, to many, like speaking a new and foreign language. It must be learned. One is not surprised that a foreign tongue is slowly and brokenly spoken at first. Prayer gains in scope and richness as the elements of spirituality increase and the habit of expression is formed.

FAULTS IN PRAYER.

Private prayer ought to be regarded as a pleasure and privilege, not as a duty. But public prayer may fitly be spoken of as a duty, since it is seldom that one would of choice pray publicly for his own devotion, but only because it is his duty to the brotherhood. No service needs more, and none is susceptible of so little, improvement by means of instruction. This is an exercise in which men cannot be drilled. It is ungracious even to criticise what purports to be an address to God. Yet, there are some suggestions which we shall venture to make.

We think it very important that the pastor, or some leading officer, should be faithful with the younger members of the church in pointing out blemishes and faults, which may easily be corrected at first, but which, if suffered to go on, will become ineradicable. One man falls into a whining tone, another prays in an inaudible whisper, another exalts his voice far beyond the natural conversational pitch, and others lose the natural tones entirely, and pray in a kind of sacred falsetto. Some talk in tenor, but pray in base; some converse in upper-base notes, but pray in tenor notes. If a brother first speaks, and then prays, a stranger, listening from the outside, would think two different men had been speaking. This habit becomes very marked in the ministrations of clergymen, many of whom come, at length, to have a conversation voice, a praying voice, a hymn voice, a reading voice, and a preaching voice.

Men are seldom entirely true to themselves and natural in their prayers. There is a certain round of topics supposed to be necessary to a symmetrical prayer. These they punctiliously introduce, whether their heart craves such utterance or not. Of all forms of prayer, extemporaneous forms are the worst. They have all the evils of written prayers without their propriety. If, when a Christian brother were in full tide of prayer along the regular succession of topics, Christ should really appear before him, how extremely impertinent would most of the petitions seem, addressed to a living and visible Saviour! Thus a man's real feeling is not expressed, and matters quite good in themselves, but almost wholly indifferent to him, constitute the bulk of petition. Reverential tones and well-connected sentences, expressing very proper ideas, do not constitute prayer. The very essence of praying is, that it conveys the real desires or thoughts of the suppliant. When a man really reveres God, how simple is the language of veneration! But if his heart is breaking with sorrow, or depressed by care, or fretted by ill-adjusted affairs, why should he leave the real strain of feeling, and strike into a false key?

It is remarkable how skillfully men will contrive to avoid all real interests, and express almost wholly those which are not real to them. A man prays for the glory of God, for the advance of his kingdom, for the evangelization of the world; but, in that very time, he will not allude to the very things in which his own life may stand, nor to the wants which every day are working their impress upon his character. The cares, the petty annoyances, the impatience of temper, pride, self-indulgence, selfishness, conscious and unconscious; or, on the other hand, the gladnesses of daily life, the blessings of home, the felicities of friendship, the joys and success of life—in short, all the things which one would talk of to a venerable mother, in an hour of confidence, are excluded from prayer among the brotherhood. Without a doubt, there is to be reserve and delicacy exercised in the disclosure of one's secret and private experiences. But this is not to be carried so far as to strip prayer of all its leaves and blossoms, and leave it like a formal bush or tree in winter, with barren branches standing in sharp outline against a cold sky.

We must enter a solemn protest against the desecration of the name of God, so very common in prayer. There would seem to be no necessity, in a prayer of ordinary length, and upon ordinary occasions, of more than one or two repetitions of the divine name. Instead of this, it is often repeated from twenty to forty times. Every sentence begins, "O Lord!" Often the middle of a sentence is pivoted upon the divine name. It is made to be a word on which, long drawn out, men collect their thoughts or gather breath. It is a word used simply to begin a sentence or to close it up. In short, the name of God degenerates into a mere rhetorical embellishment, and is the wasteword of the prayer. For our own part, prayers interlarded in this manner are extremely repulsive, and even shocking. The prayer of intense feeling, of uncontrollable sorrow, or desire, are the exception. And no one would shrink from any repetition of the Divine name, which seems like the clinging and pleading of an earnest and yearning heart. Nor can we consent, any more, to be moved by the interjections and epithets of prayer. Many prayers are rolling full of O's, and the voice runs through half a semicircular scale of gracious intonation with every other sentence. It is, O do this, and O do that, O send, O give, O bless, O help, O teach, O look, O smile, O come, O forgive, O spare, O hear, O let, O snatch, O watch—O! O! O! O! through the whole petition, with every variation of inflection. Some O's are deep and sad; some are shrill and short, some are blunt and decisive, but more are long, very long, affectingly long!

It is sometimes painful to hear men getting their prayers to a close. After advancing through the topics for a proper time, it seems as if it were thought needful to throw in a collection of very short petitions, or to come to the close through a certain cadence of petitions, until at last the gate is reached, and the man comes out in regular style through the "forever and ever, Amen!" And so habituated have men become to this, that a prayer that begins without a certain conventional opening, and closes without the regular gradations, is thought singular and irreverent. The familiarity of deep feeling, the boldness of love, the artless sentences of unconscious sincerity, are to some undevout, while the cramming a prayer with all manner of conventionalisms gives no offence, if the manner is only solemn. Solemnity is a mask behind which levity and thoughtlessness heap up endless fantasies. It is the arch-patron of hypocrisy.

The use of Scriptural language in prayer becomes often a serious vice. Of course, when fitly used, no language can be more elevated and appropriate. But when texts or scraps, and fragments of texts are strung together, or when certain favorite texts recur in every prayer, long after they have ceased to convey to the hearer the thoughts originally coupled with them, the use of Scripture, instead of edifying, injures. A prayer is not a thread on which men are to see how many texts they can string.

An improper use of figurative language in prayers, is a source of positive mischief. We take no exception to figurative language when it springs fresh from the imagination. Then it augments the tide of thought and feeling. But there are certain figures, and not all of them Biblical, which have been repeated over and over, until all sense is gone from them, except a false sense. They come to be, at length, in effect, the assertion of literal truths. And a figure that was meant simply to kindle the imagination, finds itself in a didactic position, teaching the strangest conceivable things.

Some men are always "opening the windows of heaven," "raining a rain of mercy," "laying down the weapons of rebellion." "Stony hearts," "unclean hands," "blind eyes," "deaf ears," at length transfer the thoughts to the outward symbol, and quite hide the inward and specific spiritual state. Some men never say humble, or humility, except by such expressions as "on the bended knee of the soul," and going down into the valley of humiliation." Many men have apparently forgotten the name of Christ. They always use the word "cross" instead. They pray to be reconciled to the "Cross," they exhort men to come to the "Cross," to look up at the "Cross," to lay down their sins at the foot of the "Cross." We once heard an ordination sermon of great ability upon salvation by Christ, in which that name was not once mentioned, the "Cross" becoming the synonym. Had a heathen stranger been present, he would have supposed the name of the God whom we worshipped to be "Cross." This is the more unfortunate, because it not only sinks the power of a living personality, but presents in its stead a symbol which, however precious, and historically affecting, may, by too great familiarity, lose entirely from sight the Saviour, and leave only the wood; a relic worse than any which Romish superstition has presented.

AIDS TO PRAYER.

We have always been affected by the petition of the disciples to the Saviour, "Lord, teach us how to pray." How many yet would fain address the same request, with simplicity and conscious want, to Christ! It is not our purpose to say anything to those Christians who have by long experience learned the way of prayer, and made its language as familiar to them as their mother-tongue; but to them only who are vexed with the troubles incident to beginning.

If the first moments of the morning, the very first thoughts of the day, are given to prayer, it will be found, at least in many cases, to give direction to the feelings of the whole day. The key-note of the day is struck early. And simple as it may seem, we have forced a few moments in the morning to hold the day to its course, as a rudder does the ship. Some persons, we suspect, fail of interest in prayer, by attempting to pray by the clock. They have been taught that a regular time and an appointed place are eminently beneficial. They have tried the time with so many failures, that the place, by association and memory of ill success, becomes disgustful. We are not about to say that punctuality and regularity are not good, but only that they are not alike good for all; and that when experience shows that they hinder and do not help, Christians are under no law to the clock. Persons of regulated feelings, of methodical habits, and of uniform occupations, find great advantage in stated hours of prayer. People of mercurial dispositions, who live without special arrangement and system, will find, on the contrary, that such attempts at punctuality will not help them, except as an exercise in method and regularity.

If a man should insist upon wallowing in the sand when the tide was out, because he had made up his mind to bathe in one place and at one hour, he would not be much unlike him who prays when his watch, and not when his heart, tells him the time. Christians are to remember that they are children of liberty. They are not bound up, as the Jews were, to times and seasons, to places and methods. Prayer may become a yoke of superstition, instead of the wings of liberty.

It may be briefly said, take notice of the times when prayer is refreshing. Learn from your own experience how and when prayer is best for you. You are under bonds to no man, be he minister or layman.

We think that one may very much aid himself, by taking a few moments of his brightest hours for silent prayer. The Jews were taught to present their best fruits for offerings. We should not choose refuse hours, good for nothing else, to pray in. No matter where you are, nor what you are doing, send a glance Godward from the top of every exalted hour—as from a hill top, a child, going home, would strive to catch a glimpse of his father's house. In this manner, after a little, the soul would lay up remembrances of many sweet and noble experiences, and would fight discouragements by hope drawn from past success.

We suspect that many persons mar this enjoyment by very erroneous ideas of quantity. They read of eminent Christians who pray by the hour, they hear sermons upon the wrestling of Jacob with the Angel, and above all, they are told that Christ prayed all night. They therefore attempt immense prayer. Of course they fail. A man might as well attempt to imitate the old prophets who ate in preparation of forty days' fast. If a man is moved to pray only five minutes, it is his duty to stop there. If he is moved to pray an hour, he is at liberty to do so. But in every case, prayer is to be regulated by your own inward want, and not from the outside by somebody's example. Indeed, we meet every day with persons who would be injured by long praying. They have but little to say. If Christ were on earth, and they were disciples, they would listen rather than speak. There is communion by thinking as well as speaking. There is unuttered prayer as well as vocal. Thoughts that roll silently are more significant, often, than those which can clothe themselves in words. It is possible to pray too much. That is always too much which is beyond your real want or desire.

Christians bring themselves into trouble by very false ideas of prayer. They select impassioned prayers as models, and judge themselves to be praying in proportion as they approach these examples. But what if your wants are few, your feelings tranquil, your thoughts simple, and your whole mind and experience formed upon a different basis? Is prayer some objective exercise to be copied? or is it the presenting before God of just what you think, feel, or need?

One single sentence is a sufficient prayer. There is no one who cannot command his thoughts long enough for that. If your thoughts wander, the probability is that you are trying to pray too much. Be shorter. Say just as much as there is in you to say. If there is nothing, say nothing; if little, say little; silence is better than mockery. Consider the Lord's prayer, how short, how simple. It contains the whole world's want, and yet a little child can use it.

Accept prayer as liberty, and not a bondage. Use it in any manner that will be of profit. Go often and tarry but a little, or go and tarry all night, if you will, upon the mount. You pray if there is but one sentence—God be merciful to me a sinner—just as freely as if there were a thousand besides.

FORSAKING GOD.

We have known men—upon whose grounds waved magnificent trees of centuries' growth, lifted up into the air with vast breadth, and full of twilight at mid-day—who cut down all these mighty monarchs, and cleared the ground bare; and then, when the desolation was complete, and the fierce summer gazed full into their face with its fire, they bethought themselves of shade, and forthwith set out a generation of thin, shadowless sticks, pining and waiting till they should stretch out their boughs with protection and darken the ground with grateful shadow. Such folly is theirs who refuse the tree of life, the shadow of the Almighty, and sit, instead, under the feeble trees of their own planting, whose tops will never be broad enough to shield them, and whose boughs will never voice to them the music of the air. Some of the most remarkable figures of the Bible are made to illustrate this sad truth.

The mountains lift their tops so high in the air that towering clouds, which have no rest in the sky, love to come to them, and wrapping about their tops, distill their moisture upon them. Thus mountains hold commerce with God's upper ocean, and, like good men, draw supplies from the invisible. And so it is, that in the times of drought in the vales below, the rocks are always wet. The mountain moss is always green. The seams and crevices are always dripping, and rock-veins are throbbing a full pulse, while all the scene down below faints for want of moisture. In some virgin gorge, unwedded by the sun, these cold rills bubble up and issue forth upon their errand. Could one who builds his house upon the plain but meet and tap these springs in the mountain, and lay his artificial channels to the very source, he would never know when drought cometh. For mountain springs never grow dry so long as clouds brood the hill tops. Day and night they gush and fall with liquid plash and unheard music; except when thirsty birds—to whose song the rivulet all day long has been a bass—stoop to drink at their crystal edges! And he who has put himself into communication with these mountain springs shall never be unsupplied. While artificial cisterns dry up, and crack for dryness, this mountain fountain comes night and day with cool abundance. While others, with weary strokes, force up from deep wells a penurious supply of turbid water, he that has joined himself to a mountain spring, has its voice in his dwelling night and day, summer and winter, without work or stroke of laboring pump, clear, sweet, and cheerful; running of its own accord to serve, and singing at its work, more musical than any lute; and in its song bringing suggestions of its mountain home—the dark recess, the rock which was its father, the cloud which was its mother, and the teeming heaven broad above both rock and cloud!

With such a spring, near, accessible, urging itself upon the eye and ear, how great would be his folly who should abandon it, and fill his attic with a leaden cistern, that for ever leaked when full, and was dry when it did not leak! Listen, then, to the word of God: "My people have committed two evils: they have forsaken me, the fountain of living waters, and have hewed them out cisterns, broken cisterns, that can hold no water."

Man is not made to be independent in his powers. With all his endowments he is made to lean on every side for support; and should his connections on either side be cut, he would droop and wither like a tree whose roots had been sundered.

The eye carries no light with it, but receives its sight from the luminous element without. The ear hath no sound within it, but only receives it from without. The tongue and throat beat upon the air for vibrations, as a musician strikes for musical sounds; and if hindered in their connections or broken from their dependencies, ear, tongue, and eye would fall back into voiceless darkness. And every bodily function is directly or immediately joined to the physical world in such a way, that, while man is lord of creation, he is also its subject and dependent, and must ask leave to exist from the earth, the air, the sun and the clouds.

These dependent relations symbolize the yet more important relations which the soul sustains to God. Man is not made to exist in rounded, perfect, and independent spiritual life in his own right and nature. He only is a perfect man who has himself in the embrace of God. The soul only when divinely brooded receives its power. Our faculties, like the eye that must be filled with light from without, wait for their power from above. It is the divine energy acting through the human faculty, that gives to man his real existence. Nor does any man know his power, his nature, his richness of emotion, the height and depth of his being until he unfolds under the stimulus of God's imbreathed influence.

What is that effluence? What is this spirit which acts within or upon the soul? I will tell you when you will tell me what it is in light and heat that works upon the root to bring forth the stem; what it is that works within the stem to bring forth the bud; what it is that works upon the bud to persuade it into blossom; and what that mysterious spirit is, that, dismissing the beauty of the bloom, holds back its life in the new form of fruit. It is light, it is heat, it is moisture, it is the soil, it is the plant, it is the vital energy of nature. Thus we stand throwing words at a marvellous change, whose interior nature we cannot search nor find out. "So is every one that is born of the Spirit."

But of the fact itself, it is full of blessedness to know that the soul has a relationship to God, personal, direct, vital, and that it grows and blossoms by it, while it languishes and dwarfs without it.

The body grows by its true connections with material nature; the social affections grow by their true relations to men and society; and the spiritual powers must grow by their true relations to God. In the material world, the roots of trees are in the ground, while the top moves freely above. But the soul roots upward, and so like long, pendulous vines of air-plants, that root upon tropical branches, has its liberty down towards the earth. We are the branches of Christ. "As the branch cannot bear fruit of itself, except it abide in the vine, no more can ye except ye abide in me."

But is not this a bondage and restriction? To selfishness it may be; but not to love. Selfishness grows strong by shrinking, for concentration is the nature of selfishness. But love grows by pressing outward and evolving.

That we are bound to God is as great a restriction of our liberty as it is to a plant's freedom to be held by the sun; to the child's liberty that the double-orbed love of father and mother bear it up from cradled nothingness to manly power; or to the human heart's liberty, when, finding another life, two souls move through the sphere of love, flying now with double wings, but one spirit. No man has come to himself who has not known what it is to be utterly forgetful of self in loving. And no man has yet learned to love who has not felt his heart beat upon the bosom of God. As a bird born in a cage, and singing there, amid short, impatient hops, from perch to wire, from wire to ring, and from ring to perch again, so is man unrenewed. As this bird, when darting through the opened door, feels with wondrous thrill the wide sweep of the open air, and dare not sing for joy, but goes from ground to limb, from lower limb to higher, until the topmost bough be reached, and then, stooping for a moment, springs upward and flies with wild delight, and fills the air as it goes with all its sounds of ransomed joy—so is the soul that first learns its liberty in God, and goes singing heavenward in all "the light and liberty of the sons of God."

He who forsakes God for a greater liberty, is like a babe lost from its mother. They who refrain from God for the sake of pleasure, are like men running from the free air to seek sunlight amid shadows and in dungeons. They who withdraw from God that they may have wider circuits of personal power are like birds that forsake the forests and fly within the fowler's cage, to find a larger bound and wider liberty.

A RHAPSODY OF THE PEN UPON THE TONGUE.

WHEN St. James says, "If any man offend not in word, the same is a perfect man, and able also to bridle the whole body," one is at first surprised. It would seem to place the sum of virtue in a very little thing. But a larger experience of life would change our opinion. The tongue is the exponent of the soul. It is the flame which it issues, as lightning is the tongue of the clouds. It is the sword of anger, the club of brutal rage, the sting of envy. It is the soul's right hand, by which it strikes with wasting power. On the other hand, the tongue is the soul's voice of mercy, the string on which its love vibrates as music; the pencil with which it fashions its fairest pictures; the almoner of its gifts; the messenger of its bounties!

By speech a man may touch human life within and without. No sceptre has such power in a king's hand, as the soul hath in a ready tongue; which also has this advantage, that well uttered words never die, but go sounding on to the end of the world, not lost when seemingly silent, but rising and falling between the generations of men, as ships rise and fall between waves, hidden at times, but not sunken. A fit speech is like a sweet and favorite tune. Once struck out, it may be sung or played forever. It flies from man to man, and makes its nest in the heart as birds do in trees. This is remarkably exemplified in maxims and proverbs. A generation of men by their experience prove some moral truth, and all know it as a matter of consciousness. By and by, some happy man puts the truth into words, and ten thousand people say, He got that from me; for a proverb is a child born from ten thousand parents. Afterwards the proverb has the liberty of the world. A good proverb wears a crown and defies revolution or dethronement. It walks up and down the earth an invisible knight-errant helping the needy. A man might frame and set loose a star to roll in its orbit, and yet not have done so memorable a thing before God as he who lets go a golden-orbed speech to roll through the generations of time. The tongue may be likened to an organ, which, though but one instrument, has within it an array of different pipes and stops, and discourses in innumerable combinations. If one man sits before it not skilled to control its powers, he shall make it but a monstrous jargon. But when one comes who knows its ways, and has control of its powers, then it becomes a mountain of melody, and another might well think he heard the city of God in the hour of its singing. The tongue is the key-board of the soul. But it makes a world of difference who sits to play upon it. "Therewith bless we God, and therewith curse we men." It is sweeter than honey. It is bitterer than gall. It is balm and consolation. It is sharper than a serpent's tooth. It is a wand that touches with hope, and lifts us up. It is a mace that beats us down, and leaves us wounded upon the ground. One trumpet, but how different the blasts blown upon it, by love, by joy, by humility, or by hatred, pride, anger!

A heart that is full of goodness, that loves and pities, that yearns to invest the richest of its mercy in the souls of those that need it—how sweet a tongue hath such a heart! A flute sounded in a wood, in the stillness of evening, and rising up among leaves that are not stirred by the moonlight above, or by those murmuring sounds beneath; a clock, that sighs at half hours, and at the full hours beats its silver bell so gently, that we know not whence the sound comes, unless it falls through the air from heaven, with sounds as sweet as dew-drops make, in heaven, falling upon flowers; a bird whom perfumes have intoxicated, sleeping in a blossomed tree, so that it speaks in its sleep with a note so soft that sound and sleep strive together, and neither conquer, but the sound rocks itself upon the bosom of sleep, each charming the other; a brook that brings down the greeting of the mountains to the meadows, and sings a serenade all the way to the faces that watch themselves in its brightness, these, and a hundred like figures, the imagination brings to liken thereunto the charms of a tongue which love plays upon. Even its silence is beautiful. Under a green tree we see the stream so clear that nothing is hidden to its bottom. We cast in round, white pebbles to hear them plash, and to see the crystal-eyed fish run in, and sail out again. So there are some whose speaking is like the fall of jasper stones upon the silent river, and whose stillness follows speech, as silent fish that move like dreams beneath the untroubled water!

It was in some such dreaming mood, methinks, old Solomon spoke: "A wholesome tongue is a tree of life." And what fruit grows thereon, he explains, when he afterwards says, "A word fitly spoken, is like apples of gold in baskets of silver,"—beautiful whether seen through the silver network of the sides, or looked upon from above, resting their orbed ripeness upon the fretted edge of the silver bed.

AN AGED PASTOR'S RETURN.

It was about half-past nine o'clock at night that the conductor upon the Naugatuck Railroad train called out "Litchfield!" We stepped out into the light of the brightest moon, and looked about only to see two or three snug houses, and a little bit of a station-house. The town lay four miles to the west, *i. e.*, by daylight, and with a nimble team. It was at least ten miles that night. But we did not care. Nothing is more befitting than to return to one's native place in the quiet of night, and with the witchery of moonlight, that at the same time reveals and dims old familiar places. It was thirty-one years since either of us, my venerable father or myself, had been on this road. We had been back to the town before, but had approached it from a different point. As we climbed up hill after hill, the driver, an intelligent man, gave us the names of the places, and what power was there in many of them to evoke the past, and bring up its faded scenes in a pastor's heart! Litchfield was a large township, and the inhabitants were in neighborhoods among the hills, and along the clefts and valleys. It was necessary to have preaching places in every direction. On the Sabbath, the farmers would come to the "town-hill" meeting-house, but during the week, there were lectures and conference meetings appointed, in turn, in every neighborhood, at distances from two to six miles from the centre. As we rode along, the aged pastor, who was returning to the scenes of his early ministry, was full of recollections, as one name after another was called. In this house he used to lecture; in that, he remembered an affecting funeral; yonder, he used to hold conference meetings; and all the region about was storied with religious interest. The seventeen years which Dr. Lyman Beecher spent in Litchfield, though not the most influential, perhaps, upon the whole country, were probably the most laborious and energetic of his life. Some passages of his history here would seem almost fabulous to the economical workers of our day.

It was half-past ten o'clock when we reached the mansion-house. The Rev. Leonard Bacon, jr., received us cordially—the fifth pastor who has succeeded in the ministry of the white-haired patriarch whom he now greeted. In the thirty-one years that separate these two ministries, what a history has transpired? And as the young pastor led the aged one across the old common to his house, is it strange that we followed with more thoughts than can well be put into expression?

A good fire blazed on the hearth. Blessings on wood! We should have despaired at once, had we come back to Litchfield to find a coal fire, or worse than that, to find a black hole in the corner of the room puffing out dry heat, instead of the old, hospitable fireplace, with ashes and coals, and the long-fingered blaze that opens and shuts its red palm with every grace and sleight of hand. A good Litchfield fire of Litchfield wood, even if it was only the first week of September, was the very fittest banner that could be spread out to greet us, and every fold and flicker of flame brought back from the past old shapes and long-buried scenes, that used to flit round the fireplace, years ago, before railroads were dreamed of, and when New York lay a week's journey from us; when the old red or yellow stages came once a day from the north, once from the south, and once from the east; when the drivers blew the horns as they came into town, and boys heard the curling notes go through the air, and thought that a stage-driver was the greatest man on earth, and that to hold four reins and a whip in one hand, while the other held to the pouting lips the long tin horn, noisy at both ends, was the most wonderful feat of skill ever achieved!

The next day it was sent out far and wide that Dr. Beecher was in town. Though the great body of his former parishioners had passed away, some remained that were old when he preached here. As we passed the graveyard coming into town my father, pointing to it, said, "There is the congregation to which I preached when I was here!" Silent now and without memory. The unconscious assembly gave no greeting as we passed, but kept their long Sabbath without bell or tithing-man! But some yet remained alive. Men now of fifty years were boys when my father left. Those who blushed to think of love and husband yet, now rocked their grandchildren's cradle! Those who were then in the prime middle of life were now venerable.

And indeed Litchfield is the last place one should settle in who desires to go early to his rest. It seems difficult to obtain release from earth on this clear hill-top. Men are counted very young at fifty, and sound at seventy-five, and not very old at eighty. One old man, near ninety, modestly told us that his mind had been affected by a shock; but surely he had more wit and sprightliness, after all his loss, than most men have to begin with. He was peculiarly thankful that while he was too old to do much himself, God had been pleased to give him a young wife. She was only seventy-five, he informed us.

A man past eighty, going through the streets to visit all the fathers and mothers in Israel that had been young in his ministry there, was a scene not a little memorable. One patriarch, in his ninety-ninth year, when his former pastor came into the room, spoke not a word, but rose up, and putting his trembling arms about his neck burst into tears. Did he see in that moment, as by the opening of a door, all the way he had walked till that hour, and all the companions who had walked with him? and did he feel, standing by the venerable pastor, two old men, how few there were that yet kept step with him upon the bleak way of life?

Passing his own former home, my father broke out with a swing of his arm, "Oh, how many thoughts and associations hang about that place! They fill the air like swarms of bees, and yet I cannot speak one of them!"

The particular errand which brought us hither was a lecture. A new organ was to be bought. All

Litchfield boys were permitted to help. Our contribution was asked in the shape of a lecture, and it was soon done. Then the aged pastor came forward. A crowd of old and young gathered at the pulpit stairs to grasp the hand that had baptized them, or had broken to them the bread of life. It was a scene of few words. One woman gave her name, but was not recognized in her married name. She then mentioned her maiden name. That touched a hidden spring. Both burst into tears, but spoke no words. The history came up instantly before both, but silently, which had occasioned the preaching of those "Six Sermons upon Intemperance." That volume is in every land on earth, and in many languages. It is preaching and working with unwasting vigor. Those that read it know only that it is a cry and pleading that few men can hear without deep feeling. But not many know that it was a cry of love, the utter effort of a heart of love to save a dear friend imperilled, or two friends, rather, closely related. One of them was rescued. These sudden openings of memory to scenes that included in them the strangest experiences of life, pictures painted on the past, with strokes of thought as sudden and as revealing as when the lightning at night opens the heavens and the earth with wide sheeting flash, and shuts again with obliterating darkness, cannot be drawn or described upon paper.

The second morning, also, was memorable for greetings, and conversations whose roots were forty years deep in the soil of the past. For ourselves, we hovered about as a mere shadow among those who had a right to be principals in these sacred meetings. If an angel could write all that transpires when an aged warrior in the church militant comes back to the earlier fields of his achievements, and meets the companions of his toils, where tears and prayers, hopes and joys, sorrows and deaths, and troubles worse than death, were common experiences, it would be a history of more matter and depth than all the volumes that are stuffed with empires, and buffoon kings, and prelates.

Last of all, as we departed, it was fit that we should stand silently by those stones that record mother and wife, sister and son, a lonely group! I could not forbear to think of the stream and its contents that has flooded between the two points of time, the first when I, a little babe, my father came to the burial ground, bearing the wife of his youth to her rest; and the second, when leaning on my stronger strength, his failing steps came again, and probably for the last time, to behold the grass that again waves, as it has yearly waved for forty-six years! Between these two comings hither, then and now, a great army of events hath marched.

While witnessing such scenes, it is strange that one cannot foresee a like experience. But men seldom look forward to see old age. They look into the future with young eyes. It seems very vague and doubtful to me whether I shall ever walk with trembling steps, and bedimmed eye, among early scenes, an old man, waiting for permission to go home!

LESSONS FROM THE TIMES.

"When it is evening, ye say, It will be fair weather; for the sky is red. And in the morning, It will be foul weather to-day; for the sky is red and lowering. O, ye hypocrites! ye can discern the face of the sky; but can ye not discern the signs of the times?"

Every season is indebted to that which has gone before. Yet, the first labor of the new life of grass is to push away the old and overlying growth. Many trees are obliged to begin the spring by casting off the leaves of the previous year. Thus it was in the moral world at the advent. Christ's first and last adversaries were those who represented the religion of the times. They were the men who were religiously conceited; and who, under the pretence of sanctity, of truth and the venerableness of holy things, refused to let the new growth come on which God appoints to every generation. They were the religious conservatives of that day. Clamorous about the truths of the past, and very ignorant of the truths of the present, they seemed to think that all of God's teachings to this world were already issued; and that *they* were the King's post, in which these teachings, sealed up like letters, were to be conveyed to another generation; and they supposed that their business was that of sacred mail-carriers, to convey unopened and unused the sealed messages of God to those who should come after them.

Of course, such men would scorn the ethical activity of their age. Men's business was to take care of the legacy of the past, not to plough and sow for new harvests.

It was this kind of men that met Christ at every step; that were shocked because he ate and drank like common men; because he went among common people, and thought religious truth, not in the consecrated language of rabbinical schools, but in the vernacular; because he sat in their houses at meat with them; because he gave men liberty on the Sabbath day, and declared that that day was not meant to restrict but to help men; because he let his disciples sit at the table with unwashen hands; because he preached to the outcast, and took the side of publicans and harlots against the respectable Pharisees; in short, because he took the part of religion against the religious institutions; because he took sides with religious spirit, which is always young and vegetating, against religious usages, which are always venerable in proportion as they are nothing else.

It was against this kind of religion, and these stubborn, conceited, unlearning, and impracticable religious men that he uttered these words. Men who had apparently never suspected that God had any way of teaching the world except through them; who would as soon have looked out into the street for gold and silver, as to have looked there for divine revelations; and who, when God sent armies to Jerusalem or drove them away, when he sent the yoke or broke the yoke, when he raised up world-wide commotions or gave peace to the foaming waves of contention, heard no moral lesson, saw no divinity, but looked point blank upon God's providential developments without seeing God. They were yet so attentive to that voice which sounded a thousand years before upon Sinai, that they did not hear the silent thunder of God's voice now in their own streets, and right at their own door!

Christ rebuked them. He put their conduct in a striking light, by comparing it to their habits in trifling things. The state of the weather they could judge by looking at the elements of the weather. But the state of God's kingdom in their midst, while miracles were wrought, truths wonderfully spoken, the poor relieved, the sick graciously healed, and God's law of love, which they had changed to stone, was smitten and caused to gush forth with divine water for the poor multitudes that lay athirst in the community—from all these things they never suspected that the kingdom of God had come nigh to them.

The truth to be remarked is this, that we are bound to understand God's dealings with the times in which we live.

Because by such discreet consideration of current events, we learn the nature of human conduct, and test the wisdom of various courses.

Because, by such study, we come to right apprehensions of God's moral government over this world.

It is a thing to be remarked, how little benefit men have derived in the long experience of commercial life.

The same mischiefs occur every ten or fifteen

years. Courses upon which the Bible pronounced sentence two thousand years ago, are entered upon again and again, as if nothing were known of them. God has spoken to him who hath ears to hear, upon the nature of greedy selfishness, upon unscrupulous devices in business; upon making haste to be rich; upon pride and hard-handedness; upon deceit and guile; upon the infatuations of hope, and the supreme folly of unwarrantable conceit; the blessings of contentment; the blessings of a good name; the blessings of God's service instead of mammon's bondage; all these have been proved over and over again, and yet almost without impression.

I. It is remarkable to see how much suffering comes upon men, not by any disease, but simply by difficulty of commercial breathing.

If the human body be stricken with fever or palsy; if cholera or plague attack it; or if the sword or bullet smite it; or if some weight fall suddenly and crush it; or some secret wound draw out, drop by drop, the blood—we do not marvel. There is a cause adequate to the effect. But if you put a man into an exhausted receiver, under a bell-glass, without a particle of air, the mischief is just the same. No organ suffers, no tissue is lacerated, no muscle crushed, no part is poisoned, none wasted or drained of its vital fluids, and yet the man effectually dies.

The course of affairs among us has not been disturbed by the unnatural invasions of war. The harvests have not failed, and famine has not reached out its gaunt hands among us. Disease has not striven in our midst, nor has industry ceased for lack either of legitimate enterprise or proper matter for enterprise.

And yet this great nation, in full health, with uncounted abundance of harvests, in its young manhood, stalwart, eager, hopeful, is suddenly brought up, and trembles, and staggers, as if it would lie down in faintness. What is the matter?

It is the want of air. The city cannot breathe. What, then, is this commercial air, which is so needful to life and activity? It is the faith of man in man. It is mutual trust. It is confidence. This is the air which commerce breathes. And now, in our midst, although there have been indiscretions, there have been none which the country could not bear almost without a check. Men speak of overstocking the market, or over-manufacturing, of over-importations, and of extravagance of various kinds. I do not say that there have not been mistakes in these respects, and great mistakes. But I do say that we are too strong a people to be brought into such confusion by mere mistakes of this kind. This country has such vigor, and such elements of power, that surface mistakes will never damage it seriously. There is money enough, property enough, and need for goods and manufacturing, but men are all paralyzed to-day chiefly by fear of each other. Men look at the best concerns, as in times of siege they look at bombshells, expecting that every one will burst, and that the only difference between one and another, is in the length of the fuse, and the time it will take to burn out.

But why should there be this sudden cessation

of confidence? You trusted those men yesterday to go around the globe with your money, whom now you will not trust to carry it from the bank to the store! No change has come over these men. They are just as honest now as then. Their morals are as good. Their business is as safe. On whatever foundation you stood five months ago, the materials of that foundation remain untouched to-day. Your ships are there. Your goods are there. Your shops are there. Your neighbors are not niggards nor simulating friends. They are the same men that you always knew, just as good, just as bad, unchanged either for better or for worse. But the city is under a spasm. No one will take things to be as they seem. No one trusts. Every one doubts and fears.

Now it is to the last degree important to inquire, Why has confidence gone, and gone so suddenly and so completely? Yesterday it blossomed like flowers over the field; to-day frost has fallen, and all are black and drooping! What wind has sent that withering frost?

In reply to this inquiry, I would say that in part this panic of fear is without proper ground. It is the overaction of causes, of which I shall speak, which are real. But we have not stopped at the legitimate potency of those causes, but allowed our imagination to carry our fear headlong, and with it our confidence in each other. Merchants are now like men awakened in the night by the attacks of an enemy. All scream and run, one crying out one thing, another another, all stumbling over each other with insane fear. Now there may be a cause for some fear, for some precautions, for some earnest defence. But there is, and there has been, no cause for the excessive reaction from hope which has taken place. The roots of business are sound. There never was, upon the whole, more health with so much life. And hundreds of men will be upset by nothing but because they are run against by affrighted men. Hundreds of men will go down, and lose years of toil, and the fruits of honorable industry, for no adequate reason except that men are scared, and in their unreasonable affright, like persons in a crowd, they tread each other down. It is a shame!

I am not in business. I have not one penny invested in stocks or goods, and never had. If the market touches the sun, or goes to the bottom of the slough of despond, it carries nothing of mine with it either way, and I am, therefore, not biased by my interest. And I look upon this convulsion and trouble with unfeigned amazement, as reckless, needless, wanton cowardice. The business-men of this country are suffering at this hour from a contagious cowardice! The whole continent is unstrung by nothing but fear. Nothing, I say, for that of which I shall speak by and by, and which is the ultimate of this iniquitous evil, was not of any such proportions of power as to justify any such breadth of effect: and fears have been added to real trouble in such unwarrantable proportions that it is scarcely immoderate to say, that we are all lightning-struck with fear.

And the cure, if it could but be taken, might be effectual in one day, as much as in a month or a year. Hope and trust to-morrow would set the blood going again, and bring color to white faces. For the mischief is not in the business, but in the business-men—it is not in your affairs, but in you!

The country is like a ship under a stiff gale and a rolling sea; in the watch of night, the man at the wheel and the watch think they see a ghost, and abandoning their post, they all run gibbering and tumbling headlong down the hatchway. The ship falls off and rolls in the trough of the sea, until, if some one does not help her, she will roll her masts out, or come upon her beam ends. But, if there be a heart of oak among them that can cure these frightened sailors with the thunder of imperious scorn and indignation—if they will go again upon duty, seize the wheel, set the sail, and bring the ship out of her wallowing, to her course again, all will be well! And I speak my honest conviction when I say, that all which the country wants just now is manliness. Your banks cannot cure you. The government cannot cure you. I come to your bed-side, and feel the pulse, and I pronounce the patient to be in a prostrated condition, from causeless excitement of fear, and my prescription is—Let there be *men* for nurses, and give them large doses of courage, to be taken every hour until the blood comes to the skin, and the patient can use his feet. Then turn him out, and say, Rise up, walk, and work!

II. But there was a beginning to this fright. There was cause enough for fear, but not enough for fright.

What was that cause that destroyed confidence and paralyzed hope?

A relaxation of moral integrity, and a special development of it in connection with the management of stocks, and the vast interests which they represent, have introduced an element of profligacy and untrustworthiness, which threatens to move the foundations of trust of man in man. And unless there can be the infusion of moral integrity in the transactions of business-men, in the immense interests represented in markets by stocks, unless these swamps can be drained, and a highway of moral integrity be cast up for men to walk on through the poisonous growths of this forest, the land will suffer, season by season, with malaria, and commerce will never be free from chills and fever, until moral tonics are used. The conscience of stock-dealers needs quinine!

The boards of directors, in our greatest enterprises of this kind—railroads—have permitted themselves to employ the power for selfish ends, by unscrupulous methods.

I believe myself to be strictly justified, when I say that the revelations of the last ten years show that in the management of these great and useful corporations, our most eminent business-men have not scrupled to do or to wink and connive at courses of conduct which involved directly, or indirectly, almost every crime against property known to our laws. I aver my solemn belief that most eminent business-men, banded together, and acting as a board of direction, have pursued methods which, if a single man in his private capacity should pursue, would convict him irredeemably of crime, and crush him with ignominious punishment.

The consequence has been, that one of the most important—yea, indispensable—elements of property in this land is so associated with deceit and fraud that it is likely to become a by-word and a hissing!

Now, when one by one eminent financiers, who manage these interests, all at once like a midnight house on fire, burst into conflagrations of dishonesty; when next whole corporations are detected at games of swindling, which, if practised in the park with a thimble, would send a man to the Tombs; when, yet further, it is found that banks are inveigled and are made to be left-handed partners in schemes that will not bear the sun; and when, yet further, strong business men are discovered to have stepped from their legitimate calling, and to have lent their names to devices for obtaining funds that are unwarrantable even in commerce, and utterly abominable in morals; when all these things are revealed, is it strange that men do not know whom to trust? and that men, with David, "say in their haste that all men are liars?"

Springing from this, and coupled with it, is the monstrous and over-bloated sin of stock-gambling.

There is no more sin in buying and selling stocks than in buying or selling bank bills, or any species of property. But it is one thing to buy and sell legitimately, and another to buy and sell as gamblers do.

Many honorable men pursue an honorable business in the brokerage of stocks. But it is quite notorious that millions and thousands of millions of dollars of stock are sold every month under the lawful forms of the Stock-Brokers' Exchange, which can be shown to differ in no moral or material respect from undisguised gambling. It is not necessary to enter minutely into the distinctions between right and wrong in buying or selling stocks. It is enough to say, that he who buys stock as a *bonâ fide* method of investing his funds, looking for dividends, or for some benefit from the interest represented by the stock, buys legitimately and without moral blame. But that whole scheme of buying stocks for no other purpose than to make money upon the bet that they will rise or that they will fall, is a scheme of gambling. Men that do it are gamblers. All the soft names on earth cannot be dissolved to make a varnish strong enough to cover the real wickedness. Men will resent the imputation. No man likes to be called a gambler. But the way to avoid the title is to avoid the thing.

In this gambling game the whole community have more or less participated. Some devote their time to it. Since my day, I remember, I think, one concern to have failed four times; it fails to-day, is on its feet to-morrow, in as good credit as ever. For when the business is fraud, and the customs of it are dishonesties, it does not take a man long to repair any little cracks in his reputation.

Merchants are forsaking their legitimate business,

and dabbling in this pool. Their clerks, following their example, gamble too. Simple men, seeing these marvels of success, venture their hard earnings, and go to gambling likewise. The lawyer follows suit; and that there may be no want of moral sanction, ministers of the Gospel are found, not a few I am informed, secretly buying and selling stocks.

Now when the company themselves are gigantic speculators by fraudulent and dishonest means; and when the stock of the company goes up and down the street, carrying in its hand a bowl drugged with gambling, and crowds rush to drink its intoxication, is it strange that at length the head is sick, the whole body faint, and that the commonwealth lies at length upon the ground, wallowing like one possessed, foaming, and rending itself?

It is supposed that there are one thousand million dollars invested in railway property. Can this mountain of power be used against good morals, against commercial prudence, and the country not reel and stagger? Can this prodigious weight be cast rudely hither and thither upon the deck and the keel lie level? There is not an honest man in the land patiently conducting a legitimate business, who is not in the power of these irregular forces. There can be no permanent security, if financiers can, at pleasure, draw up such enormous elements of power, and hold them suspended, like water-spouts, to burst and flood down desolation the moment they are touched with misfortune. And if commercial men will not draw tight the reins of morals upon these unprincipled men, they will have their own neglect to thank for the mischiefs which will have come upon them in some sense by their connivance.

III. Now, what lessons do these times teach?

1. We are to learn that commercial prosperity stands indissolubly connected with public morals. In their heat, men cast aside moral scruples, as one would throw off his garments in a race. Where everybody sins together, men fondly think that their concord is a law of nature. Little by little success domineers over conscience. The permission of custom, the sole condition of accomplishing, the fact of accruing wealth, with its praise and influence and power, these overrule moral considerations, and men do not hesitate to violate rectitude by ranks and multitudes. They systematize selfishness and organize injustice.

But all seeds demand time between sowing and reaping. When first sown, thistles are as good as corn. But when the reaping-time comes, they that sow grain shall carry their bosom full of sheaves, and they that sow thistles shall have their skins pierced full of spines and poisonous prickles. In commercial intoxication it is as in drunkenness by strong drink—first the pleasing exhilaration, but afterwards the bursting headache.

No class of men are more interested in a high tone of public morals than business men. Their life depends upon credit as much as their bodily life stands in air fit to breathe.

Credit demands the solid rock of integrity. It

will not stand upon the shifting sands of custom. The merchant should be a Puritan. Whoever else may permit the public conscience to be tampered with, the merchant is interested, by the whole force of self-interest, that the consciences of men touch God, and anchor there beyond the reach of temptation. To tamper with the sanctity of the divine law, to admit anything to be higher in human affairs than religious rectitude, is preparation for unfaith and untrust of man to man.

The merchant that destroys good morals plucks off the planks from the bottom of the ship which carries him and all his goods. He will founder. He will be carried down, sooner or later, by inevitable leakage.

2. Public indifference to immoralities, will be avenged as if it were participation. The bills which wicked men draw against the public treasury to pay for their crimes and vices, are always indorsed by the virtuous men of the community; and in the end, the sober always pay for the intemperate; the pure pay the expenses of the debauched; the honest man pays for the knave's debts; the working and frugal man pays for the indolent and spendthrift; and in such times as these it is seen that the headlong and swindling speculators run the commercial world into desperate straits, and then the criminals step aside, and the sound men take the burden and carry it. In prosperous times men attend to their own business and will not be troubled with public interests. This is a selfishness which God never will forget. In their

hour of distress they find out that indifference to public morals is itself a crime, and that Providence, in due season, punishes honest and good men for the misconduct of wicked men, which they could have prevented but would not.

3. These are the times for men to detect unnamed vices and crimes, and give them their place and proper designation on the list of evils.

In all vigorous communities, where enterprise attempts new things, by new measures, we may be sure that selfishness will pioneer conscience. Many things will be done, as now we clearly see they have been done, which are wrong to the last degree. But because men had not yet analyzed them or sat in judgment upon them by moral rules, they were permitted to go on as if right and permissible.

God's providence judges human conduct before men's consciences do. And we find out what is wrong by the punishment with which we are surprised, rather than by the use of our moral judgment. It is a shame that God's whip should have to be a better judge and interpreter of rectitude than a Christian man's conscience.

4. These times ought to point out the attention of men to the sure punishment of greediness. Haste to be rich comes more speedily through the stage in which they give equivalents, of skill, or benefit, for wealth received, into the always wicked and demoralizing stage in which men desire to enter without giving fair equivalents for gains. This appetite has no bounds when once planted. It is a raging fever of avarice. It is the peculiar disease

of speculators, of stock-gamblers, and of all other gamblers. A man who deliberately purposes to gain wealth without earning it by some substantial equivalent rendered to the community, is a thief. He may be called, down here, by much softer names. But above he is unceremoniously called thief. Nor is God's justice silent or motionless. While these men are ripening, the sickle is patient; but that is all that it waits for. Where now are all the eager financiers? Where are those inflated speculators that use God's great round of time and providence as a gambler's box to throw their dice with, who venture a penny, and rise from the table with uncounted gold? Where are these greedy men and their greedy associates, and where are their gains now? "He that hasteth to be rich hath an evil eye, and considereth not that poverty shall come upon him." God has written these words so high up that all financiering hands that reach around the world greedily cannot reach to rub them out. And every generation of men, whether they like the ritual or not, are compelled to say, Amen. At this time, men are affirming this truth with deep and bitter pronunciation.

The ship that was struck by this mighty gale and well-nigh overturned, is already righting. May we not hope that the worst is passed? Already streaks of light are appearing. There will yet be a struggle, but the fierceness of it is over. Some will yet go down, but those who are strong will stand; and now, if there be Christians among these thousand merchants, who can rise a little above their own selfish ness, and, though in distress, go to help their fellows, how true and devout a gospel shall such disinterested and heroic conduct be! There is many and many a friend whom you may cheer, encourage, and help; and your coming to such in this stormy hour, will be to them almost like Christ walking on the sea in the night and tempest, pressing down the waves to tranquillity with his feet, and casting serenity into the storm from the peace of his own divine face.

Not again in a man's lifetime may it be permitted him to do so much for God and Christ, by heroic endurance, by cheerfulness amid danger by helpfulness when the instincts of men would make them selfish.

Good men! true men! Christian men! all! take hold of hands, put shoulder to shoulder, stand and make others stand! After a little more trial you shall come forth as Nelson's ships came from the smoke of battle, pierced and crippled it may be, but floating still, and able to float; and afterwards, every shot, every wound and every loss shall be healed by victory, and then become insignia of glory! "The night is far spent, the day is at hand."

CHRISTIAN CONSOLATION.

During the summer, on western rivers, as you are riding or even wading across the ford, you may see, lying a little below you, great flat-bottomed boats, used for ferrying. During the summer, while waters are low, and men can cross without help and without danger, these craft lie moored to the shore with nothing to do. But when heavy rains have swollen the river, and the ford is drowned out, so that no man may dare to venture it, then travellers are glad to see the clumsy boat swung round, and by cords and poles forced across the swift running waters for the convenience of those who must pass over.

All our emergencies are like streams. So long as we can cross them without help we use the ford. But when our affairs are beyond our own skill or strength, God sends round his promises which had lain along the shore, tied up and disused, to bear us over the black swelling waters. And blessed is he who is willing and able to venture across real troubles upon God's staunch promises.

In times of trouble, every Christian man will find wonderful comfort in the psalms of David. Now their true colors will shine out. The psalms are like diamonds, which, though bright in the daylight, do not give forth their peculiar brilliance until night and artificial light cause them to flash. And so are those great lyrics of the world sung not to any lover's lute, or even Homeric harp, but sung from the chords of the soul itself when God played upon it. They are deep as human life, wide as the earth, and far reaching as immortality. And in times of trouble men ought to walk in the garden of this Book and comfort themselves with its fruits and flowers.

It is not the design of God's promises to help us so long as we can help ourselves. They are like defensive arms which men wear in a wilderness among robbers, not to be fired incessantly, but hidden for emergency, and then brought forth for self-protection.

They are like a mountaineer's staff, though good for level ground, not meant specially for that; but to be relied on chiefly among rocks and sharp acclivities.

What is a man's faith in God good for, which only holds him up when he can hold himself up without help, and breaks under him when he needs to lean upon it? What is a belief in God's special and particular providence worth, if it applies only to fair weather, and dissolves in storms of trouble?

If one will go back to the prophets, to David's experiences, he will find that God's promises were first made to men in the most bitter trials. They are not summer promises. They are not general nor indefinite. They were made to touch exactly such cases as yet occur every day.

Are hopes ever baffled? God has balm for that. Is an honest pride sorely wounded? God has spoken consolation for that. Is a man's good name shot at? That too has been done to ten thousand men before, and God girded them with promises which held them up. The men have died, but their charmed girdles are left. God's armory is full of them.

Do your enemies triumph over you? There are blessings thick as spring flowers among old grasses for those who suffer evil and bear it patiently.

Now, while men are rowing in darkness, and upon a dreadful sea, they may expect to see Christ coming to them walking upon the water. Or, it may be that he is already in the ship and needs only the uprousing of their grief and prayer to come forth upon the elements, sovereign over their wild tumult!

Methinks I hear Christ saying to all his disciples the very words which he variously pronounced while upon earth. Some are beseeching him to relieve their fear and bring back prosperity. They cannot bear the thorn in their side that threatens to reach their heart. But Christ's answer is, I will not remove the trouble, but my grace shall be sufficient to enable you to bear it.

Another bewails his misfortunes, and cries out, "Lord, why is this?" The reply is, "The servant is not greater than his Lord. It is enough for the disciple that he be as his Master, and the servant as his Lord." None of us are reduced as low as was Christ for our sakes. And it is a comfort to every penitent heart to feel, at each step down, that he is not going away from light and love but towards them.

Christ lives near the bottom of human life, and that way lies the gate of heaven. They who abase themselves are going towards God. And when Christian men are going down, step by step, nearer the bottom, let them say, "why not? why should I demand for myself what my Lord and my God gave up freely for my sake?"

Men often put questions the wrong way, and when they are bereaved, they say, Why should I be afflicted? When they meet losses, they say, Why should I have such misfortunes? But, would it not be soberer and more sensible if men should say, Why should *not* I have trouble? Am I not a man in a world of trial? Am I too good to be touched? Shall all God's elect since the world began drink of the bitter cup, and I claim exemption? What have I done that God should honor me? What use have I made of my strength and wealth, that I should demand their continuance? How have I brought up my children, that I should be surprised if God withdrew them from me, and placed them in his own bosom? Shall Christ walk in poverty, and I disdain that experience? Shall he not have whereon to lay his head even, and I complain in the midst of home, food, comfort, and love? How very good a man must be, who can afford to be surprised when God unclothes him of superfluous wealth, and makes him walk as near to the edge of necessity as the best men of the world have done before, and still do!

We are not to affect stoical indifference, and still less rail out bitterly at wealth; and seek, thus, to cover over our disappointment by a false pretence of anger. How much better is Paul's spirit (Phil. iv. 11), "I have learned, in whatsoever state I am, therewith to be content. I know both how to be abased, and I know how to abound. I am instructed both to be full and to be hungry, both to abound and to suffer need. I can do all things through Christ that strengtheneth me." Which of these extremes is the more difficult, it is not our purpose to consider. Far more difficult than either is the spirit that can play back and forth between them both. A Christian man's life is laid in the loom of time to a pattern which he does not see, but God does; and his heart is a shuttle. On one side of the loom is sorrow, and on the other is joy; and the shuttle struck alternately by each, flies back and forth, carrying the thread, which is white or black, as the pattern needs; and, in the end, when God shall lift up the finished garment and all its changing hues shall glance out, it will then appear that the deep and dark colors were as needful to beauty as the bright and high colors.

Meanwhile, as God's children are going through unwonted and bitter trials, it is affecting to see with what royal tenderness God stoops to comfort them. As a parent that convoyed his flock of children, in a flight by night, from a savage foe, would whisper words to this one, and cheer that one—now lifting up, and then for a little way even carrying some, meanwhile encouraging them, and saying, it will soon be light, hold on, and hold out, my brave children, we are almost through; so God hovers about his flock in days of sore adversity, saying, "Be of good cheer; because I live ye shall live also; I will never leave you nor forsake you. I am not angry, nor gone away from you; I chasten because I love you. Whom the Lord loveth he chasteneth. Ye are my sons. Cast all your cares upon me, for I care for you. Let not your hearts be troubled, neither be ye afraid. If God be for you, who can be against you. Think it not strange concerning this fiery trial, as if some strange thing had befallen you. Since the world began, I have scourged every son that I ever received. Blessed is he that endureth affliction. To him that overcometh I will give to eat of the tree of life, which is in the midst of the Paradise of God!"

Wherefore comfort one another with these words!

TROUBLES.

Whoever enters this world with an expectation of finding or making a life of uninterrupted joy, will enter blindfold, but trouble will quickly open his eyes. The wish to be happy is natural and normal. But the expectation of happiness unalloyed is most unreasonable. Life is a probation more or less severe with all, but severe in different degrees to different men.

Some seem only dipped into life, as we plunge children into a bath. They come for a moment within the horizon and depart again.

Some appear to have answered the earthly conditions of their existence in a few years. There is no interpreter to God's Providence, and God is silent.

Some persons appear to have an end in life which requires an even and balanced mind and temperament. They pass smoothly on, neither exalted by great joys nor depressed by burdensome sorrows.

Others are sent into life armed to resist the pressure of external things. They have hope, courage, elasticity, and they meet and vanquish assaults with almost gladness.

But others still there are to whom is appointed a much more difficult task. Their troubles are within.

As a shipmaster who carries an insubordinate and mutinous crew has his enemies in his own ship, so many men have a disposition so wild, so untempered, a mind so unbalanced, that their chief work of life is in their own souls.

Others still are children of special sorrow. God seems to deal with them as Apollo is fabled to have dealt with Niobe—slaying all their hopes.

Many persons carry their own troubles; others find them in their social dependence and connections. But there are many troubles that do not seem to bear any relation to our wisdom or to moral obliquity. They are like silver arrows shot from the bow of God, and fixed, inextractible, in the human heart.

In such a world it is folly to expect exemption. They who escape have reason to fear evil. But some there are who meet their troubles with such cheer that they hardly remember them as trials. As the sun converts clouds to a glorious drapery, firing them with gorgeous hues, and draping the whole horizon with its glorious costume, and writing victory in fiery colors along the vanquished front of every cloud, so sometimes a radiant heart lets forth its hope upon its sorrow and all the blackness flies, and troubles that trooped to appall, crowd around as a triumphal group around the steps of a victor.

Now these need not fear that they are not the sons of God. They seem but little tried because they have such singular victory. But those who have no troubles, and gain no victories, have never striven for a higher place in life than nature gave. A man without aspiration is stale indeed. But aspiration brings endeavor, and endeavor strife, and strife many grievous woundings.

It is unwise, therefore, to rear our children to avoid trouble. Instinct will do that sufficiently. It should be ours, rather, to teach them how to vanquish one part, and how to endure the other. And enduring is the greater.

Secular troubles, or troubles from without—troubles by men, troubles from affairs, troubles of business, should always be met with greater force than they bring.

Many troubles can be cut at the root and cease. Many can be strangled. Many can be overcome by direct attack. We should count worldly trouble to be only an excitant, and by it be aroused to an energy and force which otherwise we could not have felt. Such trials are only occasions of victory. Meet and resist them!

Some troubles and trials can be thrown off. Diseases are repelled by great animal vigor; and troubles may be repelled by great mental vigor. Every one perceives this in his own experience. In the morning we can carry the world like Atlas. At noon we stoop and find it heavy. At night the world crushes us down and we are under it.

The very troubles of to-day were about you yesterday, and you did not know them. For you were engaged in things that fired the mind with higher excitements. Very many troubles of life are nothing but your weakness. Stand up and they are gone

They are like gnats, which, while one is still, settle and bite, but rising up and working, the whole swarm fly off or do but buzz. But the moment the man rests, they alight. Thus, activity is exemption, and sleep is defeat.

The want of proper occupation is the cause of more than half of the petty frets of life. And right occupation will be a medicine for half the minor ills of life. A man without any proper aim in life, without moral inspiration, too rich to be industrious, and a prey to the thousand frets of unoccupied leisure, sometimes sets himself to pray against his troubles. Now a man might as well pray against the particles of sand in Sahara as a lazy man pray against petty troubles.

Therefore it happens, sometimes, that bankruptcy brings to a man what all his wealth failed to give—happiness; for he has real troubles, and trouble is a good medicine for trouble. There is a moral counter-irritation.

Many troubles, unlike the above, that are real, can be medicated by Hope. For so is it, that we can bear much when the prospect before us is cheerful and assured. If a man lets his troubles come between him and the sun, they will cast a shadow and interpose their substance too. But if he will put himself between the sun and his troubles, then his own form will fall upon the over-shadowed evil and half eclipse it. It is for this that hope is given. We are saved by hope, it is said. Hope is an anchor that holds on to the bottom while the storms handle the ship, and enables it to outride the tempest.

Happy is he that has hope. It is a heart-spring. If a man had no elasiticity in his foot, and could spring over no pool, nor ditch, nor roughness, but went leadenly through them all, how burdensome would his journey be! But by an elastic ankle he springs over a hundred hindrances, and never knows their annoyance. Many of our troubles should be oversprung.

Many troubles in life cease when we cease to nurse them. We take them up, we dandle them upon our knee, we carry them in our bosom. When they seem to sleep, we wake them up, and insist upon sharpening their point. We ruminate our cud, which was a thistle at first, and make mean and fretful martyrs of ourselves. If one *will* be unhappy, if bitter is craved by the palate, there is no need for remedy.

Many real troubles there are which will cease the moment our heart accepts them and submits itself to them as a part of a Divine Providence. For many, many troubles are but the strain which we endure when God would carry us the right way, and we insist upon going the wrong! When two walk arm in arm, if one would turn and the other would not, either they must pull diversely or else must separate. But God never lets go his children's arms, and if they struggle and hold back, they are dragged. Let them submit to be led, nor struggle, nor hold back. In that instant the trouble goes.

This is specially true of all troubles which involve loss of property and worldly comfort, as though they were necessary to happiness, when myriads live most happily without them.

Many of our troubles are instantly cured by holding them up in the light of God's countenance. They arise from seeing things in a false light, or from seeing things in the half-light of this world. When they are surveyed in the great sphere and in the light of heaven, they dissolve like snow-flakes.

This is the reason of the experience of many Christians. They go under a cloud, and finally, pressed and burdened they go to prayer, and rising into the presence of God, filled with hope and cheer, when they begin to think of their petition, it is gone. The air of heaven has health in it. There is peace in the very presence of God. They that touch the hem of his garment are often as much healed as those whom he takes by the hand!

The same is true of music; a little hymn, child-warbled, has sometimes done more for a man in one moment than all his own philosophy, his strivings, and his labor! For a hymn is like the touch given to the servant's eyes by the prophet. It opens the air, and it is full of God's messengers.

There be troubles that may be worn out. A patient endurance will destroy them. Like tides, they cannot be checked nor resisted when rising. But, like tides, if patiently waited upon, they will turn and flow out of themselves!

Nay, rather let me say that they are inundations of freshets. When God means mercy to the seasons, he sends clouds to the mountains. From their bosom all the mountain-springs nurse, and are full.

But when from the fullness of the rain the streams swell, and branch adds to branch its tribute, the over-swollen river spreads wide over all the neighboring meadows. Trees wade deep; bushes, half-hidden, seem cut in twain, and the earth is lost. But with a few days the stream sucks back its waters and drives them out to the sea. Now see the drenched earth all aslime. Mud, mud, mud! But go again in two months and see the children of the mud—grass that waves its little forest—flowers that carry heaven in their bosom—corn and grain that exult in richness and vigor. Troubles come to us like mire and filth. But, when mingled with the soil, they change to flower and fruit.

PHASES OF THE TIMES.

THE art of being happy is less cultivated in this land than in almost any other. We make extravagant preparations for it; we give no bounds to our enterprise; we heap up material; we go through an immense experience preparatory to being happy. But, in the main, it is the very thing which we forget to extract from an abundant preparation. Contentment is a quality which few know how to reconcile with aspiration, and still less with enterprise. Satisfaction, therefore, is the bright ideal of the future. It never blossoms to-day. It is always for to-morrow. Men never come up with their hope. The short and intense excitements which we misname enjoyment are paroxysms, not steady pulsations. At length it comes to pass that men do not enjoy life in the midst of heaped-up prosperity. And amid reverses they bemoan themselves when the topmost leaves of the banyan tree are plucked by the wind, and refuse to shelter themselves beneath the vast breadth of what remains.

The whole land stands in surprise and complaint at a sudden and violent revolution. Our disasters are in every mouth. The change of circumstances is the fertile theme. A little while ago and we could see nothing but brightness, and now nothing but darkness. Then it was noon all the while; now it is midnight. In neither case was there balance and just judgment. The light was too bright then, and the darkness is too dense now. It becomes us to estimate—to sit down and put one thing over against another, and to frame a judgment upon a view of all sides of our case.

There are undoubted evidences of the advance of the world in true civilization. Within the last ten years the most extraordinary wars and civil revolutions have taken place on the globe. Once such a combination and movement as we have but lately beheld, would have affected the whole globe with terror. Since the French Emperor put his bloody foot upon the steps of the throne, there have been set on foot the most wide-spread combinations of governments, the most prodigious armies and navies, such as turn the historic Armada into a mere affair of yachts. Once the globe would have trembled to the footsteps of such an unparalleled war! So much did the spirit of the past dwell in military things, that, a hundred or two hundred years ago, such a history would have drawn with it the world's nerve and blood and vitality. But now all western Europe rose up and the world did not tremble. All Russia gathered together and the Orient did not feel it. And the pounding of war in that gigantic conflict disturbed the world as little as a thresher's flail upon the barn-floor disturbs the earth beneath it. Not even the nations that carried such battle in their hands thought it heavy. Great Britain took but her left hand. Not a wheel stopped in her manufactories. Not an acre the less was tilled in France; and the world upon this side read the account simply as news. It produced no more effect than the last serial story that drags its long and tedious tail through the cheap and stupid magazines.

But now, upon these western shores, over-eager capitalists and operators have pushed their trade too far and built their plans too fast. A bank explodes in Ohio; then a line of banks gives way in Pennsylvania. This shook the continent more than all the cannonade of Sevastopol. Next, the banks of New York suspended. All business stopped. Society was tremulous from top to bottom! The tidings are borne across the ocean. That wonderful island, whose top is narrow, but whose base is broad as the whole earth, began to quiver, and that silent panic brought her down quicker than an axe brings down the ox. War could not make her plumes to quiver; but Commerce, by a look, cast her upon the ground. And it stands apparent to the world by the grandest demonstration, that in valid influence Commerce has supplanted War, and is its master. The general's sword, the marshal's truncheon, the king's crown, are no longer the strongest things. The world's strength lies in the million hands of producers and exchangers. Power has shifted. No matter who reigns—the merchant reigns. No matter what the form of government is, the power of the world is in the hands of the people. The king's hand is weaker than the banker's. War cannot convulse the world, but Capital can.

This should not be mentioned as if it were an unmixed good. It has its own mischiefs, for every event grows in a husk, which at first proserves and then cumbers the grain; and commerce has its dangers and tyrannies; but it marks the direction the world is pursuing, and the progress of the march. The growth which is everywhere to be witnessed is away from dynasties, from imperious governments, and towards the great masses of men. This is one of the signs of the times which wise men are able to discern in the present crisis. It is true, a man that was rich yesterday, but is bankrupt to-day, may not find consolation in being told that his facile destruction was one of the straws which show which way the wind blows; but, notwithstanding, it does show it; and though we are sorry for the immediate sufferers, we do not think it needful to refuse some alleviation.

The conditions of growth in our age and nation are unlike those of past times, and are not to be measured by them. Germany, France, Great Britain, began in a barbarous state, and through centuries developed their civilization. Their growth was slow; their wants did not require any ingenuity or skill for supply. Slowness gives nations a chance to be steady. Our nation had no interior infancy. Our fathers were ripe men, for their age. Society in America has begun, at the beginning, with all the wants which, abroad, came gradually through centuries.

The inevitable result of such condition was twofold: Now to give an extraordinary impulse to our people in industrial directions; and to oblige them to devise every possible means of operating. With no accumulated capital, with no past behind us, that had builded towns, roads, and structures for us—we yet had the same tastes, the same intellectual wants, the same scale of social life, the same or higher domestic needs that older nations had. It was impossible that men who were under such conditions—a quick, enterprising, industrious, ambitious people—should not be powerfully influenced, and that in the earlier stages of national life the propelling power should not be in excess, and the consolidating and steadying power relatively deficient. Never was there a people truer to their circumstances. Had they tried to live in the past they would have been like a plant trying to grow away from the light. God put their life in their future. They pressed towards it. Even the present was but one broad step, by which to go further towards the future. And all the developments among us have been those which were necessary—in the imperfect way in which the world always grows—to this answering of our people to their true nature!

The central faculty which warms, incites, and intensely influences the American mind, is hope. And while we are served and blessed by this power we must take it, with all its limitations and evils. Hope tempered a little, and judiciously combined, works out full and fruitful enterprises, and gives light and pleasure to industry. But this feeling is subject to various conditions and diseases. Gambling, in the worst sense, is nothing but the last and worst development of diseased hope. The distance and difference between the mild beginning and the terrific end of this action is immense. The risks and ventures of the stock market is another source. The element of speculation is derived from the same feeling. Hence nationally, and as a fact of our race, Hope is large. Past and present circumstances have powerfully developed and inspired it. It has given to us in our circumstances, a character of adventurousness not only, but a great part of our material prosperity has arisen from this very thing.

To construct thirty or forty thousand miles of railroad in twenty-five years could never have been done by merely prudent men. There seems an overruling element in affairs that provides tendencies to fit the exigency. If our border men were not rude, coarse, hard—nature and circumstances would be too much for them. Even when cut off they are less a loss. Living or dying they seem fitted to their place and work. And so in early periods of commercial development there is need of pioneers. Men who have nothing to lose and everything to gain in venturesome enterprises, must take the lead. We are fortunate in having such. We owe to them an immense obligation. It is the ruined men of the community who make the prosperous men. They went before. They ventured as no others would have done. They foresaw, or thought they did. They had that mind element which made it as easy for them to do this, as it would have been hard for others.

Even in the mutations and upsettings of this class of men there is to be observed a wisdom of affairs. It does not hurt a sanguine man, full of spring and hope, to be destroyed. Some men are like some of the earlier forms of worms; cutting them in pieces only multiplies them. Every fragment gathers up a head, and finishes out a new tail, and moves along. You may turn a life-boat over and it will right again; but it would not do to upset a frigate or line-of-battle-ship. Many men in New York get so used to failures that they expect them as much as ten-pins expect to be tripped up; it is part of the game. If they do not expect it, their neighbors do.

When a community is moving under such influence and pressure, there is neither legislation, nor experience, nor any other regulating power, that can prevent gradual and increasing tendency to excess. Some men will live too fast. Some will venture too far. Gradually, competitions and strivings in a large and free acting community will engender heat. Heat will carry people further than they have calculated; it will tend to develop that most powerful element—credit, which carries in its right hand blessings, and in its left curses, but ten blessings to one curse. In varying periods, ten, fifteen, and twenty years, according to circumstances, men will have ventured so far along, that a reckoning day will come. And such crises are but that relief which the great system needs. It is but a fever, arising from the reaction of nature—the throwing off of morbid matter.

In this process, sufferings of pride, honor, and even personal and bodily, tend to keep men's faces too close to their affairs to let them see the benefit of the whole operation. One would think by the exclamations of ruin, disaster, dismay, that crises are deadly! Almost the whole evil rests upon individuals, without inflicting any considerable damage upon society. And even that which falls upon individuals is temporary, and compensated by collateral benefits, which, upon the whole, in a large way of judging, are beneficial.

It should be borne in mind, and thought of with thankfulness, that although a heavy pecuniary pressure has been resting on the community, the great incalculable mercy of health, the land throughout, was never more eminent than now; that abundance for man's sustenance was never greater, and for the general national want never so available; that it is only particular points that suffer; that the average virtue, intelligence, and progress of the masses is onward, and not backward; that we are not tangled or wasted by foreign wars; that our great national struggles are pointing towards victory; that free labor was never so strong as now; and that discussion never was so free, so thorough, and so satisfactory.

It should be borne in mind, also, that with this crisis nothing perishes. No ships will rot, as under embargo; stores will not fall down; not a wheel will rust, but only rest; the railroads whose creation has cost us so much, are created, and will not go back, but thunder on. Not an acre will go again to forest; not a seed will rot. We shall hold all the substantial elements gained, losing no art, no science, no ideas, no habits, no skill, no industry, nothing but a little temporary comfort; and for that we shall receive back steadiness, safety, reality, and consolidation, worth a thousand fold.

THE FULLNESS OF GOD.

Many passages of the Scripture are like hundreds of wayside flowers, which for months and years are unnoticed by us, simply because we have been accustomed from our childhood to see them without stooping to pluck or to examine them. Many of the homeliest flowers would appear transcendently beautiful if we would take the trouble to study them minutely, to magnify their parts, and to bring out their constituent elements. And so, we were taught to read the Bible so early, in the family and in the village school, and we have so often and often walked along the chapters, that we have beaten a dusty path in them, and some of their most precious and beautiful things are neither precious nor beautiful to us, simply because we look *at* them and not *into* them. Many parts of the Bible may be compared to those exquisite creations of art which are sometimes found in old cathedrals; they have collected dust and grime and weather-stains, that hundreds of persons go past them every day, never cleansing them, never restoring feature nor color, nor bringing out the artist's embodied thought, so that they are quite unconscious, till they see them restored in the picture of some book, or till some enthusiastic Ruskin brings them out, and teaches us how beautiful are the things that we have slighted as uncomely. So the Scriptures are often overlaid, and, frequently, some of the passages that really are the most resplendent are those which seem only common and ordinary.

Just such a passage is to be found in the third chapter of the Ephesians, in which Paul says: "For this cause I bow my knees unto the Father of our Lord Jesus Christ, of whom the whole family in heaven and earth is named, that he would grant you, according to the riches of his glory, to be strengthened with might by His Spirit in the inner man; that Christ may dwell in your hearts by faith; that ye, being rooted and grounded in love, may be able to comprehend with all saints what is the breadth, and length, and depth, and height; and to know the love of Christ, which passeth knowledge, that ye might be filled with all the fullness of God." What a passage is this! But this is not all. This is a prayer; and the apostle having made a prayer which few men can climb, takes a still higher flight, and says: "Now unto Him that is able to do exceeding abundantly above all that we ask or think, according to the power that worketh in us, unto Him be glory in the church by Christ Jesus throughout all ages, world without end. Amen."

These words are, throughout, a sublime strain against despondency. Paul was in prison. "For this cause," the chapter begins, "I, Paul the prisoner." His design was to present such a view of the fullness of God's heart, and of the grandeur of his administration, as should be an offset against any possible weakness, disaster, overthrow, or trouble in life, to Christians both as individuals and as churches.

It is a presentation of God in such a light as shall enkindle praise. "Now unto Him"—the very words indicate the mood of devout ascription. He would excite joy and adoration in view of God's royal generosity and large-heartedness. The Divine generosity is measured not only by our wants, but by our thoughts and desires above our wants, and it equals and transcends both. He is "able to do exceeding abundantly above all that we ask or think."

The word "abundance" expresses the idea of more than enough. "Enough" is a measuring word. It is the complete filling of a given measure. It satisfies the demand. It just equals the want. But "abundance" is something over and above. It is "enough and to spare." A handful of berries or dried fruits given to a pilgrim who is ready to perish of hunger, might be enough to stay his strength and satisfy his appetite; but if instead of this, the kind heart of sympathy should throw open the garden-gate and the orchard, and say to him, "Go in, pluck and eat," even when the lively appetite had sated itself upon the nearest fruits, there would still be on every bush and bough, in hundreds of rows and ranks, throughout the garden and the orchard, multitudes of kinds and the utmost abundance in quantity, of sweet and delicious fruits, which he could not begin to eat nor even to taste. In the one case he would have simply "enough," in the other "abundance."

Saith the armorer, "I will not be wasteful," and he uses steel with an economic eye in forging the blade, and the smith measures his iron for each purpose. So he that pays a debt at the bank lays down the exact amount to a penny, but no more. The apothecary takes the physician's prescription, and weighing it out allows himself no generosity in measuring the ingredients of the medicine, but puts it up by drachms and scruples with rigid exactitude. So God does not measure in creating, or in sustaining, or in administering. On the other hand, the thought of God which the apostle conveys is that of a being of magnificent richness, who does everything in overmeasure. The whole divine character and administration, the whole conception of God set forth in the Bible and in nature, is of a being of magnificence and munificence, of abundance and superabundance. Did you ever take the trouble to look at a lazy bank that bears nothing for itself? It has no trees growing out of it for grateful shade, and no vines with cooling clusters, and no grass which herds may browse upon, and no flowers that lap over it, and yet the hair of ten thousand reeds will be combed upon its brow, and it will be spotted and patched with moss, of ten thousand patterns of exquisite beauty, so that any artist who, in all his life, should produce one such thing, would make himself a master-spirit in art, and immortal in fame. God's least thought in the barrenest places of nature is more prolific than man's greatest abundance. God is a being of great thoughts, great feelings, great actions. Whenever he does anything, he never does it narrowly, certainly not meanly. He never cuts out such a pattern, and then works up to it with even edge. He is a royal Creator, who says to the earth, "Let it swarm abundantly," and to the sea, "Let it be endlessly filled." He touches the sand of the shore, and it stands forth as a representative of the abundance of his thought. He spreads out the heavens, and no man can count the fiery stars. He orders the seasons, and they all speak in their endless procession of this one thought of God—His everlasting abundance!

But "abundance" is a relative word. What is abundance for a wayfarer is not abundance for a shepherd. What was abundant for a nomad, a wandering shepherd, would not be for a settled farmer, with crops and stock, with barns and houses. But what is abundant for a farmer, would not be for a merchant; and what is abundant for a merchant would be very sparse and scant for a prince; and even among princes there is great difference of degree. The abundance of a petty German prince would be poverty for the court of the royal Czar. Now put the word, with its relative and increased significance, upon God. Divine abundance! The fullness of God! It is not in the power of man to conceive it! If God might be supposed to have worked narrowly anywhere it would be on the earth, his footstool. But the earth is infinitely full of God's thought. And yet, great as the earth is, absolutely it is relatively little, and all symbols and figures drawn from earthly things stop this side of the divine idea of abundance.

But the apostle says, "Now unto him that is able to do *exceeding* abundantly." What a vision he must have had! How grandly in that moment did the divine thought rise before his enrapt mind, when he so linked words together, seeking by combinations to express what no one word had the power to flash forth. He could not by the mightiest single word express his own thought and feeling, and so he joined golden word with golden word, as if he fain would encompass it with a chain!

But Paul employs a measure of comparison even over and above all this, "above all that we can ask or think." That is, above the measure of all human aspirations. How much can a man ask or think? When the deepest convictions of sin are upon him, in his hour of deep despondency, in critical and trying circumstances, when fears come upon his soul as storms came on the lake of Galilee, consider how much a man would then ask, and how much more think! Or, when love swells every vein in his soul, and makes life as full as mountains make the streams in spring-time, and hope is the sun by day and the moon by night, in those gloriously elate hours in which he seems no longer fixed to space and time, but, springing as if the body were forgotten by the soul, wings his way through the realms of aspiration and conception, consider how much a man then *thinks!*

All books are dry and tame compared with that great unwritten book prayed in the closet. The prayers of exiles! The prayers of martyrs! The prayers of missionaries! The prayers of the Waldenses! The prayers of the Albigenses! The prayers of the Covenanters! The sighs, the groans, the inarticulate cries of suffering men, whom tyrants have buried alive in dungeons—whom the world may forget, but God never! If some angel, catching them as they were uttered, should drop them down from heaven, what a liturgy they would make! Can any epic equal those unwritten words that pour into the ear of God out of the heart's fullness!

Still more, what epic can equal the unspoken words, that never find the lip, but go up to heaven in unutterable longings and aspirations! Words are but the bannerets of a great army; thoughts are the main body of the footmen. Words show here and there a little gleam in the air, but the great multitude of thoughts march unseen below. Words cannot follow aspiration even in its tamer flights; still less when it takes wings and flies upward, borne by the breath of God's holy spirit. I see the gulls from my window day by day, making circuits against the north wind. They mount up above the masts of vessels in the stream, and then suddenly drop almost to the water's edge, flying first in one direction and then in another, that they may find some eddy unobstructed by that steady blowing blast, until they turn finally with the wind, and then like a gleam of light their white wings flash down the bay faster than any eye can follow them! So when men's aspirations are borne by some divine wind towards heaven, they take swift upward flight, and no words can follow them!

Consider what a soul thinks in yearnings for itself, and in yearnings even more for others; what a saint thinks in hours of vision and aspiration, when he reflects how all his life long, through good report and through evil report, through manifold trials of temper, of mind, of feeling in his family and out, the hand of God has led him every day, and his cup has been filled to overflowing; consider what a dying man thinks in view of death and of judgment and immortality awaiting him beyond the grave! What wonderful thoughts! What wonderful feelings! And yet the apostle's measurement is more than all these, for he says: "Now unto him that is able to do exceeding abundantly above all that we ask or think!" How true it is that God's riches are unsearchable!

This is the idea of God toward which men ought always to repent. It is sometimes supposed that repentance is drudgery. It is drudgery in a mean man, but in no one else. There is a kind of mean repentance that needs to be repented of. But when a child knows that his misconduct has really hurt a loving parent, the child is more pained than the parent. When a noble spirit has done wrong to a friend, through some misunderstanding that has sprung up between them, such a man *demands* the liberty of restoring himself more than the other demands that he shall restore himself. When we have injured a friend, it is our privilege to make it good. It is necessary to our thought of manhood that we should repair a wrong done. How much more when we have wronged Christ, our elder brother, our redeemer, our friend, our joy, and our comfort, should we make haste to repent—not as a duty, but as a sweet privilege; not with the thought that our repentance is a necessity made so by him, but made necessary by our own honor and conscience. To sit down in a corner, and to cry so much, and to feel so bad, and to mourn so long, is not repentance. True repentance springs out of the most generous feelings of a Christian heart. It is a man's better nature triumphing over his lower and meaner. A Christian should never say, "I must repent," but "Let me repent." It is the goodness of God that should lead us to repentance, not his justice and his terrors. Many persons suppose that God sits on the throne of the heavens as storm-clouds that float in summer skies, full of bolts and lightnings; and they are either repelled, or they think they must come to him under the covert of some excuse. But repentance ought to lead us to God as toward light, toward summer, toward heaven made glorious with his presence, toward his everlasting goodness. His eye is not dark with vengeance, nor his heart turbulent with wrath, and to repent toward his justice and vindictiveness must be always from a lower motive than toward his generosity and his love.

It is with such a conception of God that Christians should come before him with their wants. It is a glorious comfort that God's love is as infinite as his power. We are all apt to think of his *power* as infinite, and we call him omnipotent; but we too often forget that his *love* also is infinite. It has no end, no measure, no bound. A man's generous feelings are often like the buds at this season of the year—wrapped up in coverings to keep them from the selfishness and coldness of the world. By and by they may burst out and bloom, yet now they are circumscribed. But we do not have in ourselves the measure of the love of God. How base it is, then, when we have some gift to ask of him, to go with shrinking confidence and with piteous look, as though there were need of importunity. Is it possible, if with men "it is more blessed to give than to receive," that it is not infinitely more with God? To a true Christian heart, next to the pain of being unable to do for those who are in want, is the pleasure of being approached by them, when we have it in our power to help them. Is it not the same, and in an infinitely higher degree with God? The happiest being in the universe is God, because he has an infinite desire of benevolence, and infinite means of gratifying it. There is with him no limitation, either of heart or hand.

Such a view of God, habitually taken, will deliver us from unworthy fears, and will inspire in us great boldness of approach, and access with confidence, unto the throne of his grace. It will tend to comfort Christians who are in despondency respecting their rectitude through life, their victory in death, and their glorification in heaven; for these things are thus made to stand, not in a Christian's feeble desire for them, but on God's infinite desire and abundant grace. When stars, first created, start forth upon their vast circuits, not knowing their way, if they were conscious and sentient, they might feel hopeless of maintaining their revolutions and orbits, and might despair in the face of coming ages! But, without hands or arms, the sun holds them! Without cords or bands, the Solar King drives them unharnessed on their mighty rounds without a single mis-step, and will bring them in the end to their bound, without a single wanderer. But the sun is but a thing, itself driven and held; and shall not He, who created the heavens, and appointed all the stars to their places, and gave the sun his power, be able to hold you by the attraction of his heart, the strength of his hands, and the omnipotence of his affectionate will?

It is this view of God that the Apostles taught. We read it on every page of Paul and Peter and James and John—everywhere in the New Testament. What was the beginning? "Peace on earth, good-will to men!" And what was the last word that was heard ringing through the air before the message was sealed, and the vision failed? "The spirit and the bride say, Come; let him that heareth say, Come; let him that is athirst, Come; and whosoever will, let him come and take of the water of life freely." WHOSOEVER WILL! That is the alpha and the omega! That is the beginning and the ending! That is the offer; that is the promise. And what shall be the response of every Christian heart, if it be not those final and sublimest words of the great Revelator, "Even so, Lord Jesus, Come quickly?"

CHRIST IN YOU, THE HOPE OF GLORY.

In journeying through a hilly country we are often able to see only the objects close at hand, the windings of the road, the ravines, or the forest-covered portions of the path, hiding the connection of one part with another. Now and then we come to an open summit lifted up as a watch-tower over all the region, and the whole scene breaks upon the eye at one view. The separate steps which we made are invisible; the particular dells and hills are now but lights and shadows of a great whole which fills the eye.

It is thus that we journey through life, occupied with single hours and single days; with successive individual labors and cares; we rise over the summits of individual successes or joys, and are chilled in the intervals of trouble and sorrow. But now and then, there is some experience, whose nature it is to lift man up above all his daily round, and to flash forth to his conception the whole past of his life, the whole prospect of it. Yesterday, in his counting-room or shop, question of life to come and immortality seemed so unreal as to suggest a painful doubt of their reality, and the themes of religion, exhaling like dews, from all tangible things, seemed to hang so high in the air of meditation as to be but vanishing films—the merest fleece of vapor. But to-morrow, God's providence strikes down upon him, no matter by what implement, and he finds himself lifted up out of the drudging and insensitive habits of business, his prospect widened, and his soul made keenly cognizant of spiritual truth. Then the honors of life dissolve before him; his own ambitions seem dream-like; the domineering cares that had bent his back, and wrung out his best services, are, to his thinking, like the summer dust which the whirling wheels roll up in the highways. Then, the truths of God, of the soul's truest good, of the connection of life and after-life; of the nobleness of Justice, Truth, Purity, and Love; of the reality of a Divine Providence, and the *sense* of God's presence, as of one who listens, and observes, and influences the heart,—sink down from the recesses far up, where they had hidden, and invisible things, relations, conceptional truths become more real to him than things which have physical substance and activity palpable to the senses.

That tidings of death, or sudden losses, or the disclosure of disease in oneself, should give such projection to the mind, we can well understand. But how shall we account for such intense recognitions of spiritual truth and such wide prospects of things at other times hidden, or seen in detail, and disconnectedly, and so, unimpressively, when there is no exciting cause—no shock that electrifies the nerves, and arouses the mind to a state of exaltation? Thus one takes up some common sewer of news, and stepping over the avidity of the editorial columns—full of only flying dust—he carelessly scans the jumble of advertisements—dogs, clothes, medicines, estrays, runaway apprentices, losses and findings, meat and drink; and besides these, the ten thousand signals of quackery in every profession, the bland hints of vice for decent vicious men, and all the boastings, the promises and lures—and while he divinely sees this phantasmagoria and is half Christianly chiding himself for such a bitter contempt of life, and such a wish to be well rid of it, all at once, unbidden, without gradual transition, and with the clearness of a vision, there stands up before him a conception of the whole human family, just as they must appear to God, a vast complexity of interlaced and writhing, struggling worms! And such an intense sense of sorrow, such a pity as almost suffocates the soul!

Then, quicker than a flash over all this abyssmal darkness, in which pride, and selfishness, and lust, and cruelty, shine and make dismal outcry, there rises up a sense of God's inexpressible patience, and a foreshadowing to the soul of some great consummation of which we have as yet not even a hint; and the heart rolls all its sadness and evils away, and clears itself of the horror of distresses, as the summer vault cleanses itself of storms, and changes all dark vapors into transparent ether. Just then the boat touches the slip, you have crossed the ferry; and these thoughts, like birds that had sung in the boughs of a tree, arise out of your mind with a clap of their wings, and are gone away. You, too, rush to the bow of the boat as if there were fire behind you, and join the throng that rattle gaily homeward.

A few moments' walk clears you of the crowd, and remembering the flavor of your meditations, you put yourself into mood for them once more. Now you try to fly up again. Not a whit of it! You stretch out your thought to take the compass of life—in vain! You reach up to find those calm regions of repose where the soul rests itself as in the garden of God—they are all hidden. You implore the majesty of Divine Presence to overshadow you again, but there is no voice to your spirit, and none that answereth. Why should such a vision have had its birth from the contents of a newspaper? Why, when intermitted, cannot the will evoke them again? Do they come without willing, and refuse to come at the will's bidding?

Can any one tell why one sometimes awakens in the morning, and finds his mind harnessed from the first moment, and ready to dart off in some special direction? Why, sometimes, is there such a sense of the wickedness of oppression and injustice, such a conception of the facts of life—the strong consuming the weak, the skillful, the wise, the refined, only armed by their excellence with the means of injury to their fellows; coupled with such a grief and indignation as shakes the very soul, and makes it resound, as old castles howl to the roar of intrusive tempests?

At another time it is a distress of love. Were all that is in heaven or upon earth ours, it would not be enough to express the soul's desire of blessing all that can feel a blessing. We would ask no other joy than to put a brighter light in every eye, a sweeter hope and truer joy in every heart. That should be our everlasting reward at the hands of God, to distribute his mercies to others. Suddenly, out of this sense of the beauty, and nobleness, and joy of blessing others, there arises the stateliest thought of God, and a conception of His bliss, with such a heart of love, and such a hand of power, and with such a field, and all marching in glorious procession on—on—and forever—that the soul has a certain faintness, from very joy.

If these states arose from the presence of objects or events which naturally led to such reflections, or if they arose from any principle of reaction, or as the contrast and antithesis of any reverse actions, we should ascribe them to such influences. But often they defy both explanations. They come in season and out of season; in high health, and in depression of vital power; in solitude, and in the roar of the city; in moods that are sad, and in moods that are merry and mirthful. They are capricious as regards one's own will.

Is it only a normal activity of the soul, in a higher range, for whose solution we simply lack familiar knowledge of ourselves? Is it the potent suggestions of ministering spirits? Is it not rather God's own Spirit inflaming ours, and unsealing the soul to influences quite impossible to it, by any suggestions or volitions of its own? It surely seems to us that the promises of Christ, that He will dwell within us, that He will give us a Comforter, an Enlightener, might reasonably be expected to produce other and higher fruits than those which spring from the force of our own volition. And if such thoughts and such emotions, setting always toward God, toward Justice, toward Love, full of Hope, and Trust, and Heaven, are the things of God's Spirit, unsphering us from sensuous life, and giving us a prescience of life to come, then there is a glorious meaning in the promises of Christ. Thus we understand how He manifests himself to his disciples as he doth not to the world.

PRAYER-MEETINGS.

An unknown friend in New Jersey has written us a sincere request for a form of prayer suitable for a prayer-meeting. We should be glad to oblige him, if we thought such a form would be of any use. But a form is not what he needs. A form may do for a congregation, where it is understood that prayer is to comprehend only the wants that are general and common to all. But it seems to us that forms would destroy the very conception of a social meeting for prayer.

What is a prayer-meeting? It is a place for social religious life. It is not for preaching. It is not for exhortation. It is the place where Christian men excite each other, and instruct and strengthen each other, by the free and familiar development of their religious emotions. Every Christian brings a brand, each places it upon the altar, and the fire is the joint flame of many hearts. What would be thought of an application for a form of conversation for a Christmas-night's party? A form of bargain for doing general business on 'Change? For a form of impassioned utterance, for the use of loving hearts? A form of family greeting, to be used in vacations when the children come home? But forms would be every whit as sensible in such circumstances as in a social gathering of Christians for religious conference.

The very secret of conducting prayer-meetings, is

to force people out of their conventional ways; to break up their hereditary forms of unwritten prayer; to inspire a genial and devout familiarity; to keep off those impertinent moths called exhorters, that fly about the flame of rising feeling; to charm men into a forgetfulness, if possible, that it is a meeting, and make them talk artlessly and sensibly.

The very first step towards a wholesome meeting is *truth*. Truth is that which prayer-meetings, in numberless instances, lack. Christians go to them, assuming the sense of awful responsibility, or else trying to appear solemn; or else trying to manifest a devout spirit. But in truth, a man should go to a meeting feeling just as he does feel; and not pretending to anything else, simply because he thinks he ought to feel something else. This pretentious mood, this artificial and clumsily hutched up feeling, overlays the mind as straw and dead leaves do the soil, that nothing can shoot up.

What if men should go to parties carrying, not each one his own nature and disposition, but, one striving to be brilliant, another to be witty, another to be instructive; who could endure the sham? We need to have men willing to stand simply and only on what they are and what they have. The speaking in prayer-meetings should be conversational, and so, natural. Usually, when a man has nothing to say, he gets up and exhorts sinners to repent. Another empty soul informs the church that they are very cold, and live far beneath their privileges. When such men pray, they usually begin at Adam and go on to Revelations:

and then, sometimes, unable to stop, go back and strike in about midway, and back out both ways, through all manner of religious platitudes.

How many prayer-meetings begin a long half hour after the time appointed? First comes a hymn, then a chapter in the Bible, then the deacon prays, then a hymn; and so on, a hymn and a deacon, until the list of officers is exhausted. The pastor laments that there are few men, besides those whose ordination obliges them to pray, that take part in meetings. But why are there no more? What has been done to increase the number of praying members? Have they been encouraged to do what they could do? Or is the spirit of the church such, that no man prays to edification, who does not pray smoothly and ornately, or with a round, sonorous, guttural solemnity.

Humble prayers, timid prayers, half-inaudible prayers, the utterances of uncultured lips, may cut a poor figure, as lecture-room literature. But are they to be scornfully disdained? If a child may not talk at all till it can speak fluent English, will it ever learn to speak well? There should be a process of education going on continually, by which all the members of the church shall be able to contribute of their experiences and gifts; and in such a course of development, the first hesitating, stumbling, ungrammatical prayer of a confused Christian may be worth more to the church than the best prayer of the most eloquent pastor. The prayer may be but little; but it is not a little thing that a church has one man more to pray than it had before.

In order to this, pastors, or whoever conducts the

prayer-meeting statedly, should have a distinct conception of what a prayer-meeting is to do. It is a mutual instruction class; a place for religious feeling to develop itself through the social element; and the conductor of the meeting is to draw out the timid, check the obtrusive, encourage simple and true speaking, and apply religious truths to those wants, and struggles, and experiences which are freely mentioned there.

A few hints, gathered from experience, will be, perhaps, of some benefit to those who are young, and beginning to assume the duties of pastor.

There is no meeting for which one needs more preparation than a prayer-meeting. But it is not a preparation of thoughts, ideas, and topics, so much as of the spirit and of the soul. One should save his strength; come to the meeting with vigor and fullness of feeling, and already eager when he first sits down.

The way in which a meeting opens will often determine its whole character. If the brethren are scattered through a large room, bring them closer together. Slow and long services at the beginning increase the sluggishness which too often is brought in. A short hymn, adapted to move the feelings, sung quickly—so quickly that every one has to arouse himself to keep up—will frequently give life to the whole scene.

A church should be trained to courage. They should be thoroughly indoctrinated not to despise the gifts of the meanest member.

When there is piety in a church, and the prayer-meeting becomes the exponent of it, then it will become the most powerful and important meeting in the whole series of church meetings. A fair account, from grateful lips, of what God is doing in the hearts of a whole church, cannot but be better than the ideas of any one man, uttered from the pulpit, speak he ever so wisely.

But if our friend still wants a form of prayer, for a prayer-meeting, we must refer him to numerous churches, where forms of prayer have prevailed for uncounted years, although they are called extemporaneous; and, if he have some skill at stenography, he can soon supply himself with a book of forms of prayer.

ONE CAUSE OF DULL MEETINGS.

WE hardly know of a more unprofitable exercise in social religious meetings than what is called exhortation. Doubtless there is a scriptural warrant for exhortation. But what is the nature of the exercise? It is the persuasion of a man to accept or obey some view of truth. The force of it depends upon the force given to the *truth*. It must needs relate principally to *conduct*. If one desires to produce intellectual convictions, the way is not to exhort to them, but to present truths which of their own nature will convict. If one desires to enkindle feeling it is folly to exhort to it; for feeling arises from the view of truth, and he who wishes to thrill the feelings must employ the truths which have a power to do it: or he must impart it by sympathy, being himself full of emotion; or what is better, and the true method, he must present the right truth from a soul already glowing with the feeling which it is sought to enkindle.

Therefore, when a brother arises in a prayer and conference meeting, unmoved himself, and exhorts men to repent, without presenting powerful motives through such views of its necessity as shall incline them to it, and without any exhibition of a deeply penitential feeling in himself, he throws away his efforts, and sometimes does harm rather than good. We have heard man after man in succession arise and exhort Christian brethren with such a deadening effect that if there was a spark alive at first, it was quenched past all rekindling before the exhortation was done. During many a long, dry, sound, sober exhortation which has been inflicted upon long-suffering meetings, we have seen men exhorted into sleep, and exhorted into helpless stupidity, into yawning, and weariness; and there would be but a single truth that seemed to touch a genuine chord of feeling during the whole meeting, and that was the truth that it was time to close the meeting. A dull, unmeaning, religious meeting is simply an abomination. If a husband and wife should get together, once a week, and without a particle of feeling or earnestness, go through with an hour of affectionate etiquette, it would be regarded as a supreme absurdity. If business men should gather together once or twice a week in grave consideration of things which no one of them at the time cared anything about, and talk them over on this side and on that, each one forgetting at the door what he, and what his neighbor had said, men would say that they were fools.

Such things are seldom or never done in things in which men are alive. But for months and months together, men will gather, without a ray of warmth, without any real earnestness, and talk in a drowsy and prosing manner about the most startling truths that were ever addressed to the human knowledge, in such a lifeless method that not a single thought moved responsive, and not a single emotion throbbed!

Let us imagine a man suffering the deepest afflic

tions and pressed by trouble beyond all ordinary power of endurance standing up among a score of friends in like afflictions, and saying in a gentle voice, whose tones were mellowed by the deepest emotions, "Dear friends, the hand of God is upon us. Let us not sink. Let patience have a perfect work. We must be tried. Whom the Lord loveth he chasteneth. We are now in the fire, but God is with us. Let us be patient." Every heart would yield to such an exhortation. For conscious troubles would be *the truth*, and an exhortation to patience would have a vital relation to their living wants.

But what if, amidst great abundance, with homes, and friends, and affluence, in times of peace, and when life flowed with music, like a vocal brook between banks of flowers and fringed shrubs, a reasonably good man should commence a scriptural exhortation about patience—its virtues, it necessities, our obligations to exercise it, etc., who would be reached? Perhaps here and there a conscientious soul might reproach itself because it did *not* feel; but feeling, under such unnatural circumstances, is past all conscience-invocation.

In like manner Christians are very composedly told that they are dead and good for nothing; that they are not doing their duty. One man, with a familiar fluency evincing long practice will declare in the soberest and quietest way imaginable that he is a great sinner, and he is conscious of it, and that he feels that he ought to repent, and thinks that the brethren ought to join him in the impression. One man for the fortieth time during the year, exhorts brethren to awake because the night is far spent and the day is at hand. Another thinks that Christians ought to rejoice in God, and without a smile or one heart-swell, sets forth with frigid exactitude the duty of joy, and sits down to hear another brother say the same thing over again, in another set of words, if possible more gloomy than those in which he had enunciated it. In this manner, too, we have heard men, profoundly engrossed in the world, rise up and exhort sinners to repent; to repent before it was too late; to repent now—it was their duty; it was dangerous to put it off, etc., but not a sign of feeling had they. No heart-heaving—no deep and disclosed sense of the hatefulness of sin, none of that softening and gushing which belong to penitence. It is worse than absurd, it is monstrous for men to mouth the most solemn facts, the most profoundly affecting truths of religion, as if they were rolling marbles, or discussing some trifle to while away an hour withal. The ear of a congregation often and often has been beaten hard as a macadamized road by the weekly tramp of exhortation about truth, and to truth, and duty, and what not. Life is the characteristic of God. Life is the characteristic of Religion. Life is the characteristic of Truth. A dull assembly, with lifeless men talking about dead topics, is a scandal upon real religion.

This matter grows even worse, if possible, when one listens to the dissuasives from courses to which the persons addressed have not the remotest liability. Thus a church dead beyond all budding or blossoming, is exhorted to beware of wildfire and fanaticism; a slow-moulded methodical brotherhood, exact as a clock, are exhorted to discretion, to deliberation, and cautioned against impulses. A man of the most incorrigible literalness, whose matter-of-fact soul never had a glimpse of any quality which was not measurable by one of his senses, will descant upon the wiles of the imagination, and warn the young against fancy and fiction. A close-fisted man is in great dread of spendthrift benevolence, and thinks that Christians should always give upon principle and not on feeling. On the other hand we have heard a man of mercurial temperament greatly dreading lest he should be left to a heartless control of his judgment!

Thus men impose upon themselves; and social religious meetings degenerate into absurd formalities. If any one thinks that liturgies and set forms of worship are the only means of dullness and formality, they surely cannot have been much acquainted with prayer-meetings. They cannot have heard the same prayers substantially repeated by the same men, varying only in a growing glibness and dryness, for years and years; they cannot have heard the juiceless, tasetless exhortations about feelings, from persons without feeling to persons without feeling; they cannot have seen the hour and a half of weekly conference run the same dreary round, beginning and ending, with intermediate consistency, without a sign of life, but with an utterly lying semblance, a pretence of caring for what they did not care for; of renouncing what all the world knew they did not renounce; of asking what they did not desire, and desiring what they did not dare to ask.

WORKING OUT OUR OWN SALVATION.

There is a sense in which a man's salvation is not directly and absolutely a divine gift. It is not made over by God to man as a complete thing. A perfect title to a piece of property puts a man in possession of it just as absolutely on the first day when it is given as in twenty years after. When a man gives a flower, it is a perfect gift. But the gift of grace is rather the gift of a flower-seed. It contains within it all the elements necessary for growth, which the sun is yet to warm and develop, until it comes to blossom and fruit. When men are called effectually by the power of God's Spirit, that is purely the office of God, and not of a human power. The calling is of God, and the forgiveness and amnesty are altogether of His free goodness. The efficacious influence of the Spirit upon the heart is God's work, and not man's.

But when this has taken place, and men are awakened and brought into the number of God's children, the work is just begun. There is now to be a development of a Christ-like disposition. There is to be a life within, which is to consist in a development of every part of the mind, so that the whole soul shall be reëducated by spiritual influences. There is to be also a corresponding outward life—a course of Christ-like conduct. Every man is called, and graciously aided by God, that he may take care both of the work which respects his own disposition, and the work which respects his outward conduct. And when the Apostle says, "Work out your own salvation with fear and trembling," it is not meant with servile or painful fear, but fear in the sense of solicitude; fear, in distinction from presumptuous confidence.

But, it is added, "for it is God that worketh in you." Here is the inspiration of man's liberty, and the charter of his hope. Standing in the atmosphere of the divine heart, every one finds that his summer is come. The doctrine is not, that every man must wait till God moves him. It is a command to go forward, with a reason attached. It is an encouragement, not a dissuasion. It is wrong, by the twists of perverse reasoning, to change a divine truth right about, and put its back where God put its face.

Many teachers have made an anchor out of this text, which God spread for a sail, and have, in effect, cautioned people not to move till God attracted them; as if the chief danger of men was too great alertness in matters pertaining to religion.

When God calls men to awake, it is implied that the morning has come. When God says, Plant, it is implied that soil, air, and summer are prepared; and he speaks to April, not to January!

And when God says, Work, it is implied that there are all those conditions of providence and divine overshadowing which make it worth a man's while to work.

But many say, "How can I work if it be God that is to work within me?" Well, if a father, going out into his garden where his child is at work among the flower-beds, should say to him, "Now my son work with a will, I will help you and work with you," what would be thought if the child should suddenly look up and say, "But if you are going to work, how can I work?" Is there anything incongruous or paradoxical in the idea that, though God worketh in us, we also are to work out our own salvation? It is not said that God performs the work, but that he influences us to perform it. It is not, that God works *for*, but *in*, us!

The work of the Spirit is not to supersede, but to help our faculties. It is akin to parental training, to education, to the action and influence of one mind upon another. Not that God's mind acts upon ours, just as ours acts upon others; for we have no warrant for saying this. But the illustration is sufficient to show, that one mind may stimulate another to action without destroying its liberty. The young artist, while he sits under Raphael, or Michael Angelo, or Correggio, does not expect to have his work done by his master. He goes to witness and to catch his master's enthusiasm, that his own eye may be fired and his own hand guided. We bring up our children by the action of our minds upon theirs. Our influence over the child does not take away anything from the child's power, but on the contrary adds to it. And so, God says to us, "Work out your own salvation, for I am working in you." It is like a father saying to his children, "Here am I working among you, adding my experience, my wisdom, and my power to yours; therefore be hopeful and courageous, and enter with zeal upon your work." It is an argument of hope and ardor, and not of waiting and faltering. It is an argument to begin now, and not to delay, with the vain thought that God will finally do all the work and leave us nothing to do.

If it be asked how shall we distinguish divine influence from natural, the reply is, We cannot always do it. There is no intimation in the New Testament that anybody can tell. If a husbandman wishes to know whether he is under the influence of right farming, he must go and look at his harvests. If, therefore, a man says, "How can I tell whether this feeling is of God or of Satan?" he cannot tell by the feeling, but by its results.

It is the same act that plants good or bad seed. It is the same string and bow, whether a scraping beginner or a Paganini play. The music evolved must determine whether a master or a bungler touches the violin. The human faculties, whether acted upon by sinister spirits, by divine influences, or by natural causes, always act within the lines and limits of their own laws and nature. And it is not any difference in sensation or consciousness which can distinguish divine influence from any other. We must abide by Christ's rule of estimate, "By their fruit shall ye know them." Is the fruit good, is there enough of it, is it continuous? It is very certain that a disposition of deep benevolence, a heart of unfeigned love, will lead a man in the right direction, and he need not spend one anxious thought lest the devil should have inspired him with such influence.

On the other hand, conceited and presumptuous men are found, who, assuming that they are under the divine influence and guidance, follow out their own selfish and fleshly lusts, and attribute it all to God. But no man can have any evidence that he is moved by the Spirit of God, except so far as the fruit is divine. There is nothing in mere consciousness, nothing in sensation, nothing in any witness or inward light, nothing in any degree or kind of exhilaration, nothing in the pleasurableness or other quality of the feeling. The moral quality of the life determines whether one is a child of God, or of the Devil.

What, then, is the use of the truth of God's Spirit, if you cannot discern its presence or action? It is good for general hopefulness. It gives men courage to know that they are divinely helped, though they may not perceive the special acts. It is an exorcism to fear and superstition. For it exhibits the world, as illumined and overcome by the gracious presence of God working both in Providence and in grace, and throwing around all who will do well an atmosphere of protection and genial incitement, in which they shall thrive and bring forth abundant fruit.

TRUST IN GOD.

In a true Christian's devout aspirations, it is not from instruction or habit, but from spontaneous impulse that he exclaims "Our Father!" His thoughts go out after God. His heart yearns for him. His soul longs, with unutterable longings for his abiding presence. He comes with a truly filial spirit before God, and it is perfectly easy and natural for him to say "Our Father." And he has a right to say it. He is the child of God, and he knows it; for "the Spirit itself beareth witness with our spirits that we are the children of God." Being the child of his Father, and away from his Father's house, he yearns for it, and at times is homesick—as children that are kept at school away from their parents long for the day of vacation, that they may go home; and these yearnings are the testimony of the Spirit that we are the children of God. The man who has these feelings, and has them habitually, need not hesitate to call himself a child of God, or to address God as "Our Father."

There are some Christians who always seem to have entire and unwavering faith in God as their Father. They trust in him to such a degree as to believe that whatever may be the happenings of Providence, everything will be for the best, and that they will be taken care of, and never left alone.

They are confident in him, and seem never for a moment to doubt. Their cup always runs over, because they always think it runs over. But, on the other hand, there are others who, while they are blessed abundantly, never see or think that they are blessed at all. And this class comprises the multitude of men. They call God "Our Father," only because the Lord's Prayer begins so, and not because their own prayer naturally and spontaneously confesses that they are his children, and that he is their Father. They have doubts and glooms. They have fightings without, and fears within. They allow small things to perplex them, and great things to overwhelm them. They distrust God—not intentionally, but really. They doubt his providence, though they would hardly believe that they doubt. They habitually look on the dark side of things, and excuse themselves for it by saying that they are constitutionally melancholy; whereas, the fault is nothing more nor less than a practical want of faith. It is an unconscious skepticism of God. Men theoretically extol their faith, but practically deny it. They give way before every trouble, instead of conquering it; and in every dark hour flee for refuge, not to God, but to themselves.

Now all Christians, whether hopeful or despondent, are sometimes like the disciples on the Sea of Galilee—driven hither and thither by contrary winds. They toil all the night upon the deep, casting their nets, but taking nothing. Nay, oftentimes, their sea is without a Christ walking upon the water, and their ship without a Christ even asleep. Yet when they desire his coming upon the sea, and cry out to him, they soon see him walking to them over the waves. When they desire his awakening in the ship, they soon see him rising to rebuke the wind, saying, "Peace, be still," until there is a great calm. God hides his face only to disclose it again; and his hidings are oftentimes as full of mercy as his manifested presence. But whether to their feeble-sighted eyes he is present or absent, they may always know that "He is not far from them at any time." When there are clouds so that they cannot see him, they may look at him through faith, and discern that he is not far off. And as they that go down upon the deep, and are overmastered by storms in the darkness of the night, knowing not on what strange shores they may be thrown, cast anchor and wait for day, so in the midst of trial and temptation, when the storm is fierce and the night is dark, when the lights are quenched and the signals gone, they may at least cast anchor; and if they wait in faith and hope for the day, it will surely dawn. The darkness will always hide itself, and the light appear. There never was a night so long that the day did not overtake it. There never was a morning without its morning star. There never was a day without its sun.

God can reveal himself to his own people as he does not to the world. He can give to every Christian heart, to the timid as well as to the strong, to the sorrowing as well as to the hopeful, those divine intimations, those precious thoughts, those sweet-breathed feelings, which are evidence that there is summer in the soul. He can inspire the heart with that perfect love which casteth out fear. He can take away all doubts and misgivings, all gloomy misapprehensions, all dreary forebodings of the future. He can make sunshine out of shadow, and day out of midnight. When our fears have been like growing thorns in our side, he can pluck away the thorns, and heal the wounds; and he can turn every spear which has pierced us into a rod and staff, which, instead of wounding shall support us; so that the very things which once cast us down may be made to hold us up. He can so deal with us as to make every yoke easy, and every burden light; so that the heavy-laden may come to him to be relieved of their loads. He can touch the fountains of our sorrow, and make our tears like gems and crystals, more precious than pearls or diamonds. Our tears are oftentimes among his most precious treasures. The things that we call treasures, he counts as of very little worth. The human soul is his treasury, out of which he coins unspeakable riches. Thoughts and feelings, desires and yearnings, faith and hope—these are the most precious things which God finds in us.

He can do all things for us, whatsoever we need, and more than we need. We are too slow to believe in his generosity. We do not often enough think that as he has infinite desires to help us, so also he has infinite powers. He is able to carry out all that he can ever wish for us. God is not like man. Our means are limited. With us, wishing to possess is far from possessing; wishing to do is far from doing; but with him, the wish and the power are one. His desires are fully equalled by his means. He is "able to do exceeding abundantly above all that we can ask or think." Things that are great to us are small to him. The favors that we ask of him seem to us to be large and royal; yet to him they are very little things. The gifts he has power to bestow are not only greater than we ever ask, but ever can ask, or even think.

He is always willing to give special grace for special emergency. If men are suddenly brought into trouble, He is "a very present help in time of need." When rich men, by some unexpected reverse of fortune, are made poor, he can sustain them under their burdens, when without him they would be utterly crushed. When friends are parted from friends, when families are broken and scattered by death, when the mother loses her child, and weeps because the cradle is no longer to be rocked, and the sweet laugh is hushed in the house, God can give "the oil of joy for mourning." Whenever his children suffer disappointment, when clouds cast shadows over their path, when troubles brood heavily before them, when they are in trials of business or in greater trials of bereavement, he can take off the heavy weights. He can make the rough places smooth, and the crooked ways straight. When sorrow comes that seems to forbid all consolation, he can gently wipe away the tears, and bring back joy and hope once more.

He is a physician who only waits to be called; he is a friend who longs to be trusted; he is a helper who only wants us to ask his aid. But he wants us to ask him heartily and truthfully. He wishes us to reach up our hand, and take covenant by his hand. He desires us to cast our care upon him, for he careth for us. He commands us to confide entirely in him. He wants us to have no hesitancy in our faith.

And this is reasonable. It is what men ask every day of their own children. A father expects his child to confide in him. A child expects to trust freely in his father. And we ought to go to God, being his children, with less distrust and more confidence. We ought to take him at his word, and to have faith in his promises. If he has said, "I will never leave thee nor forsake thee," we ought boldly to say, "The Lord is my helper; I will not fear what man shall do unto me."

But when we borrow trouble, and look forward into the future to see what storms are coming, and distress ourselves before they come as to how we shall avert them if they ever do come, we lose our proper trustfulness in God. When we torment ourselves with imaginary dangers, or trials, or reverses, we have already parted with that perfect love which casteth out fear. Mothers sometimes fret themselves, and are made miserable about the future career of their children—whether they will turn out drunkards or not, whether they will go to the gallows or not, whether they will be a disgrace to their parentage or not. Now all this is simply an evidence of a lack of faith. There are many persons in good health, with all their faculties in active exercise, who, having nothing else to worry about, rob themselves of sleep at night by thinking, "if they should suddenly be taken away, what would become of their families, and who would take care of their children?" Such distrust of God is dishonorable to Christian men; and it is only because of his exceeding patience—which is the most wonderful attribute of the divine nature—that he does not signally rebuke and punish it whenever it is manifested.

When persons are taken sick, they ought to bear it with a good grace; but nine out of ten, even among Christian men, repine and murmur. When they are visited with any trouble, their first thought is apt to be, "How grievously I am afflicted!" though the nobler thought would be, "How graciously I am sustained!" When a cross is laid upon them, they cry out, "What a burden I have to carry!" whereas they might better say, "What a burden Christ carries for me!" A Christian sailor, who lost one of his legs in the battle of Trafalgar, said that he could very often measure the faith of the people who conversed with him by the way in which they alluded to his misfortune. Nine out of every ten would exclaim, "What a pity that you lost your leg!" and only one in ten, "What a blessing that the other was preserved!" When God comes into the family and takes away one child, instead of complaining because he has taken one, it would be wiser to thank him that he has left the rest. Or he may crush a man's business, and strip him of all his worldly wealth, and yet leave untouched and uninvaded what is dearer than all—the cradle of his only child. Would it not be nobler for such a man to be thankful for what God left than to murmur for what he took away? "The Lord giveth and the Lord taketh away," but he always gives more than he takes away. If God robs a man of his riches, he leaves him his health, which is better than riches. If he takes health he leaves wealth. If he takes both, he leaves friends. And if he takes all these—house and home, and worldly goods—God's providence is not yet exhausted, and he can make blessings out of other things which remain. He never strips a man entirely bare. A man may be left a beggar upon the highway, and yet be able to give unceasing testimony to God's goodness and grace!

If men were to give thanks to God for what he permits them to have, rather than to utter complaints for what he wisely and graciously withholds, he might not unlikely give to them more abundantly, if for no other reason than to increase their gratitude.

An old man, who is now without home or friends—a stranger in a strange land, who earns a scanty crust of bread, day by day, by selling steel-pens and writing-paper from store to store, and from street to street, in New York, said the other day, that though he had several times been so reduced as to be for a period of forty-eight hours and longer without a morsel to eat, he never lost his trust in Providence, and always rebuked himself whenever he complained at his lot! This man's faith was genuine! He was a hero in rags, greater than many a hero in armor!

God's goodness is large and generous; only our faith in it is small and mean. He carries the whole globe in his thoughtful providence, easier than a mother carries a babe in her arms. If we cannot see the end from the beginning, what matters it so long as he sees it? What have we to do but to seek first the kingdom of God and his righteousness, and leave the rest in faith to him?

We ought not to forget that an affectionate, confiding, tender faith, habitually exercised, would save us half the annoyances of life, for it would lift us up above the reach of them. If an eagle were to fly low along the ground, every man might aim a dart at it, but when it soars into the clouds, it is above every arrow's reach. And they that trust in God "shall mount up with wings as eagles; they shall run and not be weary; and they shall walk and not faint." Christ's invitation is: "Come unto me, all ye that labor and are heavy laden, and I will give you rest. Take my yoke upon you, and learn of me; for I am meek and lowly in heart; and ye shall find rest unto your soul. For my yoke is easy, and my burden is light."

"WE SPEND OUR YEARS AS A TALE THAT IS TOLD."

Who that goes into the garden to-day would ever dream that summer had been there? In midsummer, what covering of the earth, what abundance of leaves, what fragrance of blossoms, what tangled masses of pendulous vines! All is growth, luxuriance, ever-sprouting varieties—the passing away of short-lived things covered by the fresh growth of new kinds!

A sound comes from the north! It is the voice of Winter! In one night his nimble legions come, and the sickling frost cuts down summer to the ground. In a few weeks decay is over; freezing succeeds frost, and summer is wiped away, with all its colors, it sights, its sounds; and sad winds mourn over the play grounds of flowers!

When, in winter, we remember the summer, its glories seem like a dream; it is no longer a fact, but a thing imagined. But, when high winds walk abroad in the winter, and drive all men from the fields, and the house is populous, the family is gathered, and the night, having grown long by robbing the day at both ends, morning and evening, of many hours, the household cheer themselves with industry and study. And at evening, all gather to their various tasks—the father to his books, the mother to her children's treasures, the elder children to their school tasks, while the rosy child, with curled pate, climbs the nurse's knee—and she drones to him the long story, hundred-times told, and yet falling fresh as new upon the story-greedy ears of childhood! He laughs, he weeps—he sighs, he shudders—he glows and expands, or shrinks and cowers, till the tale is done—then sitting for a while upon the stool by the mother's foot, the child grows abstracted, gazing into the pictured embers, seeing all manner of fantastic figures and changing forms upon the opening and shutting face of coals, and the plastic ashes, till the eye sinks and the head nods, and the drooping little sleeper is borne off safe to bed.

In the morning, he wakes and hungers. The night is forgotten. A vague remembrance rests with him of the sweet excitement of the night. But the day clears off these fancies; they grow more and more dim; they lie in the mind as films of spider-web float with long thread glistening in the summer-air.

And thus, saith the Psalmist, we spend our days! *As a tale that is told!* Years, with all their vast variety of incident, are remembered vaguely—they are thin and dreamy! The *present* glows and even burns with intensity. But it is quenched when a few days are past! Days come in with form, and sound, and motion like the coming in of crested waves. Like them, they break upon the shore of the present; they cover it with a million evanescent gems; they dissolve and flow out in undertow, and are lost again in the black depths—while new days, like new waves, foam, sparkle and break, as did they!

One by one come to us days and years. Coming, they have individuality! But receding from us they lose all separateness, and the past is one indistinguishable whole.

Who can analyze and separate the years of his childhood? From birth till one is four or five, the unripe brain receives few impressions that last. It is all blank. As in a printed book, at either end, are bound up many blank leaves, without print or writing on them, so is human life, at either end, begun and ended with blank years, preserving no record—leaving no mark!

But, then come the youthful days—full of romp, of hunger, of growth, of childish exhilaration! How do they seem to you now? Are they separable? Can you thread them, and paint them by memory? Only one or two things peculiary significant remain. The days are huddled together. The very years are heaped in mass; and you think back upon twenty years as if they were but a hand-breadth!

It is as with a landscape to a traveller. Having journeyed all day, at evening reaching some high hill, he sits down to trace his path. The grass at his feet is plain enough, and the ants that run express up and down every stalk have brisk distinctness. The near bushes and the trees are so plain that the boughs, and separate leaves, stand out in their individual forms. But, as the view recedes, gradually he loses all these; and a little farther off, leaves lie upon leaves, grass is matted upon grass, and is no longer form, but only color. Yet farther, and trees begin to fade; tree stands up upon tree, and at length whole forests are to the eye but faint clouds, with not one distinct line, and hills are rubbed out, and all the inequalities of the way, which the complaining foot felt in travelling, the eye no longer discerns, and only here and there a single peak or mountain remains clear and individual against the all-bounding sky!

Thus is it in life. Our nearer hours report themselves; a little farther, and days only, not hours, are discerned; then days lapse, and weeks or months are like long aërial distances, in one line, whose continuity is measured by no prominent object. At length, years only can be seen, and not even these finally. For, as sailors leaving the harbor carry with them for a long time the sight of shore, but sailing still, lose first the low water-lines, but cling by the eye to the higher masses, which in time, in the ever sailing, fade and sink, leaving nothing but some height lifted far up like Teneriffe, which, after the night is passed, is all gone, hidden by the bend of the earth's surface!—so, even high-topped years at length are shut down from our memory by the bend of the vast cycles of Time.

How wonderfully true is it that we spend our lives as a tale that is told!

Come, go back with me.

Who were the members of your father's family? Besides your brothers and sisters, who dwelt there? Who visited? Who came and went? Who were the neighbors? These things were vivid realities to you when a child. What are they now? Mere marks. As a landscape artist plants in the foreground figures with limbs and features clear, but in the far-off distance, when he would paint a figure, taking his brush and spots down a mere dash—a formless color-mark; so to us are the living things of the neighborhood. Some, to be sure, stand up and remain! But a million are forgotten where one remains.

Who went with you to the village school? Call the roll! Who were the successive teachers—Popes of the ferule!

Who were the girls? Who the boys? *Then*, when the uproarious school broke forth in tumult at dismissal, if I had asked you, you could have given every name. *Now*, call them up! Who sat by you on the right? who on the left? Who were in the first class? who in the second? These were important things then. Who was whipped? and who was never once struck? These, to *you*, were then more important than the roar of European revolution, the burning of Moscow, the battle of Waterloo; but what do you remember of them? Some memories are more tenacious than others. A few will reproduce much; more, some; most, but little if any!

How much can you recall from the church? Who went with you? Who sat about you? Who were the old men? Who were in their prime? And who, like yourself, were young? And if these living and throbbing realities are faded out, it will be useless for me to ask you after the sermons. They were gone before they were finished. They fell upon your dissolving ear as flakes of snow upon water, and were gone in the very act of touching.

How much do you recall from the green graveyard? What memories come thence, from that populous city without a magistrate, without a law, where all who quarrelled on earth, are now peaceable dust keeping excellent neighborhood!

And thus I might go on, tracing, step by step, your entrance upon life—your early endeavors—your first hopes of manhood.

But, let us change the method, and try the truth of this description in another way.

Call up the unwritten dreams and reveries of the past! They have filled years in all. You have woven fabrics of every pattern in the loom of fancy. You have reared up castles, peopled them with heroes; you have lost and found treasures; travelled and explored, fought and conquered, loved and won, all in airy fantasies; and thus worn out the watchful night, or wiled pain from consciousness in the weary sickness. Is *that* part of your life gone? All gone!

Birds gathered for flight in autumn, rising high above snare or shot, and flying toward equatorial summer, often chance in their course to cast a feather, from the wing which carries them through the air—brilliant in color, and curved like a bow—which, wavering, and swaying, falls into some thicket, while they flock on. And when, the seasons changing, they are recalled, and fly now northward over the same ranges, they reach the spot where dropped the spent feather, can they see it, or find it any more? It is lost and hidden forever! And so our youthful fancies, which carried us far above human life and reality, are fallen, and like the downiest feather from the wing, are lost and forgotten! If a tale that is *told* fades, how much rather those untold traceries of thought and subtilest evolutions of inarticulate fancy!

Where are the admirations which set the mind all a-sparkle? Where is the record of the wonders, the surprises, the ten thousand excitements which broke the level of life, and brought interjections to the lips? That a dull routine should be forgotten, is not strange. But where are the salient experiences of life, the events which beat upon the attention like a drum, or roused up your passions like a trumpet?

Only a few of all the myriads remain! As one who goes forth from a populous town, often looking back, sees it shrinking and growing smaller, houses fading, and the complexity of streets and buildings growing to a mere spot, and at length, only beholds here and there a long spire against the sky, or single tower, all the rest confused and hidden; so, in the past, but one or two high-reaching experiences remain, while all the diverse and populous experiences besides are covered down and forgotten!

Your years of the past have been built of the same materials as go now to build your days. What rising and falling emotions, what flow of endless thought, what perpetual succession of events, which arrest the attention and occupy the feelings, what endeavors, what successes, what failures, each with its train of joy or pain, and each so important as to seem to leave indelible marks upon the memory! Yet, though there have been ten millions of these, and though they were of strength sufficient to hold you in their thrall, and excite you with pleasure, or agitate you with alarm, or afflict you with grief, sweeping the soul as wind sweeps the sea, and raising as many tumultuous feelings as the sea hath waves; yet, now the smooth memory has shed them all! The trees will sooner remember all the successive leaves whose bosoms prepared the food for the growth of the wood, than you will recall the innumerable experiences of the past which have formed and fashioned you to the shape which you wear! The burdens which you could not carry for their weight are forgotten, the sorrows that pierced you to the heart have left scarcely their name; the troubles that blocked your way, the dangers that shook your courage, and all those things which in their time wrung from you cries and prayers for relief,—you have not alone surmounted and out-lived, but mostly forgotten.

Love, alone, stands with an undiminished memory! What we have once really loved we never forget! The friendship of youth, the warm and generous confidences of true affection, the tender worship of a true heart, are immutable! All other feelings write their memories upon glass with crayons—Love writes upon crystal with a diamond. For, of all the heart's powers, this alone is sovereign. And, being sovereign, God has crowned it with immortality, and given to Memory charge to keep unwasted all its experiences! And Memory, that is tenacious of nothing else, lets nothing slip of the experiences of true loving.

Another year has passed! Its months and its weeks already are buried. Only days and hours remain. These are passing. One more sunrise only hath this year! The next morning shall shine upon the face of a new year!

Let us turn, and bid farewell to the past and the passing! Farewell to its cares, to its burdens, to its troubles! Farewell to fears, and hopes, and griefs! Farewell to its yearnings, its aspirations, its wrestlings! They are gone.

Farewell to many who walked the year with us!—to the companion, that was to us as an angel of God, and is, now, an angel with God! Farewell to the babe that was ours, and is God's, and therefore more than ever ours, though beyond the reach of our arms! But, the heart tends it yet, and cradles it more vigilantly than ever! Farewell to our Christian brethren, who have heard the trumpet before us, and gone forward! Year! thy march is ending! Thy work is done! Pass! Disappear! We shall see thee no more, until re-ascending, we shall behold thy record in the All-judging Day!

SUDDEN CONVERSION.

It is a fact somewhat remarkable that most of the conversions narrated in the Bible were rapid and in some instances instantaneous. Paul, on his way to Damascus, was struck down, in a moment by the visible presence of God. He saw a great light at mid-day, and heard a voice saying, "Saul, Saul, why persecutest thou me?" and he was so suddenly and overwhelmingly impressed by this manifestation that he could do nothing but yield to the power of God; so that from being a persecutor of the Church, he was at that moment changed to be its chiefest apostle. Matthew, the publican, sitting at the receipt of custom, was met by Christ, who said to him, "Follow thou me," and it is said that "he arose and followed him."

The conversion of the thief on the cross, during the very last moments of his life, at the eleventh hour of hope, was almost marvellously sudden, yet not on that account doubtful; for Christ confirmed it by saying, "This day shalt thou be with me in Paradise."

And there are similar instances at the present day. Sudden and unexpected conversions are not unknown to any Christian church. There is nothing whatever absurd in the idea, however some may affect to ridicule it. A conversion which takes no longer time to begin and end, than the sun to rise from day-break to the mountain-top, may be just as undoubted as though it had been the work of a month or a year. The impression that a spiritual change, in order to be genuine, must be a long and gradual process, dragging itself through weary weeks and months, during which the mind is to pass through much anguish and tribulation, until finally the light shall arise and shine, is simply foolish. Time adds nothing to the thoroughness of conversion, nor suffering to the evidence of it. In many cases much time is taken, and much suffering felt, but neither of these is to be considered as an absolutely necessary part of it.

Yet there are many persons whose conversion is a long and severe struggle, during which they alternate week after week, and month after month, between hope and fear, who, were it not for perplexing their minds with a wrong notion of what they are to do and to be done with, might go up the mountain almost without going through the valley. Such instances have occurred among the most eminent Christians. It is known that John Bunyan went through awful terrors, as a consequence of a long-continued exercise of mind, before he found religious peace; and his experiences are embalmed in some of the best writing in the English language. But it is our impression that the conversion of Bunyan might just as well have been a work of days as of months. John Wesley also went well-nigh three years before he found what he sought. This was a period of great effort, of continued urging up to duty, of watchfulness and carefulness, involving almost unutterable trouble of mind. He finally went among the Moravians and there reached those views which finally gave him quiet in Jesus Christ.

There are not only single instances like these, but multitudes of others—of persons who have for years been bound, as it were, by some invisible cord, which has kept them in this bondage. The difficulty in many cases results from an erroneous apprehension of what is to be taken as evidence of conversion. Men make a common mistake between what *is* a religious life, and certain expected *fruits* of a religious life, and confound the two things.

Now, to be a Christian is to obey Christ, no matter how you feel; but many persons think that after this obedience is rendered, there will be plunged into their souls what is called a Christian experience; and that this experience, coming afterwards, is piety. They therefore attempt to conform to the love of Christ, and then wait for a projected or interjected experience which is supposed to be a religious state. It is no doubt better to have the feeling that follows, than to be without it; but the feeling itself is not to be taken for that of which it is simply the fruit, and if there is no feeling, it is not to be taken as evidence that there is no real religious life.

When a man sits down to a piano, reading his sheet of music before him, and touching the keys that correspond to the notes that he reads, it is certainly better to be able to hear the sounds that follow. But Beethoven—one of the saddest instances in history of human greatness and suffering—becoming deaf in the latter part of his life, used to sit down to the harpsichord, and play tunes of which he heard not a single note. Even though his instrument fell into all manner of jangling discords, by becoming long out of tune, yet he still played upon it all those grand, swelling harmonies which were tumultuous in his soul. Now if Beethoven had waited till his ear could have become conscious of the playing, he would not have played at all. And it is the same with persons who try to live a religious life. There are two things which they must avoid confounding. They should mark the difference between following Christ, and the sensations which come in consequence of following him. If a person trying to come into the discipleship of Christ, expects to do so by sitting down and waiting for a certain preconceived state of mind to come to him, as he might wait for a pair of wings to sprout out of his shoulders, he must not be surprised if he is disappointed. But many earnest-minded persons—who are near the kingdom of heaven, and desire to enter it—hinder themselves by just such difficulties. They deny to their own minds the evidence of their own conversion, simply because they do not experience the feelings which *other* persons are known to have experienced. They are nearer than they think to their Father's house, yet not believing that they are near, they do not go in. Being so close to the gate that if they were closer they must certainly enter, they yet sit down and tarry without—mourning all the while that they cannot see their Father's face. Such a mistake is one of the saddest that can happen a man's life, and should be guarded against by more careful discrimination and better teaching.

"TOTAL DEPRAVITY."

OUR attention has been called to some remarks in *The New York Examiner*, a Baptist religious journal, in which we are called to account for certain words said to have been uttered by us in a recent lecture in Boston, and also for giving the lecture at all in the "Fraternity Course."

Although several other religious journals, as I am informed, have commented upon the same topics, I select *The Examiner's* editorial for reply, for two reasons:—first, because I have not seen the others; and secondly and especially, because its tone is in the main kind. And we desire to say, that if all papers were as fair and frank as *The Examiner*, there would be more pleasure in the public interchange of views than is usually the case. And we beg the editors to understand the earnestness of our reply as applying more to the subject than to them.

"Mr. Beecher is not to be held accountable for a newspaper report of his words—unless, having knowledge that certain words are publicly attributed to him, he acquiesces in the report. *The Boston Journal* quoted him as saying to the Fraternity, that 'every selfish man believes in total depravity,' and added, that the remark was loudly cheered. Now, every man who has discretion enough to speak in public at all, is bound to consider, not only whether a given sentiment is true, but whether it is true in the sense in which it will inevitably be understood by his audience. There are objections to the phrase 'total depravity.' In the sense which would, perhaps, be most obvious to ordinary minds; in that sense, certainly, which Unitarians have diligently labored to associate with the words, they convey a falsehood. There is no wrong in discountenancing their use, for the purpose of substituting a phraseology less liable to misrepresentation. But that is a distinction which not one in a hundred of those who applauded Mr. Beecher would ever think of making. If he did say what is attributed to him, he must have been understood as denying and vilifying that doctrine of human nature, without which there can be no logical or reasonable necessity for a supernatural redemption. If he has been falsely reported, we should be happy to know it."

We admit in many cases that a man is to be considered as accepting words attributed to him if, when widely published, and brought to his notice, he permits them to stand uncontradicted. But it is plain that this must not be formed into a rule, and that much must be left to the discretion of the persons concerned.

If there are a thousand little things trumped up for the sake of provoking an answer; if men lie in wait, and watch how they may catch a speaker, strewing words and speeches along the way of controversy, as corn is strewn toward traps—is a man to run into the snare?

Life would be a perpetual flea-hunt, if one were obliged to run down all the innuendoes, the inveracities, the insinuations, and the suspicions which the style of modern honor permits many religious papers to indulge in.

But, even where there is no unkindness meant, and when no meanness employs religion as a cloak, and even where words or opinions are attributed to a man which have some importance, it is a serious question whether he is *always* obliged to contradict, and whether he may not be allowed to employ his own discretion in denying some without implying any responsibility for all which he does not choose to deny.

Since we have been called before the public, we must be allowed to say, frankly, that it would be utterly impossible for us to look after all the erroneous reports and the inaccurate statements which are continually made in our behalf. Hundreds of reports made for "substance of doctrine" by reporters not versed in religious literature, of sermons reported by letter-writers, and not a few more formal collections of sayings, and descriptions of things done or said, are sent abroad. Is a man obliged to put everything right in all these? Is he to be held responsible for sentiments or expressions sent all over the land by letter-writers, unless he every week comes before the public with formal disclaimer and reiterated explanation? If we did so, then, next, the very papers which require it would be the first to blame us for conceit in keeping before the public endless personal explanations!

But there is another side to this question. Have editors, religious and honorable men, a right to aid in the circulation of uncorrected statements, and hastily reported addresses, when they above all men know how seldom rapid speakers are correctly reported, and when, moreover, they have the *means of inquiring at head-quarters* as to the accuracy of any report? How long would it take to cut out a paragraph, inclose it to the person represented as uttering it, and say, "Is this correct?"—"Do you hold yourself responsible for this?" If it is not worth this trouble, then it is not worth inserting in the paper. But again and again, the most serious misstatements have been put in leading religious newspapers, whose editors almost passed my door daily in going to their office. But, while they reconciled it to their honor to give injurious reports a very wide currency, they did not deem it their duty to take the least pains to ascertain the truth of the statements!

But we have become so used to seeing misstatements and misconceptions that we scarcely lift our eyebrows any more at the most astounding things. Indeed we kill them by silence; having found that they thrive more vigorously by the notice of a denial. There was a story started some years ago that we began a sermon by the startling impropriety of the sentence, "It is damned hot." We took the pains to give this the most unequivocal contradiction, declaring it to be a lie out of the whole cloth, without the vestige or shadow of foundation of any kind whatsoever. But, since this denial, the story not only goes a good deal better than before, but more and more persons are, every month, reported to me as declaring on their personal veracity, *that they were present and heard the speech.* Of course, such persons do all, without exception, tell a willful falsehood; but we dare not say so publicly, for fear that they will fall into spasms of affidavits, and convert their guilt into permanent form, past all repentance.

Now we beg to have it understood, hereafter, that all reports which represent us as saying what we ought not to have said, are undoubtedly erroneous! Whereas if the thing reported is good, wise, safe, and eminently proper, let it be taken for granted that we said it! With this general rule we shall be content.

We now proceed to examine the allegation that we employed the term *Total Depravity* in a manner which produced upon the audience the effect of a fling at the doctrine of man's sinfulness before God.

1. Even if the term Total Depravity were one deserving of respect, the use made of it by us, on the occcasion referred to, could be tortured into an offence only by the most unreasonable theological jealousy. And those *who heard* the lecture do not seem to have felt any impropriety. It was the *report* of it, published the next day in the newspapers, and read in the study or editorial office, that excited so much anxiety.

We were illustrating the fact that a powerful feeling in action tended to produce the same feeling in other minds. We instanced the selfish man whose selfish feelings awakened like tendencies all around him, so that he roused up and surrounded himself with men's worst traits. Such a man is very apt to inveigh against his fellow-men. They seem to him exceedingly wicked. To the selfish man all men seem desperately and only selfish. And here it was that we said that a selfish man always believes in Total Depravity. Though he believes nothing else, he is always a firm believer in human wickedness.

Now we really think that one must be extremely anxious to be offended to find occasion of offence in this remark. And if the gentlemen who watch against the many-headed serpent of heresy had heard the context with the remark, they would have been saved from the assertion that it was cheered as a fling at the orthodox view of man's sinfulness. It was the whole hit at a selfish man's experience that drew applause—not any supposed subtile intimation of a doctrinal laxity on our part.

2. But although we did not employ the phrase *Total Depravity* in any opprobrious sense, at the time mentioned, we do not hesitate to say now, that we regard it as one of the most unfortunate and misleading terms that ever afflicted theology.

It answers no purpose of definition or of description. It does not convey the sense in which the great majority of churches hold the doctrine of man's sinfulness. Instead of explaining anything, it needs explanation itself. Every minister who employs the term usually begins his sermon by saying that he does *not* mean the very thing which the words *do* mean. For, *Total* signifies a degree beyond which there can be no more. A total loss is one which cannot be increased; a total bankruptcy is one which could not be more complete; a total destruction is one which leaves nothing more to be destroyed. Men have a right to suppose that Total Depravity signifies a depravity beyond which there could be no more—nothing worse. This *is* the popular understanding of the term. The people go with the language, and not with theologians. But this is not the theological meaning of the word. It is taught that universal man is depraved; and not that each man is totally depraved. No man who uses the phrase believes men to be totally wicked—*i. e.*, so wicked that they cannot be more wicked. If they can be more wicked, then they were not totally wicked before. And, just as *The Examiner* does, so do all sensible men. They do not use the term. They regard it as infelicitous. And yet, when any one handles it roughly they are full of anxiety for the truth!

This word is an interloper. It is not to be found in the Scriptures. We do not believe that it is even to be found in the Catechisms and Confessions of Faith of Protestant or Catholic Christendom.

We do not feel called upon to give the mischievous phrase any respect. We do not believe in it, nor in the thing which it obviously signifies. It is an unscriptural, monstrous, and unredeemable lie.

3. But, on the other hand, we do believe, with continual sorrow of heart and daily overflowing evidence, in the deep sinfulness of universal man. And we believe in the exceeding sinfulness of sin. We do not believe that any man is born who is sinless, or who becomes perfectly sinless until death. We believe that there is not one faculty of the human soul that does not work evil, and so repeatedly, that, the whole human character is sinful before God. We believe man's sinfulness to be such that every man that ever lived needed God's forbearance and free forgiveness. We believe that no man lives who does not need to repent of sin, to turn from it; and we believe that turning from sin is a work so deep, and touches so closely the very springs of being, that

no man will ever change except by the help of God. And we believe that such help is the direct and personal out-reaching of God's Spirit upon the human soul; and when, by such divine help, men begin to live a spiritual life, we believe the change to have been so great that it is fitly called a beginning of life over again, a new creation, a new birth.

If there is one thing that we believe above all others, upon proof from consciousness and proof from observation and experience, it is the sinfulness of man. Nor do we believe that any man ever doubted our belief who sat for two months under our preaching. Nothing strikes us as so peculiarly absurd as a charge or fear that we do not adequately believe in men's sinfulness. The steady bearing of our preaching on this subject is such as to plough up soil and subsoil, and to convict and to convince men of their need of Christ's redemption.

But our belief of this sad truth is purely practical. We have no sympathy with those theologians who use Time as a grand alley, and roll back their speculations six thousand years, knocking down and setting up the race, in the various chances of this gigantic theologic game—what is the origin and nature of sin? Poor Adam! To have lost Paradise was enough. But to be a shadow endlessly pursued through all time by furious and fighting theologies—this is a punishment never threatened. Or, was the flaming sword of the angel a mere type and symbol of theological zeal, standing between men and Paradise for evermore! We take men as we find them. We do not go back to Adam or the fall to find materials for theories and philosophies. There is the human heart right before my eyes, every day throbbing, throbbing, throbbing! Sin is not a speculation, but a reality. It is not an idea, a speculative truth, but an awful fact, that darkens life, and weighs down the human heart with continual mischiefs. Its nature will never be found in the Past. It must be sought in the Present.

WORKING WITH ERRORISTS.

We now print the entire first part of the article from the *New York Examiner*, the last part of which it was more convenient to dispose of first:

THE 'FRATERNITY' AND MR. BEECHER.

"In the congregation administered to by Theodore Parker, at the Music Hall in Boston, known as the 'Twenty-eighth Congregational Society,' there is a literary association styled the 'Fraternity.' Said Fraternity has got up a series of 'Fraternity Lectures,' an avowed object of which, if a newspaper announcement may be credited, was to give to the 'ideas' of Mr. Parker a freer scope than the Lyceum platform allows. But whether that was the purpose or not, it is manifest that the effect would be, so far as any impression was made on the public, to give increased popularity to the man and his 'church.' If the lectures prove, as has been claimed, 'the most successful course of the season,' they will reflect a certain lustre upon the 'Twenty-eighth Congregational Society,' and upon the man whose infidelity is its pervading spirit. Such an effect, we should suppose, would be deprecated—at least, would not be even constructively aided—by a sincere friend of evangelical religion. But the pastor of the Plymouth church in Brooklyn has appeared upon Mr. Parker's platform, to lend to it his popularity. Mr. Beecher has asserted his right to do in all things what is right in his own eyes, and we are not disposed, even if we were able, to abridge his liberty. But it is utterly incomprehensible by us, how he reconciles with his love for the Gospel such open aid and comfort to its bitterest enemies. To appear with Mr. Parker, contemporaneously or successively, upon a platform which represents neither him nor his 'ideas,' is one thing; to assist in giving *éclat* to an infidel enterprise is a very different thing —and that is what every Fraternity lecturer, and every purchaser of a Fraternity ticket has done."

Of course we believe in newspapers, and in editors. Yet, even an editor may be mistaken and a newspaper may fall into misstatements! And the *Examiner* has in this instance been misled by a too confiding trust in religious or secular newspapers.

It is true that the Fraternity Course was under the supervision of members of the Twenty-eighth Congregational Society of Boston, but it is not true that it was got up for the sake of giving Mr. Parker's "'ideas' a freer scope than the Lyceum platform allows"—if by *ideas*, the *Examiner* means Mr. Parker's characteristic religious views. On the contrary, it is known that Mr. Parker was preparing four historical discourses, on Washington, John Adams, Jefferson, and (we believe) Franklin. But such was the ill odor in Boston of Mr. Parker's religious notions that a studious care had been exercised to keep him from Boston lecture platforms, though history, art, or belles-lettres were his theme, lest the influence of anything that was good in him should "reflect a lustre" upon that part of him which religious men so much deprecate.

But, on the other hand, the attempt to suppress a man, and to silence his speech, on the great topics which are common to men of *all* religious views, must produce, not only among his personal friends, but among honorable men who utterly differ from him in religion, a determination that he shall have a chance to *speak*, at least; and then, if people do not wish to hear an "infidel," on secular topics, of course they can stay at home. In other respects, this Lecture Course was like ordinary courses. It was not neld in Mr. Parker's church, nor on his platform—though it would have been no worse if it had been—but in the Tremont Temple—a Baptist worshipping-place, where the Mercantile Library Association and other principal lecture courses are held. The only respect in which it was peculiar was, that Theodore Parker was to deliver four lectures in the course, upon Washington, John Adams, Jefferson, and Benjamin Franklin. Besides him, the other lecturers, six or eight in number, were those gentlemen whose names dignify and enrich the roll of all principal lecture-courses in the Union.

The funds, over and above the expenses, if there should be any, were *not* designed to support either Mr. Parker or the Twenty-eighth Congregational society, of which he is the minister. They were to be employed in charitable purposes, and for the most part among the poor and unfriended!

And if the young men of the Twenty-eighth Congregational Society of Boston judged that we were one who would be glad to coöperate with Theodore Parker, in all honorable ways which did not imply approbation of his theology, for objects common to all good men; and if they judged that we should be forward to aid all measures, among all sects, which have for their object the improvement of the young, and the relief of the suffering, they judged rightly. We believe in the right of free speech even of men whose opinions, when delivered, we do not believe!

Did the *Examiner* think that the young gentlemen of Mr. Parker's society got up a course of popular lectures for the sake of covertly propagating infidelity, and invited me, without disclosing the inward scheme, to garnish the course, and to lend my influence, blindfolded, to such an aim? Or, did it never enter the head of the *Examiner* that a man might associate with men from whose theological tenets he utterly dissented, because he sympathized with the special benevolence which they would perform? because he had an *ethical* sympathy with them in spite of their theology? because he believed that a good man ought always to seek occasions of working with men, rather than of working away from them?

We should be sorry to suppose ourselves singular in this matter. Are we to take the ground that no orthodox man shall encourage the young to self-improvement and to works of benevolence, unless they are sound in the faith? Because Mr. Parker teaches a wrong theology to the young men of his charge, are we to hold off and refuse to help them when they endeavor to live a great deal better than we should suppose their theology would incline them to? But this is the very case in hand. The young men in Mr. Parker's society undertook to do good by a course of general lectures; we lectured in that course; good papers are full of grief; and the *Examiner* regards it as "utterly incomprehensible." We must be still more incomprehensible then, when we say, that though we would earnestly desire men to believe aright in religion, yet, if they will not, then we hope that their life will be better than their creed. And, if we see men of a heretical turn of mind practising Gospel virtues and charities, we shall certainly encourage and help them. For men do not derive the right to do good from the Thirty-nine Articles; nor need they go to the Westminster Confession for liberty to recover the intemperate, set free the bound, feed the hungry, clothe the naked, educate the ignorant, and give sleigh-rides to the beggars' children that never before laughed and cuddled under a buffalo robe! It seems to us a great deal better business for a Christian man to encourage his fellows in well-doing than to punish them for wrong thinking!

But the *Examiner* thinks that the success of this course of lectures will "*reflect a certain lustre* upon the Twenty-eighth Congregational Society, and upon the man whose infidelity is its pervading spirit." Well, what then? Are we to punish an infidel for his infidelity by refusing him all credit for personal goodness, for active benevolence, for practical humanity?

If anybody does right he *ought* to be applauded. If Mr. Parker *does* well he deserves the credit for well-doing. If the young men of his charge do well, they deserve all the "lustre" of it. Or shall we take ground that no man who is not of sound orthodox faith is to have any "lustre" for practical virtue? Must nobody be counted ethically right until he is theologically sound? Such a doctrine would be monstrous! Every just and generous man in the community ought to rejoice in the good conduct of every man, without regard to his speculative views or theological affinities!

If a man institutes a temperance movement, must I refuse to help him because, being perhaps, a Universalist minister, his zeal and fidelity in that cause would "reflect a lustre" upon him and his sect? If a man would establish and endow a hospital, must I refuse to co-work with him because, being a Unitarian, its success would reflect a certain lustre upon that faith?

When, in the pestilence in New Orleans, the Sisters of Charity did not count their lives dear to them, but night and day, fearless of death and defiant of fatigue, gave their utmost being to the care of the miserable sick, must I, a Protestant, refuse admiration or fellowship for fear a "certain lustre" would shine upon the Roman Catholic Church?

If a Jew does nobly, he deserves the lustre which right-doing ought to confer; if an Atheist or an Infidel live virtuously and act honorably, he should have the "lustre" belonging to virtue and honor!

Does the *Examiner* think that we do not care for our own theologic views? We care a good deal. We shall yield them to no man's dictation. We shall not indorse any man's theology which differs from them. We have enough of the old disciple nature left to feel very desirous that folks who will cast out devils, should do it in our train, and as we do. But if they will not—why, then, we will help them to do it in *their* way! No ways can be very bad that succeed in getting rid of the devil. But, if we were to help an Episcopal movement for general benevolence, would any man say that we indorsed high-church notions? If we were affectionately and urgently invited to Princeton, to examine the senior class in theology and give them some tender cautions on parting from Turretin and entering the life of realities, would anybody be so cruel as to say that we believed in high Calvinism, or were indifferent to all woes of conscience produced by that energetic system? Bishop Hughes will never invite us to speak in his new cathedral, and we not promptly accept it. But we affectionately appeal to the *Examiner* whether, on such an interesting occurrence, he would think it his duty to pierce us with such remarks as are now puncturing our peace from his words?

If I had gone to Boston to buy carpets or books; or if I had gone to Boston to help the Republican cause, if I had gone on any of those secular errands, in which all men of every shade of belief are wont to unite without criticism, no question would have been raised. In selfish and worldly interests men are allowed coöperation for common ends. But if I divest myself of all selfish or secular aims, and rise to a higher plane of benevolence, and seek to raise the fallen, to restore the lost, to purify the vicious, to elevate the ignorant, and to cheer the poor and neglected, Christian ministers and editors will not let me coöperate for such divine objects with every man who will sincerely work for them; but I must pick for men of right philosophy, for men right in all theology! Thus we allow selfishness to go with flowing robes and a loose girdle. We make her feet light, and her hands nimble. But upon religion we put iron shoes and steel gloves. We burden her with mail, and underneath it all we draw the girt of conscience to the last hole. Then she goes slowly forth, scarcely able to walk or to breathe!

I have long ago been convinced that it was better to love men, than to hate them; and that one would be more likely to convince them of wrong belief by showing a cordial sympathy with their welfare, than by nipping and pinching them with logic. And although I do not disdain, but honor philosophy applied to religion, I think that the world just now needs the Christian Heart more than anything else. And, even if the only and greatest interest were the propagation of right theology, I am confident that right speculative views will grow up faster and firmer in the summer of true Christian loving, than in the rigorous winter of solid, congealed orthodoxy, or in the blustering March of controversy

Does anybody inquire why, if so thinking, we occasionally give such sharp articles upon the great religious newspapers, the *Observer*, the *Intelligencer*, and the like? Oh pray do not think it for any ill-will! It is all kindness! We only do it to keep our voice in practice. We have made orthodoxy a study. And, by an attentive examination of the *Presbyterian*, the *Observer*, the *Puritan Recorder*, and such like unblemished confessors, we have learned that no man is himself truly sound who does not pitch into somebody for being unsound in the faith; and that a real modern orthodox man, like a nervous watch-dog, must sit on the door-stone of his system, and bark incessantly at everything that comes in sight along the highway.. And when there is nothing to bark at, either he must growl and gnaw his reserved bones, or bark at the moon, to keep up the sonorousness of his voice. And so, for fear the sweetness of our temper may lead men to think that we have no theological zeal, we lift up an objurgation now and then—as much as to say, "Here we are, fierce and orthodox: ready to growl when we cannot bite!"

But the *Examiner* says: "The pastor of the Plymouth church in Brooklyn has appeared upon Mr. Parker's platform, to lend it his popularity." I neither borrowed nor lent. I went before an audience in the Tremont Temple, a Baptist meeting-house, the place for the chief part of public lectures, to give my own ideas, and to exert whatever power I had by my thoughts and by my feelings upon such audience as pleased to come together. If they were good men they needed me less: if they were bad, they needed me more. But either way, I was responsible for my own testimony, and for nothing more; and this was not lent to Mr. Parker, but to the audience. Yet, whenever Theodore Parker does what is right and noble, if it were possible for me to lend him anything I would do it gladly. I have nothing to lend, however, but good will, and that I never lend, but give, free as God's air!

But, it will be asked, will the public understand your position, and, however you may design it, will not the impression go abroad either that you sympathize with infidel views, or are indifferent to them? No. The public especially will not misunderstand. There is formed and forming a moral judgment in the intelligent part of the community, that popular Christianity needs more love in it. Men at large will be a great deal more apt to say that I have done a more exemplary Christian act, in daring to avow an *ethical* sympathy with Theodore Parker, between whom and myself there exists an irreconcilable theological difference, than if I had bombarded him for a whole year, and refused to touch his hand!

What a pitiful thing it is to see men, who have the chance of saying what they believe, who do say it two hundred times a year, who write it, sing it, speak it, and fight it; who, by all their social affinities, by all their life-work, by all positive and most solemn testimonies, are placed beyond misconception,—always nervous lest they should sit down with somebody, or speak with somebody, or touch somebody, and so lose an immaculate reputation for soundness! Therefore, men peep out from their systems as prisoners in jail peep out of iron-barred windows, but dare not come out, for fear some sharp sheriff of the Faith should arrest them!

If we held Theodore Parker's views, we should not wait to have it *inferred.* Men would hear it from our lips, and hear it past all mistaking. And we are not going at our time of life to begin to watch over our "*influence;*" to cut and trim our sentences lest some mousing critic should pounce upon an infelicity and draw upon us a suspicion. We have never sought influence, and we never shall seek it. Any that we have now, came to us because we went straight forward, doing whatever was *right,* and always believing that a *loving heart* was a better judge of what *was* right than a cold and accurate head. Neither is infallible. Both make mistakes. But the errors of the heart dissolve in the kindness of men's natures as snowflakes dissolve in warmbosomed lakes, while the errors of cold intellect pierce and stick like arrows. If I cannot make my people understand my belief, in fifty-two Sabbaths of the year, I shall not mend the matter by refusing to follow the generous sympathies of my heart.

No. The common people will not misunderstand. Nor will practical Christian ministers. They may differ from my judgment, but they will understand my deed. It is only those professed defenders of the faith, who, having erected suspicion into a Christian grace, practise slander as a Christian duty, that will be liable to mistake. And it makes no difference whether such men understand or not. These men are like aspen-trees growing on rocks. In conceit and arrogance they are hard as granite, while they tremble all over like aspen leaves with perpetual fears and apprehensions of dismal mischief to come!

When Theodore Parker appears in his representative character as a theologian, I am as irreconcilably opposed to him as it is possible to be. The things that are dear to him, are cheerless and unspeakably solitary and mournful to me. The things which are the very centre of my life, the inspiration of my existence, the glory of my thought and the strength of my ministry, are to him but very little. I differ from him in fact, in theory, in statement, in doctrine, in system, in hope and expectation; living or dying, laboring or resting—in theology, we are separate, and irreconcilable.

Could Theodore Parker worship my God?—Christ Jesus is his name. All that there is of God to me is bound up in that name. A dim and shadowy effluence rises from Christ, and that I am taught to call the Father. A yet more tenuous and invisible film of thought arises, and that is the Holy Spirit. But neither are to me aught tangible, restful, accessible.

They are to be revealed to my knowledge hereafter, but now only to my faith. But Christ stands my *manifest* God. All that I know is of him, and in him. I put my soul into his arms, as, when I was born, my father put me into my mother's arms. I draw all my life from him. I bear him in my thoughts hourly, as I humbly believe that he also bears me. For I do truly believe that we love each other!—I, a speck, a particle, a nothing, only a mere beginning of something that is gloriously yet to be, when the warmth of God's bosom shall have been a summer for my growth;—and HE, the Wonderful Counsellor, the Mighty God, the Everlasting Father, the Prince of Peace!

And this Redeemer of the world, this Saviour of sinners, I accept, not only as my guide, my friend, my deliverer, but as an atoning God, who bore my sins upon the cross, and delivered me from their penalty. And, since my life is spared to me by him, I give to him that life again. This hope of Christ is the staff of my ministry. First, highest, and in measure beyond all other things, I preach Jesus Christ. And all other topics are but arrows, shot out of this Divine bow. And this has been so for twenty years, eleven of which I have labored in Brooklyn. And yet the *Examiner* is pleased to reproach me, as if, against the sweep of my life, and the current and testimony of my being, I had gone to Boston to give "éclat to an infidel enterprise," and only because I gladly helped men who do not agree with me in theology to do deeds of mercy in which all good men should be united!

What must be the condition of the public mind, on the subject of Christian charity, when the simple coöperation of a man, on a ground of common benevolence, is made to signify more than his whole regular life-work?

The disposition to find some common ground of kindness and benevolent work, with those from whom we are known to differ, will be a real preaching of the Gospel to tens of thousands who are unmoved by dogmas or doctrines. It is Love that the world wants. When Love goes abroad in the full worth of its nature, and endures, and suffers, without reward except the sweetness of suffering borne for another, then men begin to see what is the heart and spirit of Christ, and to have some motions towards faith in him!

If tears could wash away from Mr. Parker's eyes the hindrances, that he might behold Christ as I behold and adore him, I would shed them without reserve. If prayers could bring to him this vision of glory, beyond sight of philosophy, I would for him besiege the audience-chamber of heaven with an endless procession of prayers, until another voice sounding forth from another light brighter than the noon day sun, should cast down another blinded man, to be lifted up an apostle with inspired vision!

But since I may not hope so to prevail, I at least

will carry him in my heart, I will cordially work with him when I can, and be heartily sorry whenever I cannot.

While we yet write, word comes that Mr. Parker, broken down by overlabor, seeks rest and restoration in a warmer clime. Should these lines reach his eye, let him know that one heart at least remembers his fidelity to man, in great public exigencies when so many swerved, of whom we had a right to expect better things. God shield him from the ocean, the storm, the pestilence; and heal him of lurking disease. And there shall be one Christian who will daily speak his name to the heart of God in earnest prayer, that with health of body he may also receive upon his soul the greatest gift of God,—faith in Jesus Christ as the Divine Saviour of the world.

MISCHIEVOUS SELF-EXAMINATION.

THE term, self-examination, is applied, not to the consideration of one's outward conduct, but to a review and analysis of one's hidden feelings; to the motives, and to the moral complexion of one's emotions. In this matter, as in many others, those who most need it seldom practise it, and those practise it most who could best do without it. Thus if a man have a strong practical cast, a natural sagacity in matters of form and substance, a ready knowledge of men and things, he will tend to cultivate that outward direction of his mind; and to regard introspection as unpractical. This opinion is confirmed by the few paroxysmal attempts at the study of himself. Made upon impulse, without skill, or practice, upon too large a scale, with the heat of new zeal, the result is confusion and disgust. He reverts to his *practical* life, and always speaks of himself as not adapted to metaphysical meditation. Yet, this man especially needs to study *himself*, because he is by his nature so strongly drawn away toward outward and material life.

On the other hand, a reflective, sensitive mind, dwells upon its own states too much, and lives so much in introspection, as to have but a slender sympathy with the outward world.

A special form of this last mentioned danger is frequently found in young and conscientious Christians.

They attempt to maintain a habitual watch over their minds. They check every budding feeling till they know what fruit it will bear. They stop every swelling emotion till they have "examined" it. They treat the religious feelings, as an officer would a person suspected of having stolen goods about his person —stripping off its cloak, and scrutinizing sharply. The mind, thus badgered, is like a steed whom you whip with one hand and hold in with the other; it becomes restless and chafed. The poor victim does not know "how he does feel." He wishes he knew his own motives. He will be heard inquiring much after his "evidences." "How can a man tell whether he has faith or not?" "How may I know whether I really *love* God?" "How do I know whether all my motives in seeking religion are not selfish?" Such questions will identify the victims of narrow self-examination.

The moment a feeling becomes an object of *attention*, it ceases to be a feeling. Emotions change to ideas. The real process of what is called, by many, self-examination, is but the transmutation of an emotive state into an intellectual state; for feeling perishes where analysis begins. They burn the flower that they may analyze its ashes, and then are discontented that, raking in the ashes, they find neither root, stem, nor flower.

This course is every way unnatural, and inflicts upon the mind a long train of mischiefs. There can be no such thing as a current in the mind, a free sweep, a generous momentum, where every state of feeling is stopped for examination. The mind becomes restless. It begins nervously to break out in one direction or another, seeking by violent reactions that natural liberty which has been denied it. If the causes continue, the results will vary according to the peculiar temperament and structure of the mind. Some will retract in disgust from all attempts at religion, except as a scheme of morals. Others will grow despondent, and all their lifetime be subject to bondage. Others still, will come to a degree of morbid sensitiveness, which will only stop short of superstition. They will have a thousand questions starting up; they will feel pangs of remorse upon the slightest occasion; they will be thrown off their guard by a text suddenly presented, by the remarks of clergymen or of Christian friends, and brood in perpetual disquiet over a chaotic and gloomy experience.

In such states, every effort of the sufferer being a stimulus upon a jaded or morbid condition, will aggravate the suffering and put relief yet further off.

Such mischiefs are not imaginary. Every year we meet them in repeated instances. Some five within a week, have come to our notice.

WHERE CHRISTIANS MEET.

A PRAYER-MEETING is a place for social religious life. It is not for preaching, nor is it for exhortation. It is a place WHERE CHRISTIANS MEET to instruct and strengthen one another by a free and familiar development of their religious experiences and emotions. It is an altar—for whose fire every Christian brings a brand, and where the whole pile is made up of the added fagots of many enkindled hearts.

This is the primary idea of a prayer-meeting. It is evident, therefore, that the first step toward a wholesome meeting is truthfulness. Yet it is this important element which is apt to be most often lacking. It is thought necessary, even by advanced Christians, to assume a sense of awful responsibility, to put on an air of profound solemnity, and to manifest an eminently devout spirit. But these feelings are never proper, except when they are real. They should never be assumed. They should never be put on and worn as a kind of appropriate dress, becoming to the occasion. Men should not lay aside their naturalness before God, any more than before men—and even less, as God can see through the guise when men may not. They should not pretend to be what they are not, any more in a prayer-meeting with their brethren, than alone in their own private closet. Any pretentious mood, or any forced and artificial feeling, will always do harm, for it will overlay the mind as straw and dry leaves overlay the soil, so that nothing is able to spring up.

No man should utter a word in a prayer-meeting which is not spoken in sincerity. It is a great and grievous sin for a man to utter prayers to God, when his heart neither suggests, nor enters into, the petitions. It is a piece of mockery that no man would endure, much less God. For any creature to bow before his Creator, and say prayers, whether they be long or short, printed or unprinted, which do not engage his heart, but which he utters from a mere sense of duty, or from superstitious fear, or from habit, is an inexpressible audacity. Yet it is often done. And it is said, "If you do not feel like praying, pray till you do." Now there certainly are degrees of interest; and a man may be blameless for experiencing less fervor at the beginning of a devotional period than at the end of it. But for a man to employ prayer as a mere exercise, or as a mere mode of giving himself a stirring up—to stand before God and assume the tones, the language, the manner of feeling, for the sake of coming by and by into the feeling, is a desecration of prayer almost blasphemous.

If it be asked, "What then shall a man do? Shall he neglect prayer until he does feel? Shall he refuse to take part in a prayer-meeting until the glow is upon him?"—the answer is that such a man should not neglect prayer, neither in his closet, nor perhaps in the prayer-meeting. But he must prepare himself for prayer. He must watch and study for the disposition. He should refresh his mind with Scriptural truths, and should consider his own wants and sinfulness. This he should do apart from noise and excitement, if possible; and he may be aided in doing it by employing hymns and psalms, which will oftentimes speedily carry his mind out of a dull and dead frame into some beginnings of life. He may thus come into a state in which prayer will not be a stupid act, or a dead form, but the glowing expression of a living feeling.

This is a proper preparation for prayer, whether public or private. If prayers in a prayer-meeting cannot be genuine, they might better be omitted, and hymns sung in their place. If but a single sentence is uttered, let it be real; and let utterance cease when the heart no longer prompts—and the heart will often have ceased its promptings long before a recitation of fifteen minutes is concluded. One moment of real communion with God is prayer, but a whole hour of recited words, without feeling, is not prayer, and is worse than none.

The way to kill a prayer-meeting is to make it conventional, and the chief secret of conducting it so that it shall minister to edification, is to force people out of conventional ways; to break up hereditary and stereotyped unwritten forms of prayer; to keep off those impertinent moths called exhorters, that fly about the flame of rising feeling; to charm men into forgetfulness of the machinery of the meeting; and to make them talk artlessly, naturally, and sensibly.

But above all, let all pretence, all mock solemnity and devotion, be put away. Let no man suffer himself to appear to his brethren to be what he is not, for this is part of the injunction, "Let every man speak truth with his neighbor." If this rule be not observed, and the frequent tendencies to violate it be not corrected, the prayer-meetings will degenerate, and people will lose first all profit and then all interest in them. For, what if people should go to an evening party, not in their natural character, but, one striving to be brilliant, another to be witty, another to be instructive, another to be profound? Who could endure the sham? There is need in prayer-meetings of men who are willing to stand simply and only on what they are and what they have.

The speaking in prayer-meetings should be conversational, and so, natural. The words spoken should flow naturally from the heart's experience, or else it were better to be silent. Usually, however, when a man has nothing to say, he gets up and exhorts sinners to repent; or, another, whose heart is empty, informs the church that they are very cold, and live far beneath their privileges. Such prayers or exhortations may be very glib and fluent, but they are as dry of sap or juice as last year's corn-husks. They are not only profitless but damaging. On the contrary, there are oftentimes prayers, humble, timid, half-inaudible, the utterances of uncultivated lips, that may cut a poor figure as lecture-room literature, that are nevertheless not to be scornfully disdained. If a child may not talk at all till he can speak fluent English, he will never learn. There should be a process, going on, continually, of education, by which all the members of the church should be able to contribute of their experiences and gifts; and, in such a course of development, the first hesitating, stumbling, ungrammatical prayer of a confused Christian may be worth more to the church than the best prayer of the most eloquent pastor. The prayer may be but little; but it is not a little thing that a church has one more man who is beginning to pray than it had before.

The conductor of a prayer-meeting should have a distinct conception of what such a meeting is to be and to do; and as it is a mutual instruction class, a place for religious feeling to take the social element, his chief duty should be to draw out the timid, to check the obtrusive, to encourage simple and true speaking, and to apply religious truths to those wants, and struggles, and experiences which are freely mentioned there.

THE DAY AND THE DESK.

It is no small thing, as it regards the education of the community, that from their youth up they have been taught to discuss all questions from ascertained and authoritative moral grounds. The rhetoric or argument of ancient civilization was secular, both in its spirit and aims. The intellect and the imagination were trained, not the conscience or the affections.

To have the whole, or the greatest part, of the community gather together every week for the religious discussion of life questions, cannot fail to establish a public mind which no other known causes could produce. The family educates the affections. Secular affairs train and sharpen the business faculties. Public affairs give general information; but where is moral training to come from?

The moral element in man has but a sorry chance against his selfish faculties and his passions. A few, in every community, are so endowed as to stand up, men of integrity and of natural religion, without or even against training. They may not be Christians. But they are men of a strong religious nature, and of slender passions, to whom justice and an imperfect spirituality is congenial. Such cases are single and isolated. The mass of men are not just nor religious, unless in a fragmentary way in exceptional instances

Take men as they rise, and their selfish and animal instincts are more active, more influential than their religious feelings. The habits of life are founded upon current selfishness. The character is shaped by the influence of three or four feelings,—the love of property, of power, and influence, of praise, and by the love of animal indulgence.

Benevolence, as an overruling power; justice between man and man, as a controlling force; a love of God and a salutary reverence for him, as an atmosphere in which the soul breathes, these are not common. From the beginning of life, the conscience is apt to be uneducated, or overlaid by selfishness, or drugged and silenced. Men are good-natured, or generous, upon occasions. A few are benevolent.

In the most select and best communities not one in a thousand is benevolent. Not one in a hundred is generous. When their own interests or wishes are not to be sacrificed; when kindness runs parallel with selfishness; when good service costs nothing, and is even easier than its opposite, then, one must be either a dyspeptic, or a very bad man, if he be not kind and generous. But in such cases the good feeling is a very narrow valley between very high mountains on either side. Of all the men that are regarded as respectable in New York, how many act from such deliberate convictions of conscience, that it may be said of them they are governed by a sense of Right? How many are benevolent—not in the sense of being good-natured when they are pleased, or kind when everything is to their mind, or generous when it costs them nothing and is easier than selfishness—but when to be so requires self-denial and moral principle? Our own convictions, founded upon observation, are, that very few have such benevolence, either by nature or by grace. Our impression is that religion has hitherto developed reverence toward God, carefulness of one's own life and conduct, and benevolence when it does not cost too much.

We see nothing in the ordinary influences of society which tends to rectify this: nothing in secular institutions; nothing in the course of business. Schools and seminaries cannot frame the man's habits, nor train the moral nature. It is in this view that we regard the Sabbath and the Pulpit as indispensable to society. The Sabbath is a day of bodily rest, doubtless; it is a day for social culture; it is to be advocated for reasons, therefore, of secular expediency.

There is a ground higher than all these. It is the day for religious education. There is no substitute for it. The work which above all others man needs to have done, cannot be done except through the force and observance of some such institution.

The Pulpit is the popular religious educator. Its object is to stimulate and develop the religious feelings. All subjects upon which men think or act, all relations and duties, all observances, amusements, occupations, and sympathies need to be discussed by every man from the ground of religious principles. Left to themselves, few men will so discuss them. Week by week men should hear their daily life discussed, not from selfish principles, not from a ground of expediency, not from popular points of view, but from the highest religious grounds. Tc have the whole, or the greatest part of the community assembling for the expression of reverential feeling is beneficial doubtless. This should be an element of Sabbath observance. But this very feeling will itself depend upon a previous education and development of the whole religious nature. That development will take place most healthfully and rapidly by such a system of education as shall lead men habitually to look at all things from the religious stand-point. When a whole community are wont to have their social life, their secular business, their public duties, taken out of their low and selfish attitudes and lifted up into the light of God's countenance, and then measured, judged, repressed or developed, and wholly bathed or inspired by the spirit of conscience and of love, then they are receiving a moral education, for which there is no other provision except the Sabbath and the Pulpit. And we regard the Day and the Desk to be as needful to the refined and philosophic as to the rude and unlettered, though for different reasons. Great culture is liable to take a selfish and subtle pride, which, though not as destructive to the animal economy, are fully as injurious to religious purity as vice and appetite.

IS CONVERSION INSTANTANEOUS?

A LETTER TO A FRIEND.

My dear Sir: I am glad that we are of one belief as to the reality of that momentous change which is usually called conversion or regeneration. We agree, too, that such a change does not require violence to be done to the mental organization. A man has the same faculties, intellectual, moral, social, and animal, before conversion as after. Neither are the constitutional functions changed; nor the laws of mind, under which all mental life exists. The change is analogous to that which happens to a thoroughly and chronically diseased body, when it becomes decidedly convalescent. All the vital organs, and every minute vessel throughout the system is changed from a morbid to a natural condition. There is neither increase nor diminution of the organs of the body; there is nothing taken from, and nothing added to the normal functions of the organs. In like manner, the change of mind is not one of faculty but of function; and in function, the change is only from a disordered to a normal and healthful state.

Is such a change instantaneous? You think that it is not. Many devout Christians agree with you. Indeed, taking the world through, I presume that you are with the majority. Nor is it to be denied that you have many apparent reasons for such doubt. Yet, it seems to me that both facts and analogies are against you when the matter is critically searched.

Every serious change that befalls the mind may be said to have three stages—the preparatory stage, the stage of actual change, and the after stage. It is of neither the first, nor the last, but of the middle one, that we affirm instantaneousness. We say that the act of volition, or of voluntary transition from one purpose or condition of mind to another, is always instantaneous, although the circumstances which led to it, and the results which follow it, may be long-drawn and gradual. A man may determine to change his secular vocation. The reasons inclining him thereto may gradually arise, and grow in force from day to day for months, and even years. But the determination, at last, is a sudden, momentary act. After the decision, months may be required to carry it completely into effect.

So that there are in a change of religious feeling two gradual stages and one instantaneous. The mind may become gradually, and, more and more, deeply serious; the perception of neglected truths may be progressive; the motives to a decision for or against a religious life may be long accumulating; but, at length, there is a time of choice; and whether perceived or not, that decisive choice will be instantaneous. Then comes the after stage—the carrying out of the determination. The eradication of bad habits, the development of right feelings, the reduction of conduct to religious principle; in short, the formation of religious character, is gradual.

In the popular mind conversion improperly includes all the stages which we have discriminated; and of such a conversion it is rightly said that it must be gradual. But conversion, as a mere act of choice, is instantaneous. We affirm all volition to be instantaneous. While one weight after another goes into the scale you are preparing for the counterpoise; but when the index passes the centre, it passes at once. In like manner, when the mind holds a change in view, it may be long in coming toward a decision; it may vacillate and swing first to the one and then to the other side. But when each faculty but the last one has consented, and at length, long resisting, that faculty coincides with the rest, the decision is instant and decisive.

The recognition of this change, by the individual, will depend upon the character of his mind. Those who have strong emotions, all of whose changes follow or are instantly followed by the intellect, will perceive that a transition has been made.

Those who have strong and positive emotions, but are not wont intellectually to inspect them, will *feel* that there is a change.

Those with an even and gentle, emotive temperament, will not intellectually recognize the mental transition, but will first be conscious of it from the results that begin to appear.

From these statements we should be led to expect that religious changes would be most apparently sudden among uncultivated minds, which being uncontrolled, act under emotion, with extremes of flux and reflux; among men of violent passions; among those who have been the most entirely destitute of moral sensibility. We should suspect, also, that such changes would be, at the time, perceived by all minds, robust or feeble, positive or gentle, in times of great general excitement, in which the mind is more active and moves more strongly than alone, by reason of sympathy with other minds. Facts corroborate such expectations.

The distinction between a real instantaneous change of mind, and the instant *recognition* of that change, should not be forgotten. As the change of mind may be induced or prevented with great facility by the degree of knowledge possessed of the mind on which influence is to be exerted, by the nature of the means employed, and by the skill with which such means are applied to the mind; so, the recognition of that change will depend in part upon one's emotive temperament, and upon the habits of decision which one possesses; in part, upon the condition of the mind at the time, and in part upon the instructions received, directing the mind's attention to such phenomena.

I imagine that you will say, of all this disquisition, "It may be curious, but is it of practical importance? Its merit is metaphysical. It will do no good in actual life."

On the contrary, though it is metaphysically true, its chief importance is that it takes hold so earnestly and efficiently on practice. A mind taught to believe in the reality and necessity of an instant choice will act with directness and brevity. The belief in gradual conversion goes hand in hand with procrastination and mere promissory amendment. Neither can the efforts of Christians nor of ministers be the same under the two systems. Those who trust to a gradual amelioration cannot in the nature of things work with that directness, with that sharp activity, and strong hope, which they have who expect an immediate result. To labor for a future, indefinite, gradual change, is like growing acorns; to labor for an immediate change is like growing wheat. In the latter case, the appointed months are so definite, the harvest so near, and the result so sure, that all have hope, and faith, and industry; while few are found sowing acorn seed for forests, which other hands, in another generation, shall fell and use.

NATURAL LAWS AND SPECIAL PROVIDENCES.

THE human mind tends to pass from one extreme of truth to the other. The mind of communities touches both extremes before it settles down at the intermediate point of truth. There is no great truth which, being pressed far enough in one direction, will not meet another bearing up against it from the opposite. There is, for instance, the truth of man's liberty; press it far enough and it will be met and restrained by the equal truth of man's dependence. The truth of man's individuality; press it to a certain distance, and it will meet another truth, equally certain—man's associated life. There is the truth of the necessity of helping men, and the other truth, just as important, that if you help them you will destroy them;—for there is nothing worse than help which impairs the disposition of men to help themselves, and nothing so bad as not to help them when they need help. There is also the doctrine of free agency, and the counter doctrine of dependence upon God. There is no one great line of thought which, being pursued at length, does not meet another coming from the opposite; and a man's mind should stand at the centre of the wheel, and all truths should come to it from every side as the spokes of one great wheel.

It is on this account that men vibrate between two extremes; and only after wide investigation that they take in all truth.

Before men had learned much of the globe, and of physical laws, they were guided, in assigning causes for the effects which they witnessed, by their veneration and imagination. When the imagination, instead of reason, guides ignorant men, they are almost always wont to ascribe effects, whose causes are not visible, to spiritual influence, infernal or supernal. The progress of observation and investigation drives men from these superstitious notions, and one effect after another is wrested from the supposed agency of spirits, and becomes affixed to its natural cause. This was the case with celestial appearances—the comets, the Aurora Borealis. This was the case also, in a great measure, with diseases. It is not long since pestilences, plagues, and many special forms of disease, such as leprosy, and many varieties of convulsive disease which affected the nervous system, were regarded by the medical faculty, and by the church itself, as the results of spiritual or supernatural causes. It is only since the art of printing that these notions have been in a measure done away. I remember, in my own day, very long sermons to prove that the cholera did not depend on natural agencies, but that God held it in his hand, and dropped it down upon the world.

There is no doubt that there are moral results to be wrought out by all these natural phenomena, but it was held that they were produced by preternatural means. It is not many ages since a man would have been expelled from any sound church, if he did not believe that diseases resulted from the direct exercise of divine power, instead of intermediate causation; and that healing was to be effected only through some form of spiritual incantation.

The same was true of the common events of familiar life. Men saw evidence of the agency of good and of bad spirits around them, at all times, and in every minute event. Since the world began this has been common; and it is no commoner now than ever before. Men have always been watching with superstitious fear, lest, some charm being forgotten, lurking mischief should gain advantage of them.

The growth of natural science has tended very much to sweep away such views; first, from philosophical minds; gradually, as general information increased, from the minds of all well-informed common men: and now, in the immense progress of science and the diffusion of a knowledge of it among the common people, there is a very marked tendency to go to the opposite extreme, and not only to refer each special effect to a corresponding natural cause, but to deny that there are any effects which are the results of divine volition. Some men are ready to say that all things are effects of physical causes, and that there is no immediate divine volition exerted upon natural laws. This is as monstrous in science, as it is absurd in religion. If men take the premise that all effects to be expected in this world are provided for in organized natural laws, and that there are none which result from divine efficiency, they must go through with all the conclusions. They must hold that human intelligence is our only guide in this world, or, in other words, is the only God of natural powers; they must argue that no man will be helped in this world except so far as he helps himself, by finding out the paths of nature and walking in them—a falsehood which is all the worse because it is half true. For in making an axe, the head is of iron and the edge of steel; but the head is the larger and heavier part, while the edge is but a narrow strip. So, with such a falsehood; the greater part of it is true, but this is made only to add weight and power to the cutting edge, which is false. They must declare that the belief in a special and particular providence is a superstition; that God works by laws, and that he never interferes with or uses them. They must believe that, consequently, prayer is a mere poetic exercise; good to those that like it, only because it reacts upon their feelings, and soothes and calms them. They must suppose that prayers which the heathen write, and which the wind offers up for them by turning a wheel, like a mill, are as effectual on the laws of nature as an humble Christian's prayer. They must hold that the doctrine of miracles is to be given up, as nothing but a superlative superstition. And, for this matter, such men usually do teach that miracles always happened in dark ages, among ignorant men; that many of the same results can now be produced by scientific causes; and that a belief in them, as effects divinely produced, is unworthy of an enlightened philosopher.

I need not say how far men have drifted away from the New Testament, who have reached this ground. Such a man is not only not a Christian, but whatever natural religion he may have, if he be consistent, he must reject the New Testament altogether, as an authoritative guide, and give himself up to Nature and Reason. For, if there be one truth more especially taught in the Bible than another, it is the fact of God's activity and influence in human life. If there ever comes a day in which it can be shown by science, that there is no active interference of the divine creative will in the special affairs of men, science in that day will demolish the New Testament. When it can be scientifically demonstrated that no more effects are wrought in this world by the intentional interposition of divine volition, than those which fall out in the way of ordinary and unhelped natural causation, in that day, I am free to say, the New Testament will be overthrown. It will be regarded as an amiable book, but one whose doctrines have been refuted, and are passed away.

This doctrine of the presence and actual interference of God in the world, producing effects which would not have fallen out otherwise, is taught in the Bible as against idolatry, as against naturalism (in the early chapters of John), as the argument and foundation of prayer, of courage, of patience, and of hope, and as a special development, among others, of the incarnation of Christ to bring to light the reality of God, who wrought invisibly in life and nature, both before and since.

It is to be admitted that this globe and its inhabitants are included in a system of physical laws; that these are, in their nature, unchanged and unchangeable; that they are incapable of increase or decrease; that they are sufficient for all ordinary purposes of human life; that the welfare and happiness of men depend largely upon a wise employment of them; and that the progress of the race is largely to be effected by their wise application of them. Not only would I cast no obstacle in the way of scientific research, but I hail it as the great almoner of God's bounty. Men should be instructed to become better acquainted with the laws and influences which operate upon both the body and the mind, and upon the natural world. Men will never be as good Christians as they ought, until they know more perfectly how their bodies are put together, and what is in their own minds, and the natural laws of the one and of the other. Science is yet to interpret Scripture, in many respects; and I am persuaded that all the most characteristic elements of revealed or inspired truth will in the end be corroborated and not harmed, by the progress of natural science. I believe in everything that is true. I am not necessarily to believe in everything that pretends to be true; but when anything is proved, whatever it overturns, I am bound to it by the allegiance with which I am bound to God! He that denies the truth in or out of the Bible, denies God!

The progress of science lays a surer foundation for a belief in God's active interference in human affairs than has existed without it. When maturer fruits of investigation shall be had, there can be no doubt that science itself will establish our faith in prayer, in miracles, and in special providence.

There are respects in which natural laws are beyond the reach of all human interference and control. There are spheres in which light and heat cannot be touched and controlled. There are various attractions which perform in their own way their own work, beyond man's guidance or reach—such are the great laws which bind together the stellar universe. Great currents and passages of natural powers are put entirely beyond man's hand. But it is just as certain that there are, also, in God's system of nature, another class of laws which come close to us, and whose office is, or seems to be, to minister to human life. They are either modifications of great laws, or they are separate laws. And in respect to these, I affirm that they are not fructified, and do not perform their function, till they are controlled by human volition. God has made the agencies which concern human life, to be of such a nature, that the *human mind is necessary to the full development and greatest fruitfulness of natural laws.* It is supposed by many that a natural law is perfect in itself; whereas it is perfected, in many instances, only when it is permeated by human volition.

Electricity, for instance, plays a round of its own. It has its own pastures, and its own great running grounds. It performs a large function unknown—beyond our reach, and without our knowledge. But so far as ordinary purposes of civilized life are concerned, electricity does nothing till we have taught it how to serve us; then it runs swifter races for human convenience than ever were run before. When the mind takes hold of it, electricity becomes a patient drudge; so that we now work by lightning, which would never have done a single thing for us if it had not been harnessed by the human mind. But now, above the sea, and under the sea ere long, it shall carry the messages of nations, flashing from the East to the West, proclaiming war or heralding peace, and performing the great offices of civilization. When man takes it by the head and says, "Receive my bridle," and throws over it the saddle, and says, "Take me for your rider," it becomes patient and submissive, and acknowledges man as its master.

Light performs a great amount of work,—whether we are waking or sleeping; in its vast journeys through the universe—in its sun-flashes and moon-reflections; but man's mind seizes this law, and does what Phæton could not, *drives* it. We have it in our dwelling. We make it work along our coasts. We divide it, and set it at work in the garden and on the farm. We give it the power of a living pencil, and make it draw artists' pictures. And yet we are in the midst of a carping set of philosophers who say that we can obey natural laws, but cannot control them. We do control them.

Water has a certain round of grand effects, and these are performed whether a creature looks on, or not. The ocean never asks man what it may do with its own waves and upon its own domain! The old Polar Sea—the only mystery now left among the oceans of the globe—has rolled for ages, by day and night, by summer and winter, with no eye to watch it—except from above! That mighty unexplored wilderness of mysterious water!—It does what it will, and is not dependent upon man. But water *is* dependent upon him for doing many things which it never could do otherwise. While it works in nature and on the globe, it is not subject to his will; but when it works for human life, it immediately becomes his disciple. Man seizes the law, and canals shoot forth, mills live, irrigation turns barren heaths to gardens, tides dig out channels, and the patient hydrostatic pump drives down to her element the vast Leviathan. Water could do none of these things without man's help. The things which natural laws can do, without human volition, are not so many nor are they more wonderful than the things which they do only by the life-giving touch of man's mind.

Heat, in the sun, produces the seasons. How vast is the great fire-place of the universe! Yet, compare it with the sphere in which fire works under the dominion of man—in the forge, in the furnace, over the blow-pipe, serving the domestic range, warming the house, and pouring summer throughout the year within the dwelling!

Look at Nature's Fruits. There is but a *beginning* in natural fruits, and they never, when left to nature alone, reach beyond that point. When a man finds a crab-apple in the woods, he would not willingly find it more than once; yet, brought to his own orchard, it becomes a fine fruit. But did nature make the pippin? Nature had been trying her hand for years and years, and had never been able to get beyond the crab-apple. Man says to her: "You are a bungling apprentice; *I* will make you a journeyman."

Nature can make iron, but she never made a sword. She never made a jack-knife, a steam-engine, a knife and fork—nothing but bare, cold, dead iron.

Now, is this a course of specious metaphysical reasoning? Is not this truth reasonable? Are not these facts alleged conclusive? And if they be true, what is the result? Nature has a certain crude, general function which natural laws perform of themselves, without any regard to men. But these laws are made to be vitalized and directed to a higher development by the control of the human mind and will. The laws of the globe are to be taken hold of by man's will, as really as the laws of the body are. The secondary effects of natural laws are just as much a part of their nature as the primary, and are of equal importance. In fact, it is these that constitute the elements of civilization. While natural laws, in a certain way, influence and control men, yet they are, in the effects which they produce, just as much controlled by man, and just as dependent on him. If nature should abandon men, *they* would die, and *it* would become poverty-stricken. Let nature forget us, and the heart would cease to beat. The pulsations of endless electrical currents would cease. On the other hand, let man forget nature, and the city would crumble, and go back to a wilderness; the garden which had grown up from a thistle-ground, would return to its native condition; cultivated seeds would shrink back to their original poverty; and all domestic animals would rebound to their wild state. Nature needs man to keep her at work.

It is this view that settles all questions about man's

necessity to obey. God has not put us before nature to make us only its pupil, but also its master. We are not alone to look up and take, but to look down and control. We are not only to obey, but also to rule. We are to obey for the sake of ruling. The whole talk about the absolute and inflexible government of natural law has no foundation except in fools' brains. It is a divided empire, and man's part is more than nature's. When God made man, he made more of nature in him than he did in all the rest of the world besides!

The question now arises—Is there a moral or scientific probability that God ever produces results by natural laws, in this world, which otherwise would not have been produced?—If we drive natural laws, cannot God do it? I hold, because the Bible teaches it, and now I hold it more because nature and science teach it, that there are millions of results that never would have fallen out in the course of nature, that are now continually happening on account of God's special mercy. The doctrine of a special providence is this. God administers natural laws—of the mind, the body, and the outward world—so as to produce effects which they never would have done of themselves. Man can do this, and why not God? By a wise use of natural laws man can make the difference between comfort and discomfort. He can till the farm, and make the seasons serve him. He can take natural laws, and gird himself about with them, so that they shall make him rich, and wise, and strong. Men can do it for themselves—why cannot God do it for them? Men can do it for their children—for their neighbors' children—for scores and hundreds of persons. A farmer that administers his estate wisely, will have enough, not only for himself, but for others. His children will be fed, the neighborhood supplied, and the veins of commerce swollen by the overplus of his sagacity. A man can say to the light, to the water, to the seasons, "I will, by you, make a special providence for this whole town," and he can do it; for if he falls back, there will not be abundance, but if he goes forward there will be. That is not all. A man may be put at a point where—as Napoleon was, or Wellington in Spain, or Sir John Moore in the north of Portugal, or Clive in India—he can make a special providence for a nation, for a race, for an age, for one land or for the globe! Now God can do a great deal more than man, and a great deal better. Is there any objection to such a doctrine?

In regard to the doctrine of prayer, many men say, "Do you suppose that God will make any difference, whether you pray or not?" The reply is, that God can, if he chooses. But whether he will, or not, depends very much on how I pray, and what I pray for. I can give my boy a book or a bow every day in the year, but whether I will, or not, is another thing. God will not do for men what men can do for themselves. Nor will he do for them at present, what they, after a proper course of development, will by and by be able to do for themselves. But a man has a right to go up along the path of his weakness, and say, "I have done what I could; now hear my prayer, and do for me what I cannot do for myself." And if it is a thing that is needed, God will answer the prayer. For he loves to give needed things better than earthly parents love to give good gifts to their children. Suppose you have been travelling in the cars, with your child, and it becomes restless with fatigue. Its rest has been broken by night-travelling, and it is hungry and asks for food. But a bank of snow lies across the track, and the train cannot go on. It waits. Anybody would feel pity for such a child—even if it were a negro's! But how much more if it were his own? And if it be my child, and says, "Pa, water, water,"—it cuts me to the heart to hear it! But by and by, with double and treble elements of iron, the track is opened, the way is cleared, and we are hurried on to the next station. The first bolt I make is into the hotel; for I am hungry, not for myself, but for the child; and I break through the crowd back again into the car, with bread in my hands for the child. Ah, do you suppose the bread is half so sweet to his mouth as to my eyes that watch his eager eating? But this is God's figure and not mine. He declares that he is more willing to give good gifts to them that ask him, than parents are to give to their children.

Have you ever prayed on this principle and found your prayer unanswered? Not prayer for amusement; for some men pray, who begin with Adam, and come leisurely down all the way through to "thy kingdom come," and then wind up with the "power and glory, forever and ever, Amen." That is not prayer; or at least it is not such praying as will be answered. But did you ever, under the pressure of a real want, go to God and say, "Thou, Father, canst help me; give me thine aid," and not have your prayer answered? Glorious old Martin Luther knew how to pray. He used to take one of God's promises, and laying it down, would say, "Now, Lord, here is thy word! If thou dost not keep it, I will never believe thee again." This may be called audacious, but it was not audacity in such a Christian as Luther.

What is needed is, that we should take a larger and broader faith, and we shall then have no difficulty with special providences, or miracles, or prayer; but all their problems will be solved, and their mysteries cleared away.

THE DEAD CHRIST.

No one conversant with Christian art is ignorant of the multitudes of pictures and carvings of the Dead Christ. Every name of eminence has attempted the subject; and the great masters have again and again repeated their conceptions.

One of the most affecting that ever came under our eye, is that in the National Gallery of London, by Francia, we believe. The Saviour is extended across his mother's lap, an angel sustains his head, and another his feet. We gazed long at the sublime face, now motionless and cold, pale and silent. All the majesty of his life, the scenes of his wonderful sorrow, came back to us; and, whether it was our imagination or the real expression of the picture, we certainly felt that we beheld the sorrow that slew the Saviour and the love which conquered the sorrow, both together; so that it seemed to us that his thorned head was overspread with sadness, only that upon it victorious love might stand forth more evidently triumphant. It was not a boisterous triumph, nor even a radiant victory that was expressed, but the calm, serene, silent victory of patience and unutterable affection. We are not fond of this class of subjects. But this one seemed to be redeemed from the weakness of death, and to suggest no thought of the crushing of power, the dishonoring of life, but only of a struggle in which Death was the opening of a gate for a spirit to march forth to victory!

In art, and merely as art, the Dead Christ is but barely tolerable. In religion, and as a part of religion, it is altogether to be disallowed. And yet, in the preaching of Christ, how many preach a Living Christ? It is a suffering Christ, a tempted Christ, a dying Christ, a buried Christ. Some mysterious benefit is hoped from a devout contemplation of such a moving theme. But is the mere natural relation of such scenes to the human sympathies, to be compared with the presentation of Christ—risen, glorified, triumphantly reigning; and reigning not for his own enjoyment, but for the succor, the teaching, and the perfection of his earthly children? Our Saviour does not live behind eighteen hundred years ago. We are not to be pilgrims along the misty track of Time, waiting for him in Jerusalem, and lingering in the garden. That he might not be local, a being of one age and nation, he arose to that blazing centre which knows no periods, no epoch, no time, but is the eternal Now. He is to every age a Present Saviour —to every soul a Living Saviour! To our mind he is clothed with attributes then exhibited, when he wore his earthly form; but, having gained a clear conception of what Christ *was*, that he *is*, and that we are to transfer in our thoughts to the invisible One, perpetually hovering near us. The hope and the joy of Christians are not in the past, but in the present. It is believed that Christ knows them, that he knows them as individuals, by *name*, in all their personal peculiarities; that he feels that living and efficient sympathy for them which their daily necessities require; that his heart yearns, that his eye follows them, that his pity enfolds them.

Christians are glad of a Saviour suffering and slain, because through this experience they are able to form a conception of what nature is in Him now. And their great and peculiar need is a Christ who knows all their weaknesses of disposition without feeling disgust; who knows all their sins without bitterness; who knows their faults and foibles without contempt; who knows their daily practical difficulties, their cares, their family troubles, their business perplexities, and who knows just how all these things, acting on the peculiar temperament which each possesses, hinders his piety, mars his joy, fills him with doubts, and afflicts him with burdens.

It requires no great stretch of faith to believe that Christ has opened up a way to save those who come to him already converted out of their sins. But to come blushing from the commission of some sinful thing, full of conscious meanness, and half-despairing, inasmuch as, a hundred times before, you have promised to renounce evil, and have broken the promise;—when in the quick and stinging confusion of shame and grief and discouragement, you can raise up the vision of a merciful Christ, looking intently upon you, and saying, "Son, now above all other times, come to me, for I am the only one that hath the patience and the power to bring thee out of all these passes and temptations;" this it is, indeed, to have a Living Christ! Do we enough preach a Living Christ? Do we not stumble, just as the Roman Catholic often does, by laying hold of the earthly form of Christ, the life and symbols of his love; and by endeavoring to extract from the past, that which the grave shall never give, nor the dark past, but which shall come, if at all, right down from the Living Heart of the Companionable Saviour, who though glorified in heaven, is none the less the earthly Guide of his people?

The faults of preaching, when such faults exist, are magnified in Christian experience. Few persons look up. Many look back, and wonder that seeing the place where Jesus lay, they see no angels there, and hear no voice. Their Christ is the Dead Christ. Some persons long for a tender heart, for impassioned experience, for more earnest love. They wander in Gethsemane. They linger on the mount beneath the olive trees. They shudder upon Calvary. They search the garden for the grave. But Gethsemane that once heard the groans, now hears them no more. The olives yield their fruit, but no Saviour sits beneath their covering shadows. The hill, if one might hear its silent voice, would cry out "Here He was, but is no longer." The grave would murmur, "Come see where He lay—He is not here, He is arisen." And all the scenes of the past have now but one office, to instruct us how to imagine and to lay hold of a Living and a Present Saviour.

AN EXPOSITION.

"Whereby are given unto us exceeding great and precious promises: that by these ye might be partakers of the divine nature, having escaped the corruption that is in the world through lust. And besides this, giving all diligence, add to your faith virtue; and to virtue, knowledge; and to knowledge, temperance; and to temperance, patience; and to patience, godliness; and to godliness, brotherly kindness; and to brotherly kindness, charity. For if these things be in you, and abound, they make you that ye shall neither be barren nor unfruitful in the knowledge of our Lord Jesus Christ. But he that lacketh these things is blind, and cannot see afar off, and hath forgotten that he was purged from his old sins. Wherefore the rather, brethren, give diligence to make your calling and election sure: for if ye do these things, ye shall never fall: for so an entrance shall be ministered unto you abundantly into the everlasting kingdom of the Lord and Saviour Jesus Christ."—2 Pet. i. 4–11.

This is a passage keyed to the note of encouragement. It sets forth the virtues which cost us most, but which we are most easily tempted to dispense with; and shows that these very qualities have a special relation to our future wealth and glory. The line of thought is this—as if the Christian graces presented themselves to the apostle's mind as so many golden links in a chain or necklace, which can never have too many, which is rich and valuable not alone by the quality of each link but by the number of them—he urges us to add one to the other in consecutive order. To faith, add the golden link of virtue; to virtue, knowledge; to knowledge, temperance; to temperance, patience; to patience, godliness; to godliness, brotherly kindness; and to brotherly kindness, love. These qualities shall make the life blessed; that is, truthful. They shall not be like ragged and weary pilgrims in a barren and unfruitful desert, but like men that walk in orchards and gardens, with abundance on every hand.

But besides the present blessing, the apostle enunciates the blessed truth that these virtues, by their number and richness, will have a determining influence upon our reception into heaven, and our condition there.

The force of this statement is lost in our common version, because there are no latent meanings and associations attached to the English words such as belong to the original. Among the ancient customs of Greece, none is more eminent than the expressing good will to society by providing public entertainments. These are to be distinguished from feasts. They were entertainments or spectacles, exhibitions in theatres and circuses, magnificent processions, public adornments, arches, wreaths, and the full wealth of music. These exhibitions took place on memorable days, commemorative of public events. They celebrated victories, they were especially prepared as honors for public benefactors: and when citizens who led the nation's armies returned from war victorious, the scale of the entertainment was commensurate not only with achievements of the victorious general, but with the gladness and exhilaration of the public mind.

Now, the preparing of these entertainments and receptions was not the business of the government but of private individuals.

Rich men, who desired to win popularity, were permitted to bear the expenses of them. And this was a kind of inferior philanthropy. Among us men build hospitals, found libraries, endow colleges, establish funds for various charities. But such things were not known then. And these popular exhibitions stood in their place, as the way in which rich men expressed generosity, munificence and philanthropy. And as these entertainments were in their nature expensive, so they grew more and more so, by the desire of men to rival each other, each one endeavoring to surpass all that had gone before. The verb employed here is *epichoregethesetai* (επιχορήγεθήσὲται.) It is from *choregos*, (χορήγος) a *choir-leader*, a *band-leader*. Now as the charge of these enormous choral exhibitions, in which scenic effects were added to the utmost wealth of music, was the means by which men exhibited their liberality, so, in time, the prodigality with which rich men did spend their means became proverbial; and it introduced a new word into the language; for the verb, derived from χορήγος, came to signify *lavish abundance*, profusion without limit. Just as Epicurus has given his own name to be a word of force, epicurean; so this name *choregos*, the name of a class of men, came to signify that which these men were wont to do.

It is not a little remarkable that the apostle should have selected this word. It is one of those flint words, which being struck, flash forth with a hundred sparks of association.

When he would encourage Christians to endure hardships, and to persevere in all virtues, he begins to tell them how blessed it would make them here; and then glancing forward, and beginning to speak of the effect which it would have hereafter, there rose up in his view a great city, like Athens in the days of her integrity; a city that glowed with marbles as the north glows with crystal mountains; whose temples glittered on every street; and from whose grand portals, as when Alcibiades or Pericles returned from victory, the whole population poured out, with chaplets of flowers on their heads, with wreaths in their hands, with costly sacrifices led by white-robed priests; with chanting choirs in some part singing peans; and vast bands of instrumental music interluding, or carrying forward the patriotic anthem alone. And, with this vision before him, Peter cries out, If ye do these things ye shall not be barren even here; and hereafter a universal choral outbreak from the city of God shall meet you. And you shall be received by the whole glorified throng, amid every demonstration of gladness, triumph, and honor. All this, historically, lay buried up in the word *επιχορήγεθήσέται*.

There is one other element that may be noted, and that is, that as the care and conduct of these ancient public receptions were allowed, as an honor, to stand upon the wealth and generosity of some public benefactor, so the apostle, carrying out the figure, means to say, that when we are arriving at our home in heaven, when we are drawing nigh to the open gates, and are about to enter, it is through the riches of the goodness of God that we shall not go in unnoticed or alone, but shall be met and greeted by a great and innumerable company whom He shall bid to come out, clad in the white robes "which the saints do wear," with harps in their hands, and with songs and salutations of joy upon their lips, to conduct us in triumphal procession into His Throne, that so "an abundant entrance may be ministered unto us." This is the meaning of the passage. The word *abundantly* is not happy in its function here. The true meaning is, For so a choral and processional greeting and entrance shall be given to you, by the goodness, or wealth, or abundance of Jesus Christ. In other words, the magnificence and costliness of the reception shall be according to the wealth of Christ's heart.

And what a thought! That the virtuous lives, the heroic deeds which men perform on earth, are not unheeded, though they may be performed in obscurity, and buried in the consciousness of the heart of the actor; that human life lies open to the inspection of heaven; that a cloud of witnesses behold our strife, our defeat, or our victory; that though, to all intents, we may be far off from heaven, since we are distant by the number of years that lie between—by the separation of time rather than space—that yet heaven is near to us; that it broods us, watches us, sympathizes with us; that though the holy and just have gone home to heaven, they are not separated from the struggling company on earth; that they look down upon us here, beholding our journey thither, and await our arrival that they may greet us with the surprise of triumphal entrance! This is the grand idea that rose before the mind of the apostle, which is so dimly conveyed in our imperfect translation.

THE EPISCOPAL SERVICE.

The *Churchman* of this city has a kind notice of some remarks made by us in the *Independent.* We are anxious that our parishioners and readers should reap what benefit they can from reading it, and we spread it before them:

"Among the miscellaneous matter of the present number [Feb. 14th] will be found part of an article on "Churches and Pulpits," communicated to the *Independent* by the Rev. Henry Ward Beecher. It contains much that is sound on the subject of the place where the preacher is located, and the description of box in which he is ordinarily confined. It is good as far as it goes. But the truth is, that in the early Church the present style of pulpit was unknown. Sermons were originally delivered from the steps of the altar. Bingham, in his 'Antiquities of the Christian Church,' tells us that the ordinary place of preaching was the altar. While quoting from Mr. Beecher, it may, perhaps, not be uninteresting to our readers to know what a 'High Puritan' thinks of the Choral Service of the Church."

The *Churchman* then extracts a portion of a letter from Stratford-on-Avon, published in the Star Papers, and proceeds:

"It is gratifying to read an extract so entirely commendable as this. We trust it may have its influence on Mr. Beecher's congregation. It would certainly be a perfectly orthodox proceeding for Mr. B., when he gets into his new church, not only to have an altar, from the steps of which to speak to the people, but to have a choir of boys, properly surpliced, to make the responses and the Amens in the service, which, of course, would be that of the Episcopal Church, of which Mr. Beecher's mother is said to have been an exemplary member. Congregational churches in England do this; why should not Mr. Beecher? We have before us the last number of the *Musical Review and Gazette*, published in this city, which contains the following extract from the private correspondence of an American lady (the daughter of a New England clergyman) now absent in Europe. 'A few Sabbaths ago we attended service at Surrey chapel, the place formerly occupied by Rowland Hill. Rev. Newman Hall is now the pastor, an interesting preacher, though in nothing remarkble. Though a Congregational church, the service of the Church of England is still used, and is chanted by the whole congregation with so much taste, fervor, and devotion, that it is really heavenly. If the service would always be performed in such a manner, I should never wish for any other. I only wish you could hear it. I find congregational singing is everywhere the custom, and I think I shall soon become so fond of it that I shall not enjoy any other. It does seem much more hearty and much more devotional.' If the service of the Church of England is deemed sound in a Congregational church in England, why would not the service of the Episcopal Church of this country be equally acceptable and 'sound' in Mr. Beecher's church in Brooklyn?"

1. We have never had a doubt as to the excellence of the Episcopal service in public worship. We do doubt whether the constant repetition of it as the sole method of worship, is the best for all. But we are quite willing to leave that to the judgment and experience of each person for himself. And if, on trial, this service is found sufficient for their religious wants, not only would we not dissuade men from its use, but we would do all in our power to make it more useful to them. And this we say without respect to persons. Should our own children find their religious wants better met in the service of the Episcopal Church than in the Plymouth Congregational Church, we should take them by the hand and lead

them to its altars, and commit them to God's grace, through the ministration of the Episcopal communion, with unhesitating conviction that if they did not profit there, it would be their own fault!

Whether the Episcopal Church is one that builds up men in holiness is not an open question. There are too many saints rejoicing in heaven, and too many of the noblest Christians yet laboring on earth, who have derived their religious life through the teachings and offices of that Church, to leave any impartial mind in any doubt. We have not a word of controversy with Christian men who accept the service of that Church as the best means of enriching their faith.

Nor are we unmindful of the debt of gratitude which we, and the whole Christian world, owe to the scholars, the teachers, the divines, and the bishops of that Church. Whatever historic faults may be raked up against it, we firmly believe that few bodies of Christian men, in so long a succession, can look back upon so many noble Christian teachers, or so much fruit of Christian living! And no man can excite in us any unpleasant feeling by a just eulogy of the Episcopal Christian brotherhood. Their merited praise brings unalloyed pleasure to us: and when, in prayer, we ask God's blessing on his Church on earth, we mean that Church as much as our own. We mean every brotherhood of Christian men who are, according to their best light, worshiping God and loving men.

2. But, now, will our Christian brethren of the *Churchman* accord to us, as Christians in Congrega-

tional church-fellowship, the same charity and liberty which we accord to them? We claim that, for ourselves and for the most of those who consort with us, our method of Christian worship is more useful, more edifying and therefore better than any other. Not better for everybody, but better for us. While we say frankly and heartily to child, friend, or parishioner—"If Christ is revealed to you better by the worship and service of the Episcopal Church, do not hesitate or fail to accept it,"—will the *Churchman* say the same to its friends, in respect to the Christian service and worship of the Congregational brotherhood?

We take this broad ground, that every man is at liberty to employ whatever form of religious worship is best adapted to develop and maintain in him the true Christian life. And we hold that each man must determine this for himself; and that when it has been determined, every Christian is bound conscientiously to respect another's conscience! Let every man be fully convinced in his own mind.

3. As to the altar, we agree with the *Churchman* that it would be entirely orthodox to have an "altar" in the new church. To those who wish them, and who can make them serviceable, there is no reason in our day why they should be denied. So might the ark of the covenant, and tables of shew-bread, and the high priest's breast-plate, and many other things of a symbolic use, be employed. But is it a duty to have an altar? Can we not offer service, without these symbols, acceptably to God? If an education makes them a hindrance and not a help,

are we to have them intruded upon us as necessary parts of worship?

We believe in Christ as a sacrifice, once offered up for all and forever. We need no visible altar upon which to lay our invisible sacrifice. Faith is to us better than sight by means of symbols.

As to "surpliced boys"—we have them already. The whole congregation is a choir, and our boys, bright and happy, unite and respond with their elders. The surplice which they wear is just that thing which their dear mothers threw over them when they left home. And angels' hands could do no more than mothers' hands do for darling children!

And now, in respect to this whole matter, we accord to our Episcopal brethren everything that they can ask, except the right of making their liberty our law. When we are satisfied that their service and method are better adapted to us than our own, and more certain to promote piety, we shall unhesitatingly adopt them; but so long as we believe, under the circumstances, that our method of worship is better for us than any other, which shall we follow—the judgment of other men in our behalf, or our own judgment?

CONGREGATIONAL LITURGY.

The discussion of the question of Liturgies in Congregational churches is sufficiently novel to attract general attention. It ought not to be supposed, however, that this is a discussion which has arisen upon foregone facts. It has been begun for the sake of producing facts.

If any church, or churches, had gone forward in the exercise of their own rights, to frame a liturgy and to employ it; if it had been said that such church or churches had no right to do so; and if this discussion were in the nature of an examination of such churches on the one hand, and a defence of them on the other, we need not say on which side we should stand. Every true church has the right to determine the method of conducting its own public worship. If they are satisfied with their own services, no one has a right to call them to account. But, in such cases, no one is bound to feel an interest in them, in spite of his own taste. If one church loves a liturgy, the neighboring church is not bound to love it, nor to relish the use of it, nor maintain that fellowship which can stand only in common sympathies.

The use of a liturgy, then, ought not to work ecclesiastical disfellowship. But, on the other hand, there is no cause of complaint if it does morally and socially alienate brethren of coördinate churches from sympathy and coöperation in worship.

But the case, at present, is far less serious than this. All that has been done, so far as the public know, is this: Some Christian brethren suspect that a great advantage would often accrue to Congregational churches if a change were to take place, by which the whole body of worshippers were made to take a more active part in the public services; and they believe that certain fixed forms of worship, to be used by the whole congregation in common, or responsively, would do much toward enlisting a more active participation of the whole people in public worship.

We certainly think that much needs to be done to inspire the services of our churches with more interest; and that, in some way, the whole congregation should become coöperative in public worship.

But we are clearly of opinion that a liturgy in whole or in part, will be of very little service. The trouble in our churches is the want of vital Christian feeling. A liturgy will not produce that.

We do not think it needful to discuss the merits of liturgies. They are, under some circumstances, useful. But they belong to a system of helps which the whole history and spirit of Congregationalism disowns. And it is not to be supposed that the Congregational churches will change the whole spirit of their economy for any slender advantages which may be supposed to linger within fixed and prescribed forms of worship. For our own part, if we were ready for a full liturgy, we should prefer the Episcopal, which has the extrinsic merits of age and long usage, and various historic associations. But it is not proposed to adopt a full liturgy. It is not, we believe, proposed to advocate a common and general form. A mixed service, in part liturgical and in part extemporaneous, it is thought, would be serviceable in some single churches.

We have no objection to the trial by any church that chooses to do it. But we are sure that the experiment will fail. The free element will overrun the fixed forms and choke them; or else, if the forms are clung to, they will expel the extemporaneous elements, and end in drawing the church over to a full liturgical service. But both of these elements, the movable and the fixed, the voluntary and the prescribed, the extemporaneous and the formal, can not coexist. The one will kill the other.

The experiment is not new. Several denominations have already tried it, the Moravians and the Methodists being of the number. But of what degree of benefit in the Methodist Episcopal service, is the partial liturgy which is in the Book? Not half of their people know that there is such a thing. It is not compulsory. It is interpolated by extemporaneous offices of devotion; and the result has been that the forms stand empty and soulless, while the life and power of the Methodist worship lies in the extemporaneous fervor of minister and people.

We think that this would be the case still more among Congregational churches. And one or two things would, in time, happen. Either the liturgy would wither and hang upon the service like a last year's dried blossom dangling upon the vine, or those churches which retained liturgies with benefit, would shrink away wholly from extemporaneous services. In this last case, a gradual division would take place, and some Congregational churches would be wholly liturgical, and some anti-liturgical; and two effectual policies of worship would soon strike division through the brotherhood of churches.

There need not, however, be the least excitement about this matter. No one need to fear that the old Congregational churches are in danger of flying off like a flock of birds into new trees. The old Congregational churches are not in danger of accepting an innovation against which they have educated instincts and hereditary historic prejudices as high as the walls of Jerusalem.

Here, then, we stand. A great want exists in our worship. Half liturgies will never remedy that want, and whole liturgies are just as bad. But, good or bad, the churches will never accept them. It seems to us, then, a waste of time to attempt feeble and uncongenial expedients. The stately simplicity of Congregational worship resents all patches and incongruous interpolations. We must abandon the whole method, and go over in a body to real, earnest, thorough liturgical services; or we must accept the Congregational idea of extemporaneous worship in all its fullness, and seek a remedy for lifelessness in a more hearty use and proof of our own system. Any cross between Congregational worship and liturgy will be mongrel, and can neither live with health nor propagate itself at all.

If then, it is said, that our public services are barren, we reply, they are. But not for want of common forms of devotion; for, churches which employ these forms, with every conceivable means of making them effectual, are just as meagre as ours. Indeed, if the Methodist, the Baptist, the Presbyterian and the Congregational churches be taken together, as having practically an extemporaneous service, and the Episcopal Church be regarded as liturgical, we are not unwilling to have a comparison made between the two methods of worship, in the very respect of producing a common feeling of devotion in the whole congregation.

If any single church—having tried the simplicity of Congregational worship and failed, or, not having failed—yet, if from some peculiarity of the congregation—some decided predilection for prescribed services—if such a church believes that it can do better by half liturgical worship than by our usual methods—then we would not put a straw in their way. We would say, Go on; make your experiment. And when enough time has elapsed to form a ripe judgment of the result, we will accept the trial for what it shall have proved itself worth.

But it does not seem to us well to urge such a course upon the Congregational churches before any trial has been made. We do not think it needful to ask hundreds of churches to embark in an enterprise which must be regarded, even by its warmest advocates, as but an experiment.

Some who plead for an addition to the old Puritan customs of public worship, do so because they believe the present methods to be very fruitless and meagre. It is said that the services of the Sabbath-day, in the church, are barren, and especially deficient in this, that the congregation, as such, bear no sufficient part. They are sung for, prayed for, and preached to; but they themselves have nothing to do. They are literally an audience; they are hearers. They are not participants but recipients. It is thought that forms of prayer, recitations of Scripture, and responsive utterances, would go far toward producing in the whole congregation a common interest in the religious worship, by making the whole to bear a part.

So earnest are we that the whole people should unite in public worship, that, if there were no better way, we should certainly advocate a liturgy. But we do not think that we have to go a step out of our own system to find means for arousing and thoroughly developing the religious feelings of the whole congregation in public worship.

The fundamental idea of Roman Catholic worship is, that the priest and the ordinances are depositories of Divine grace—that the people are simply recipients.

Protestant Christianity makes Christ the soul-fountain, and each individual Christian is his own priest. A Catholic church has its public service administered by its priests; a Protestant church has its service administered by its priests—which are THE PEOPLE.

The social religious element is the distinctive peculiarity of Protestant Christianity. Our churches will never fulfill their own social idea of public worship, until it becomes the joint act of the whole congregation. Not the separate worship of individuals sitting together, but the mingling and harmonizing of the individual devotion of the whole congregation.

The preaching meetings of our churches on the Sabbath day, do not represent our whole idea of the worship of Protestant churches. The prayer-meetings, the conference-meetings, the Bible-classes and Sabbath-schools—these, together with the Sabbath services, are to be regarded as composing the worship. We are to look for the full expression of our peculiar ideas, not in that part which the Sabbath day and the public assembly affords, but in all that the church does in its minor meetings. And it will be found that any well-instructed and rightly-trained church is a body whose power resides in its whole membership; that its worship is ministered to it by its own members; and that the legitimate end of the ordained ministry is to evolve a social religious ministering power in the congregation.

We may now suggest some reasons why our churches do not to a greater degree fulfill their design:

1. One of the most obvious reasons is, that ministers of the Gospel have not a clear and proper idea of their functions. They know generally that they are to preach to the community, and that they are to edify the church. But to be a preacher of sermons, a mere teacher in the pulpit, is not half a minister's work. He is set to drill a body of Christian men, so that they shall individually and collectively be a witnessing and ministering body. The voice of the whole church, and not the voice of its ministry, is

that which God appointed for the preaching of the Gospel. If now a minister only preaches—and so preaches that his brethren wish to hear no one speak but himself—if, instead of inspiring life-power in them, which he then guides and trains them to fitly express, he extinguishes their zeal, and fashions a public sentiment so rigid and exacting that no man in the church dare utter his feelings, his thoughts, or his experiences, unless he can do it for edification, (*i. e.*, do it in rhetorical fluency, with logical precision, and with a certain finish of literary good-breeding), he defeats the very end of his ministry, and practically disowns the Congregational idea of a minister.

Thus we see that many churches are nothing but listeners to a preacher. The society has an organic life and function; but the church, in such cases, is but little better than a roll of names of persons baptized, initiated, permitted to partake of the Lord's Supper, and expected to enjoy a good sermon. But to have a real life and function of their own, to have a social, loving atmosphere into which each one develops the blossoms of his religious life, to be a body competent to edify itself, to build itself up, and to stand, by its own vital power, as a multiform instruction in the community—such an idea is scarcely thought of. And hence it is that ministers come to be mere instructors. They do not educate. They do not train. They are not seeking to develop the gifts of the individual members of the church—to drill them in the suitable exercise of those gifts. They seek to do good to their flock as individual Christian men. But they do not group these individual Christian men into a community in such a way that they give utterance as a church, by their own voices, to the truth of Christ, or to their experience of God's guidance and goodness. So that the church is not an epitome of God's multitudinous teachings; it is not the harmony of all the voices with which Christ speaks to the souls of his children. It is a mere class, coming together to hear what a teacher shall say to them, and then going away and profiting as best they may. Now a minister of the Gospel should be a preacher of ideas, of the connection of ideas (which is theology); he should be a teacher of duties, *i. e.*, he should apply principles to the experiences of life—he should strengthen, comfort, inspire, and warn his people; but all these things should be but a part of a system of drill, by which the whole church shall become in like manner a teaching body. He is to see that his members are taught to pray—to pray with each other; to speak—to speak to edification. He is to develop the gifts of each in such a way as that the whole church shall have the benefit. One man is fitly a thinker; another man is a man of observation and experience. One has zeal and native power; another has richness of heart and blessed simplicity. One has courage, another has the power of consolation; one is powerful in prayer, another in conversation. It is the duty of the minister to bring forth these gifts and make them the *property of the whole church. A church has a right to the gifts of every one of its members*, and the minister is set to disclose and develop them. He is not to lean upon the strong; to avail himself of the service of those already developed. It is his office to take hold of every individual man, and to educate him, so that he may bring forth the one, or five, or ten talents which are committed to him, for the use and profit of all his brethren.

A man of books, a man of ideas, a man of sermons, is not Christ's idea of a minister. Follow me, and I will make you *fishers of men*. A minister is a man of men. He is an inspirer and driller of men.

Is it a marvel that churches take little part in public exercises? They are not expected to do it. The minister does not expect it. It is not for that that he preaches. He is a sermon-preacher, not a church-trainer. The people understand it so; they go to church to have him pray for them. He is to preach to them; he is to visit the sick, bury the dead, marry the affianced, baptize the children, live in a social relationship to a round of families, preach twice on the Sabbath, keep the church free from speculative heresies. But the power that lies in so many hearts dormant, the united power of such a body of witnesses as the church would be if it had a real voice, if it rose up and spoke, week by week, to the people—that is scarcely dreamed of.

Now, the church ought to be a hundred times stronger than the minister. The pews ought to have more power than the pulpit. No minister has done his duty who is himself the central power in a congregation. He is to be a power-producer; he is to see the success of his ministry in the church which he builds up. And as the architect stands dwarfed and trembling in the presence of the cathedral which he has himself builded, when all its walls and columns have gone up, and all its arches are completed, and all its pinnacles and spires lift up their heads to God everlastingly—so a pastor should stand in a vast disproportion of strength before the fullness of the power of his own church. For, can any one heart, either by original gift or by study, ever equal all the gifts which God bestows upon a hundred men? Is not all the work of Christ in a hundred souls more rich and wonderful than ever can be a single individual's experience? Is there one flower created equal to a whole prairie or garden, sheeted with the light and perfumed with the fragrance of a hundred flowers growing in profusion?

God's work in the human soul, day by day, is the most illustrious of all the events which history chronicles. Other events are more obvious, and more impressive to our vulgar senses, that love the flash and sound of physical deeds. But the watchings, the fears translated to victory, the faith and glow of love, the aspirations and achievements, the visions of heaven, the peace of God descending thence —there are no other things of such dignity as these, nor, when simply uttered, of such power. Indeed, the supremest power of Divine truth is not when it is uttered in idea-form, or as apprehended by intellect, but when exhibited in heart-forms, or as it is evolved in actual life-experiences. And there is something sublime in the conception of a great assembly of men —holding forth some one truth, first by the voice of its teacher, and then reflecting upon it from a hundred hearts that light by which God taught it pecu liarly to them; so that at length each should behold the glowing truth, not in the narrow line of his own experience, but in the clustered fullness of the experience of multitudes. Such preaching by the voice of the whole church would have a power with the community of which now we have no idea except from analogies. Let a hundred merchants and eminent mechanics—known and trusted men—gather in some vast hall in New York, and testify in regard to some new method of gaining wealth. Let them, one by one, declare the reality of the riches, exhibit his own winnings, declare the facility with which thousands more could acquire, and that joint testimony of a hundred honest men would strike a fever through a city in a day, and the veins and arteries of every occupation would throb with impatient desire. Such is the power given to a truth when many men, corroborating it, give it a blessed panic-power. A truth borne forth upon the power of a single heart is great; but what when it is sent forth upon the blasts of a thousand hearts? We have made proof of truth-power only in narrow lines. There is to be a development, of which we suspect little, of the power of truth swept along the tide of enthusiasm which sympathetic multitudes give. Conversions, then, will be like lightning strokes. For it is not enough for a man to have an idea of truth—he needs to have a moral shock, a soul-stroke, that shall electrify his being, and give to the truth instantaneous and overwhelming power. This enthusiasm comes from God. Like other gifts, it comes instrumentally. The simultaneous preaching of the Gospel by communities will be an instrument of such results.

The first step, then, toward a larger participation on the part of the congregation in public worship is to begin in the minister's own heart and design. And so superficial a thing as a common form of prayer, or a joint confession, or a psalmic response, will not train a church. There must be a common life in the church. It must be a minister's conception of his office and function, not merely to impart ideas; but by an impartation of ideas, and feeling, and personal social influence, to impart a real, COMMON religious life to the church. When that exists, there will be no more trouble about unity and interest in a congregation. They will be like a rich soil full of roots and seeds, that shoot up in exuberant richness, and though differing through genus and species, yet growing in perfect harmony. But a dead church with a liturgy on the top of it is like a sand desert covered with artificial bouquets. It is bright for the moment. But it is fictitious and fruitless. There are no roots to the flowers. There is no soil for roots. The utmost that a liturgy can do upon the chilly bosom of an undeveloped, untrained church is, to cover its nakedness with a faint shadow of what they fain would have, but cannot get.

CHURCHES AND ORGANS.

When a church is to be built, the question usually is from the outside to the inside, and not from inside to out. It is not said, "Here are a thousand people; in our system of worship the effects to be produced require such and such conditions for the congregation, and the church building must go up around these uses and be but an instrument of them." It is much more often the case that the question takes this form: "Where shall we put it? In what style shall it be built? Who shall be the architect? How high shall the steeple be, and how fine can we afford to make the interior?" Then, when these questions are settled, it is also, incidentally, a matter of consideration how to seat the people, and whether the building can be made available for hearing. As to the pulpit, but one thing is usually considered necessary, and that is, that it should be put as far as possible from all sympathetic contact with the people to be influenced by it; that it should be so constructed as to take away from the speaker, as far as it can be done, every chance of exerting any influence upon those whom he addresses. Therefore the pulpit is ribbed up on the sides, set back against the wall, where it looks like a barn-swallow's nest plastered on some beam. In this way the minister is as much as possible kept out of the way of the people, and all that is left is his voice. Posture, free gesture, motion, advance or retreat, and that most effective of all gestures, the full form of an earnest man, from head to foot, right before the people; in short, the whole advantage which the body gives when thrown into argument or persuasion, are lost without any equivalent gain. In this sacred mahogany tub or rectangular box, the man learns every kind of hidden awkwardness. He stands on one leg and crooks the other, like a slumbering horse at a hitching-post; he leans now on one side of the cushion, or lolls on the other side. And when a man, thoroughly trained by one of these dungeon pulpits to regard his legs and feet as superfluous, except in some awkward and uncouth way to crutch him up to the level of his cushion and paper, is brought out upon an open platform, it is amusing to watch the inconvenience to him of having legs at all, and his various experiments and blushing considerations of what he shall do with them!

Is it any wonder that so little is done by preaching, when, in a great church, with a small congregation, so scattered that no two persons touch each other, the bust of a man, peering above a bulwark, reads a stale manuscript to people the nearest of whom is not less than twenty-five feet from him? The wonder is that anything is ever accomplished. Daniel Webster is reported to have said, that no lawyer would risk his reputation before a jury if he had to speak from a pulpit, and that he considered the survival of Christianity in spite of pulpits as one of the evidences of its divinity.

We do not vouch for the truth of this as an anecdote, but we indorse it as a truth in philosophy.

Next comes the question, shall we have an organ? What do they want an organ for? We suspect that it would be difficult for the most part of the congregation to say, unless it were that other fashionable churches had organs; or, that it formed a cheerful and pleasant interlude to the tediousness of other parts of worship.

But, Young America means to have an Organ! And the question is not, how large a one is needed; but, how large a sum can be raised to buy it. If an organ of ten stops is good, it is innocently reasoned, an organ of twenty would be twice as good. As soon as it is known that an organ is to be built, down come the agents of various organ establishments, each one proving all the rest to be mere pretenders, and their work trash. Then comes bidding and underbidding. The builder that will give the most for the money is to have the job. One will, for the said number of dollars, give fifteen stops, another twenty, another twenty-five, and so he gets the organ. Now, a stop, in the understanding of a church committee, is a small piece of wood sticking out of the organ by the side of the manuals, with a piece of ivory on the end of it, with some name cut and blacked in, as "Pedal," "Coupler, Swell, and Choir," "Op. Diapason," "St. Diapason," etc. Of course a skillful builder can easily multiply stops fast enough, if the church committee are only ignorant enough. To cut a stop in two, and give two registers to it, makes two out of one in a manner very inexpensive to the builder, and quite satisfactory to most church committees. Or, to let a stop run only half way through the organ, speaking only either in the upper or the lower half; or better yet, to let stops run in separate pipes through half the organ and then flow together into one series of pipes for the bass, so that, like a river, many small streams meet and go out to sea in one channel—these and many other methods enable a skillful organ-builder to gratify the vanity of a church and the solidity of his own pocket at the same time.

But, when the organ is bought, put up, paid for, then comes the tug of war. What is an organ good for, at any rate? To what end is it put into the church? Can any one tell us? Or, must we come back to the subject, and give our own notions?

PATRIOTISM AND LIBERTY.*

In any other place, fellow-citizens, I should have claimed for myself to-day personal liberty and exemption from public service, but from my own city I can claim no such exemption, since I believe that every man ought to hold his services subject to the will and control of his fellow-citizens upon such an occasion as this, in every way that shall conduce to virtue, to public spirit and to patriotism.

We have returned from the laying of the corner stone of a City Armory—a circumstance not of so much interest in itself as in the historic incidents connected with it. For, that structure is to stand upon the site of the old Free Library, the corner-stone of which was laid some thirty-three years ago with imposing ceremonies. Officiating upon that occasion, and dignifying it by his presence, was that immortal man and true patriot, Lafayette, one of the few men whom we can afford heartily to praise—not his head at the expense of his heart, not his heart at the expense of his head, but head and heart and hand—the whole man together. His life will bear searching in youth, in middle age, in old age, and after his departure from life. You need hide nothing in the grave.

* Address delivered at the laying of the Corner-stone of the Brooklyn City Armory, on the Fourth of July, 1858.

We should speak well of Lafayette. He was one of those few men in whom the most romantic sentiment for liberty in youth, ripened, in manhood, into a moral principle enduring as life! He was a man without guile, without selfishness; a man whose very bread it was to love his fellow men. In his own land, and, in this, his second home—as much his own as France, and more—he devoted himself freely to the welfare of the people. He never retracted what he had said or done, nor marked dark lines of inconsistency across his clear record. While thousands like him declared for liberty, when liberty was still in a state of fermentation, he, almost alone, among thousands of prominent men in Europe, remained its firm votary, sacrificing for liberty almost everything dear to manhood.

That name is fitly associated with the name of Washington in the annals of our American liberty, and I count it a good omen—since so large a portion of our citizens are immigrants, and for years must continue to be—I count it a good omen that in looking back to our Revolutionary heroes, there is scarcely a nation on earth that cannot point to some distinguished officer, and say, "That man, who bled with your fathers for liberty, was of our blood."

It may seem, fellow-citizens, that the laying of the corner-stone of an armory is scarcely a fit occasion for me to dwell upon, or the day of the national independence a proper time to call out the enthusiasm of a man of my profession. But I was a man before I was a minister. Whatever any man should feel, I feel. Whatever any man should say, I ought to speak; I am a citizen, a Christian citizen. Is anything higher than that? I feel, therefore, that it is just as fitting that I should speak some words congenial to such an occasion as that any other man in the citizenship of this city should speak them.

If it shall seem a bad auspice that a free library should give place to an armory, you will remember that the library found itself too strait, and so removed otherwhere, and the building had been appropriated to civil purposes, and finally had been abandoned even for these. Nothing, therefore, is sacrificed.

We may well take this occasion of the founding an armory, to consider the great difference between our modern free cities and those of former days. They were beleagured with walls; our walls are the bodies of free citizens! movable walls, pedestrian walls. Wherever there is an enemy there is a wall, made up of citizens. Unlike other cities, in other lands, we have no forts and citadels, if we except the household forts commanded by fathers and mothers, and garrisoned by them and their children.

There never were more peaceful places than our citizen armories, where our citizen soldiers assemble to carry on the picturesque part of war, without risk or peril.

Build, then, these peaceful Castles of Indolence for our citizen soldiery, and let them have a home among us. The very differences between our armories and those abroad are the differences between free cities in free America and the cities of the old and oppressed nations.

But let me take occasion, upon the erection of this building, to speak of the better armories which have been long building among us, for I hold that our best armories are the houses which stand along our streets.

Wherever you shall find a father and mother, and a houseful of children, there is the best commander, the best drill-sergeant, the best soldiers. The free and well-conducted families—these are our armories. Wherever you shall find an intelligent laboring population—a population who labor, not drudge; whose labor is not compulsory, enforced, stolid, but whose heads work first, and then animate their hands with brains to work more skillfully afterwards—cheerful, unrepining labor—these are our industrial armories. And at every point where you can congregate a band of these laborers, men who sing while they work, and come from town wiping the sundown sweat from their brows, to be cheered with the comforts of home, and wife, and children—these are our armories.

Again, we have our schools, to which all our children have access. No matter how poor a man may be in money, if he is rich in children, those family jewels, his children shall have the benefit of our schools. They teach all alike, the children of all religious faiths, nationalities, ranks and conditions; they teach them all the common ideas and duties of American citizens. These are our truest armories, and the cities which have these are inexpugnable.

I might go on to point to our churches, whence, as from a fount, we draw our truest notions of personal manhood, of personal liberty, of municipal privileges and municipal rights. These are some of the institu tions which supervise our domestic armories and make them efficient.

The occasion of laying the corner-stone of the Free Library by the patriotic Frenchman, Lafayette, called together by diligent drumming and large counting eight thousand people. This was the population of Brooklyn thirty-three years ago! Who then had the prescience by which he could have suspected such a day as this? And if one had dared to say then that in thirty-three years two hundred thousand inhabitants would have lived upon this side of the river, he would have bid fair for a berth in a lunatic asylum.

Yet how has our population augmented beyond all anticipation! Instead of that little cozy neighborhood village, we have become the third city in the Union. The third not alone arithmetically—for though a city requires men and women, men and women alone do not make a city. By their heads, and hands, and hearts, their institutions, their homes, their industry, the men and women of Brooklyn have constituted a city of which men may be proud and boast. I think the sun does not upon earth shine upon a more fair and beautiful city.

You may say that this is the adulation of a fond son, and that I think it meet to praise the place of my residence. Nevertheless, if I am deceived I am deceived, for I verily believe there is not upon this continent a site so beautiful, and so well adapted for forming a large permanent city.

It cannot be many years (for we may look forward as well as look back)—I think it cannot be many years before there will be half as many people living in Brooklyn as there were in the whole country when our war of Independence began. I think it not extravagant to say that if we go on prospering as we have for a few years past, our borders extending, that in a few years we shall become the city second, perhaps, to but one on this continent. I do not know that I should make even that exception, for Brooklyn seems to be nearer to New York than New York is to herself. These cities, twelve miles long, on long, narrow islands, are not the cities to grow like your circular cities, which have room to spread in every direction, and we may yet swell our population beyond that of New York! We are destined to be an immense city, and it becomes us to lay well the foundations of these institutions which are to make our memory precious in time to come, and hand down to our children a legacy better than that our fathers handed down to us. We have begun well in our schools and churches, already renowned, but there is still in our institutions a work for you and for me. We shall not be true and faithful to our city and to the time in which we live if we do not hand them down more noble and richer in all the elements of civilization and progress than we received them.

Standing here upon the day set apart to commemorate the achievements of our fathers, we ought not to forget that we are citizens, not only of this city, but also of this great republic. We remember and praise the sufferings and achievements of our fathers, but they suffered and struggled willingly. For some years past, it would seem that the celebration of this day has been growing into disrepute, and it is well to revive the custom. Some man surely can always be found to speak worthily, wisely, and well, on the great subject of human rights and human liberty, to which the day is sacred.

What is the Fourth of July? Is it only a day for explosion of powder, a day for outside show and celebration? Is it not the day that stands for the establishment of liberty and for the rights of man? The soundest and truest doctrine ever promulgated was that sustained by our fathers in the achievement of our independence. It is that which makes us what we are; which makes this day the Sabbath of Liberty.

Let me say a few words respecting our country, than which a fairer and nobler God never made. Methinks he hid it for ages behind the heap of ocean waters, that he might here at last build up a mighty Christian civilization, that should realize the fondest hopes and expectations of prophets and seers. So broad a land, so diversified in its treasures, so fertile in its soil, partaking the boon which every climate has to confer, stretching through so many lines of longitude in the West, so many of latitude in the North and so many in the South—so fair, so large and so rich a land, methinks the sun nowhere else beholds in his daily journey. God has poured a mixed people upon this land. Races mingled together make a better population than consanguineous stocks. God has poured in hither lavishly from every nation. Some men leave their country, it is true, for their country's good, but all do not. They that are too restless and enterprising to remain at home fly to the

New World. They whose young blood cannot walk the old paces and take the old stale customs; they are the men who fly their country for their own good, and pour upon these shores for ours. We take them as a tribute from every nation under the sun—the young, the earnest, the best blood, the motive power of the nation.

Such blood mingled with ours, if educated and Christianized, will give stamina, variety, genius, and all the elements of national power and progress such as were never before brought together. This is our population now. The Atlantic greets us on the East, we wash our feet in the Pacific, we dip our hands in the Gulf, we bathe our brow in the northern lakes; on every side God gives no other boundaries than mighty oceans. Enclosed in this vast area, this nation is to make a mark in history which no other nation ever made.

But this variety of climate and diversity of interests is one great cause of danger;—as ships built too long and not strong enough, are in danger of breaking in the middle, so we, with conflicting interests upon one side and upon the other, our citizens so separated by distance as to lack personal sympathy and frequent intercourse, are in like danger of parting somewhere.

Besides this, there are men who would sacrifice their country for their own advancement, and there is nothing that can save this nation from the perils that surround it but a spirit of true religion and of that patriotism which true religion inspires, a spirit that loves country not for self but for the country's sake.

I am most happy, here at least, to claim for the Union, as most heartily I do, our undivided allegiance. For there is no sacrifice too great to pay for the union of these States, unless we sacrifice that for which the Union was first made—Liberty. We will suffer much for the sake of the Union—we will give up many sectional points of pride, but when we are asked to give up the spirit which animated the men of the Revolution—the spirit of Liberty—that we can never give up.

We declare that any true patriotism must be a patriotism which shall include in itself the knowledge and love of those principles well embodied in the Declaration of our Independence—the rights of man—the declaration that all men are born free and equal. Patriotism without that is not patriotism in America. It may be patriotism in Austria, but not in America. The patriotism that does not include within itself the doctrine that every man has inalienable rights to life, liberty and property—the patriotism that leaves that out, is like a man without a heart or a head—a hollow corpse.

We have had patriotism of all shapes and forms. Sometimes it goes up and down the country preaching Union and patriotism, but with everything of liberty left out. Our fathers embraced in their patriotism everything pertaining to sacred liberty, and by their sufferings and struggles they maintained their declaration. Our patriotism must be a patriotism that takes in Maine, and New Hampshire, and Vermont, and Massachusetts, and Rhode Island, and Connecticut, and New Jersey, and Ohio, and Pennsylvania, and Virginia, and Delaware, and Maryland, and North Carolina and even South Carolina. Yes, and Georgia, Alabama, Louisiana, Mississippi and Arkansas, Tennessee and Kentucky, Ohio and dear old Indiana, and Illinois, and Missouri, bound for freedom, and Minnesota and Wisconsin, and I know not how many besides. [A voice, " Kanas."] Yes, Kansas and California, and all the States, named and unnamed, that are and are yet to come. A patriotism it must be that shall take in every State that stands within the confederacy—a patriotism not for party broils, party spoils, squabbles, contention, wranglings and base ambitions; but a patriotism that shall give to every one of the States that very foundation laid by our revolutionary struggle—liberty, liberty, nothing else than liberty!

What are our Fourth-of-Julys from which these great truths are left out? What is that patriotism which ignores, or daintily touches and passes by this greatest thought, this most noble heritage of civilization—liberty for every man? This is a patriotism which will save our great country. I am not an ill-omened prophet: I do not believe we shall go to wreck; I believe God built his temple on these shores. Although, like temples in other times, it may have been occasionally delayed and marred, in some parts at least, yet the temple is reared to Christ and to Liberty. I believe it will be perfected and God will preserve this nation by the instrumentality of your hearts, your hands, your heads, and by your fidelity to our original Revolutionary principles. But, amid broils and high conflicts, be sure that it is safe to stand firmly upon the old truths. It is never safe to abandon our profession of faith in liberty. It is never safe to put this nation upon the shifting sands of expediency! And whatever storms arise, whatever fierce winds blow, there is no other anchor for us but that goodly anchor of Liberty! Never be ashamed of it. Speak it out, openly, boldly, sincerely, and let your life corroborate your words.

Remember that discussion should ever be free. Let us remember the duty of toleration of men that differ in the extremest points from us. Let us accord to them that right which we assert for ourselves—the right to believe what we will—the right to defend what we think—the right to express what we believe. Their rights and ours are the same, and if upon that common freedom Liberty cannot stand, let her go to the ground. I am not afraid to venture. Give us freedom of speech and action, and this land will shake the dust of oppression from her garments and stand forth the virgin daughter of God, free, blessed and blessing!

I have been asked by those concerned in a benevolent movement to mention to you the ladies of America, who are now engaged in the work of purchasing the grounds and tomb of Washington, at Mount Vernon; and with this I shall fitly close. Is it fit that women should rise up in the perturbed state of the Union, and should everywhere, as they do, beg for peace and honorable conciliation. You will remember that when Christ had slept three days, and many thought the world was empty of him, that it was the women who went to the sepulchre, asking as they went, who shall roll away the stone, and that, when they reached the tomb, the stone was rolled away, and an angel sat upon it. Now the women of America go to the tomb of Washington, and who will roll away the stone? God grant that they may find the stone rolled away and the living spirit of Washington, which is the spirit of liberty, sitting upon it, to hail, to cheer and to bless them.

PURITY OF CHARACTER.

Over the beauty of the plum and the apricot, there grows a bloom and beauty more exquisite than the fruit itself—a soft, delicate plush that overspreads its blushing cheek. Now, if you strike your hand over that, and it is once gone, it is gone forever; for it never grows but once. Take the flower that hangs in the morning, impearled with dew, arrayed as no queenly woman ever was arrayed with jewels. Once shake it, so that the beads roll off, and you may sprinkle water over it as carefully as you please, yet it can never be made again what it was when the dew fell silently upon it from heaven! On a frosty morning, you may see the panes of glass covered with landscapes—mountains, lakes, trees, blended in a beautiful, fantastic picture. Now, lay your hand upon the glass, and by the scratch of your finger, or by the warmth of your palm, all the delicate tracery will be obliterated! So there is in youth a beauty and purity of character, which, when once touched and defiled, can never be restored; a fringe more delicate than frost-work, and which, when torn and broken, will never be reëmbroidered. A man who has spotted and soiled his moral garments in youth, though he may seek to make them white again, can never wholly do it, even were he to wash them with his tears. When a young man leaves his father's house, with the blessing of his mother's tears still wet upon his forehead, if he once loses that early purity of character, it is a loss that he can never make whole again. Such is the consequence of crime. Its effect cannot be eradicated; it can only be forgiven. It is a stain of blood that we can never make white, and which can be washed away only in the blood of Christ, that "cleanseth from all sin!"

HOW TO BEAR LITTLE TROUBLES.

There is a kind of narrowness into which, in our every-day experiences, we are apt to fall, and against which we should most carefully guard. When a man who is in perfect health has a wound inflicted upon him—a wound in his foot, a cut on his finger, a pain in his hand—he is almost always sure to feel, even though it be only a small member that suffers, and the suffering itself be unworthy of the name, that the perfect soundness of all the rest of his body counts as nothing; and a little annoyance is magnified into a universal pain. Only a single point may be hurt, and yet he feels himself clothed with uneasiness, or with a garment of torture. So, God may send ten thousand mercies upon us, but if there happen to be only one discomfort among them, one little worry, or fret, or bicker, all the mercies and all the comforts are forgotten, and count as nothing! One little trouble is enough to set them all aside! There may be an innumerable train of mercies which, if they were stopped one by one, and questioned, would seem like angels bearing God's gifts in their hands! But we forget them all, in the remembrance of the most trivial inconvenience! A man may go about all the day long—discontented, fretting, out of humor—who, at evening, on asking himself the question, "What has ailed me to-day?" may be filled with shame because unable to tell! The annoyance is so small and slight that he cannot recognize it; yet, its power over him is almost incredible. He is equally ashamed with the cause and the result.

We may fall into such a state merely through indifference, and remain there simply because we have fallen into it, and make no effort to get out. When a man starts wrong early in the morning, unless he is careful to set himself right before he has gone far, he will hardly be able to straighten out his crookedness until noon or afternoon—if haply then; for a man is like a large ship; he cannot turn round in a small space, and must make his sweep in a large curve. If we wake up with a heavenly mind, we are apt to carry it with us through the day; but if we wake up with a fretful, peevish, discontented disposition, we are apt to carry that all the day, and all the next day too! I have comforted myself, and risen out of this state of mind, by saying to myself, "Well, you are in trouble; something has come upon you which is painful; but will you let it clasp its arms around you, and shut you in its embrace from the sight and touch of all the many other things that are accounted joys? Will you suffer yourself to be harnessed and driven by it?" It is well to remember that there is a way of overcoming present troubles by a recognition of present or promised mercies. The apostle Paul knew this, and so exhorted us to "look unto Jesus, who, for the joy that was set before him, endured the cross, despising the shame." All that Christ had to bear he bore patiently—he carried his sorrow about with him as a very little thing. Why?

Because of the "joy that was set before him!" Oh! let us apply the exhortation faithfully to ourselves; and when we are worried, and tempted to give way to vexation, let us seek a sweet relief in the thought of the blessedness that is set before us to be an inheritance forever!

"SIN REVIVED AND I DIED."

The apostle Paul says, "I was alive without the law once, but when the commandment came, sin revived and I died." A man walking in a beautiful field on a bright summer morning, when the sun is golden and makes everything it shines upon golden too, asks himself, "What field is this?" He thinks, "Perhaps this field, in the old Revolutionary struggle, was deluged with gore; and perhaps there are now at the roots of these flowers, and of this grass, the very instruments of war that were used in the conflict, and the bones of those who fell in wielding them." Suppose, as he walks, thus musing, and looking at the clouds and the sunlit face of Nature, all at once, in the places where he saw flowers and shrubs, there should be protruding bones!—the gaunt bones of an arm, or of a hand!—or that a skull, ghastly and appalling, should break through, and that all the hideous carcasses of the men who fought and died in the old battle should begin to stir themselves in every part of the field, with terror in their forms and figures, and greater terror still in their movements, and that they should utter again the shriek of war, horrible and sepulchral! This would be like unto that which the apostle saw, and which he meant when he wrote these words. They are as though he had said, "I was alive once without the law; and all at once God touched me by his living commandment. Sin revived, and all the corruption of my old transgressions, all the ghastly remembrances of my old folly and iniquity, all my former deficiencies, all my pride and vanity, all my self-righteousness, all my lusts, all that was wicked in me, suddenly rose up in baleful resurrection before my eyes, and I fell stricken to the ground with horror at the sight!" This is not the experience of Paul only; it has been repeated more or less vividly in the lives of thousands and thousands of persons, from that day to this; for men, while they are proud, and vain, and ignorant, are contented with their own condition, and conceited in their own favor; but when the revealing touch of God's Spirit is felt within them, and they see and understand the law of God, "Sin revives and they die!" Things change with the rule by which they are measured. A low moral standard will content men with conduct and motives, which, in the light of a higher law, would seem detestable. Human conduct, which, judged by custom and unenlightened human opinion, seems guiltless, when measured by the law of a pure and holy God, appears full of guilt. And no man has judged rightly of either his character or his conduct, until he has held them up in the light of God's countenance and measured them by God's law.

HUMILITY BEFORE GOD.

I THINK that a view of what we are before God, of our leanness, of our littleness, of our weakness and imperfection, is enough to keep down the risings of any man's pride. There are times when, if a man should receive a full, clear view of what he is himself, in comparison with what God is, all hope and almost life itself would be crushed out of him! And it is only when God reveals himself in the person of Jesus Christ, pardoning sins, and overlooking our errors and imperfections, that we are enabled to have hope! But while, in the view of God, every Christian feels that he is not only sinful, but ignominiously so, and degraded beyond all expression, yet there is in his experience of the love which Christ has for him, notwithstanding his weakness and impurity, a certain boldness that lifts him up and gives him confidence to stand in the very presence of God!

Did you ever see a child, which through a period of days and weeks had little by little been gathering mischief and disobedience, and seeming to be aching for a whipping? By and by he comes to a state in which it is plain that there must be an outbreak; and an occasion occurs, perhaps, from some trifling circumstance, in which he is brought to a direct issue with the parent, and the question is, who shall conquer, the mother or the child? She expostulates, but the child grows red and swells with anger; she pleads with him, and uses all her power to bring him to a reconciliation on the basis of justice; but nothing will do; and at last, when everything else has failed, and she has been unable by gentle means to subdue his haughty pride—if she does what she ought to do, she gives him a sound whipping! He is quickly subdued, and filled with shame, yet not entirely humbled; but when he sees the much-loving mother, who has wept with even more pain and suffering than the child himself, going about the room—a kind of living music to the child's unconscious feeling!—taking her seat at last in some window-nook, with sorrow upon her face, he comes to himself, and, thinking a moment, feels that all the old dark flood of ugliness has gone away, and an entirely new feeling begins to take possession of him. He looks at the face of the mother, with love swelling in his heart, and wishes that he were sitting at her feet. And when she says, "My child, why do you not come to me?"—with another burst of tears, not of pain and wounded feeling, but of joy and love—he throws himself into her arms, and buries his head in her bosom! Ah! if I remember aright, I can recount many similar experiences in my own early life; and I am brought back into the remembrance of such childhood's scenes, because the relation of my own disobedient heart to my mother when she punished me, is the best illustration which I can give you of the relation of the soul of a rebelling child of God to his chastising hand! When after being puffed up with pride and vanity, from being engaged in worldly pursuits, and being contented with mere worldly moralities, I am suddenly, by afflictions or disappointments, or by the direct visitation of God's Holy Spirit, humbled and brought to the very earth with contrition; oh! who can tell how sweet it is to take hold of the outreaching hand of the Lord Jesus Christ, and go up into the confidence and embrace of his love! I am nothing myself: I am entirely humbled and subdued; only I feel his love in my heart, and my heart swells with love in return. These are days of sweetness! These are days of heavenly joy! These are days of true humility! Oh! how lowly a man bows, and how lowly he walks, who has a view of his own littleness and emptiness in comparison with the greatness and the fullness of the ever-living and ever-loving God!

WHO SHALL HELP THE UNFORTUNATE?

THE importunities of various want at our door, remind us that the summer is gone and winter is coming. Work and wages are growing less and less; expense is growing daily more and more. Besides, in the change from season to season, sickness revels. Winter takes away from thousands the little strength they had. Colds, consumptions, in their endless varieties and stages, are plucking away health, energy and hope, and preparing the bosom for the last and deadly stroke of Time.

WHO HELP THE NEEDY? Not misers or stingy men. They regard poverty as a crime; importunity is worse than an insult. They button up their hearts against solicitation, and doggedly say, "No, I will not," or drive off the beseeching face with bitter advice, "Go, work, sir! I have to work for my living—you must work for yours."

"Oh, sir, I should be glad to work: will you give me work to do?"

"Give you work? Do you suppose I have nothing else to do but run about hunting work for such vagabonds as you? Haven't you got legs, and a tongue in your head? Why don't you get your own work?"

Sometimes these men are just as bad as they seem, just as heartless, selfish, and cruel. Sometimes they are very kind men in their families, and to their relatives. But they think that no one ought to be poor in this country, and that if they are, it must be from negligence, or indolence, or spendthrift vice; and so a poor beggar is presumptively a knave, who thinks that he can deceive you; and the man blusters fiercely at him, in part to let him know that he cannot dupe him.

Next, are those whose kindness depends upon their mood. Slamming the door in everybody's face to-day, and profuse and indiscriminate in kindness to-morrow. Their charity is a mere firing into the air, a *feu de joie;* they do not aim at a mark, or take sight at all.

There are some whose hearts are so tender that they never refuse until nothing is left to give. We cannot help loving such amiable fellows, whose hearts flow down with generous elements. But they are the godfathers of swindlers. They encourage and breed a race of beggars who feed unworthily upon the bread which belongs to the modest poor.

Then come a large class of men who are excellent citizens and exemplary Christians; but who have never really studied their personal duties toward the unfortunate. Some think that they are doing their part toward society by the energetic and successful conduct of their business; some contribute to charity by aiding various charitable institutions, asylums, hospitals, etc.; others throw into the plate a five dollar bill when the collection for the poor is taken up in church; or they send round a sum to their minister asking him to distribute it; or they subscribe to the City Relief Society, and so on.

All of the last-mentioned persons would unite in saying, We are willing to give our money, but we cannot give our time and attention to the poor.

There is a division of labor possible in the relief of the poor and the unfortunate. There ought to be men who should make it their business; there are others whose dispositions and whose circumstances qualify them to visit the abodes of misery and dwell much with the unfortunate; but there are others whom business so much absorbs as to make much personal attention impossible.

But after every allowance has been charitably made, we are every year more and more satisfied that no man can afford to dispense entirely with personal service toward the unfortunate. The moral education involved in Christian charity, is not gained by a mere donation of money, no matter how generous, or how often repeated. Our hearts need the discipline of sympathy with the poor and the afflicted, just as much as their hearts do. We need to put ourselves in the places of needy men, to hear their sorrows until they come home like our own; to look at life through their experience, to study their wants, and to exercise patience, forbearance and gentleness while dealing with their misfortunes, or full as often, with their faults. And no man can tell the fullness of blessing which God means for him, when he sends to him misfortunes which he adopts as his own, and studies to relieve. It was the revelation of God's nature, indeed, when it was said of Christ that he bore our griefs and carried our sorrows. If Christ dwell in any heart, this will be one of the first and most unmistakable evidences of it.

Now, the men who plead occupation, unfitness, etc., as a reason for not giving time and personal attention to the poor, are the very men who most need the discipline of such a course. They are in prosperity and need something to temper it; they are absorbed by their own cares, which seem to them heavier than anybody else's and sharper. They need to have their burdens lightened by knowing that their cares are often trifling in comparison with others.' A man who is steadily going up in the world cannot afford to lose sympathetic acquaintance with men that are steadily going down. Our softness of ease, our luxuries, our scope and power of wealth, are as deadly enemies as can intrench the heart, unless we extract the quality of selfishness from them.

The change from kindness to selfishness is very insidious. Few men are aware of what is going on in them as they rise in life. Others see it. It passes into remark among those who know them. But few men have friends who are friends, that dare tell them their faults. There are very few who will tell a man, "You are growing much more imperious than you used to be; you are more difficult to approach; you carry yourself as if you felt your importance in the world." There are not many friends that will risk their peace by saying to a man, "You are more ostentatious, but less generous than you used to be. You may give away more money, but you show less sympathy and kindness. You are more worldly. You are growing very selfish; and you spend twenty times as much upon yourself for the sake of effect, as you used to do ten years ago."

But all prosperous men need faithful friends. "Open rebuke is better than secret love. Faithful are the wounds of a friend." There are enough that will flatter those who love to be flattered, and enough that will criticise, and enough that will be silent, and sorrowful. But there are few that will tell a man the very things which it most concerns him to know.

But if a man employs his prosperity as a garner, in which are gathered the seeds of other men's advantage; if when he is lifted up he will often let himself down among those who are struggling; if he will oblige his heart to go out of its own courses, to enter upon the story of other hearts, to think, feel, plan, and achieve for them, he will rob prosperity of its sharpest danger, and put himself into that very school where God teaches us how to be like Christ—a school in which our Master was once himself a scholar, for "though he was a son, yet learned he obedience by the things which he suffered; and being made perfect he became the author of eternal salvation unto all them that obey him."

PLYMOUTH CHURCH.

We give place to a communication upon the pew-renting in Plymouth church. We have seen several like comments in print:

"It was with pain that we saw in the papers that the pews in the Plymouth church had been rented for about $25,000. Is this the way to fulfill the command of our Saviour, to make his Gospel known to every creature? Who are the men that have bid off the pews at a great premium, to the exclusion of 500 church-members, and many others, who desired the benefits of the pastor's labors? Are they such as most need his instruction? or do they secure the best seats for their own personal gratification? Ought not many of those to be laboring with feeble churches in unfavorable localities, under the belief that it is more in accordance with the spirit of Christianity to do good than to get good? We, who do not live in large cities, cannot believe that it is right or Christian for one congregation to expend $25,000 for themselves, while many feeble churches are struggling for existence, and many self-denying ministers must rely on faith for the supply of their daily bread."

The writer asks, "Is this the way to fulfill the command of our Saviour, to make his Gospel known to every creature?" Well. Does our friend wish no more churches built? The apostles built none. They never preached in a church in their lives. For hundreds of years, it is probable that preaching was mere exposition of Scripture; and performed without regularity, from place to place, in houses, in public resorts, market-places, and wherever a crowd collected.

Buildings for the church were of later date than the apostolic era. And to undertake to regulate modern preaching by the exact imitation of apostolic practice, would be the stupidest striving after an absolute impossibility. No exact form was prescribed for church organization, none for church order and government, none for public worship, and none for the external and material elements of church use. No doubt, much more attention should be given to the carrying of the truth to men who will not come to church. But is there to be no centre, no organization, no building, and no regular and formal stated preaching? And if so, is there or is there not to be a secular arrangement for maintaining such an institution? There is no one way of giving Christian truth to the people. It must include every feasible method. And central among them, and the fountain and motive power of all other ways, is the regular and organized church. Now, if the church is to buy land, build a house, buy coal for warming, gas for lighting, pay the sexton for caring for the property, and support the minister who is set for watch and teaching, then there must be money raised to do it. And a church, when it deals with material things, is subject to just the same commercial law as any other body. Buying and selling in a church are just the same as in a store. Both should be honest and equitable, and if they are, it is all sham to talk of the church being too sacred for worldly things.

Whenever a church comes to that part of its business which is secular, and requires commercial wisdom, then it must stand just like any other honest concern, subject to all the equitable laws of matter and money. The pews must be sold and taxed, or rented every year; and this must be done publicly, that all may have a chance. And if the pews are not much sought after, there will be but little trouble or complaint. But if the pews are fewer than the applicants; if ten men want seats when but one can be accommodated, how are we to select which shall have them?

Shall there be a perpetual scramble? Then the strongest will get them. Shall they be rented privately? Then the alert and shrewd will get them. Shall they be rented openly and in fair competition? Then, inevitably, they must follow the commercial law, and the man who wants them most, and has the means of paying the most, must have them.

Now, it is very easy to stand off and rail. Will any one suggest a plan by which 5,000 men can be put into a church that will hold but 3,000? If only a part are to be accommodated, will some one tell a better method than open competition upon fair commercial principles? For the secular affairs of a church are just as commercial, and just as subject to right commercial laws, as is the business of a bank, a manufactory, an academy or college.

It has been proposed to let the church-members have a chance first, and then give the world what remains! This is eminently and exquisitely evangelical! Let Christians take care of themselves first, and then give sinners the crumbs! Let converted souls become insiders, and have a first chance at the feast, and sit with a preëmption right, around the

Gospel luxuries; and when they are sated, let the outside sinners gnaw the bones! If a church after ten years' preaching has got along only so far as to be individually and corporately selfish, it might have done that without the trouble and expense of preaching and organizing. Selfishness thrives very well without means of grace to help it!

It is thought by some, and by our correspondent, we presume, that the poor should be first provided for. The poor should be held in lively remembrance. Every church ought to keep Christ's feelings for the poor and ignorant burning in the heart and sanctuary, like a fire that never goes out.

But ought we to provide for the poor in a way that shall punish those who are not poor? Are we to exclude men from churches, whose industry, patience and frugality, have made them affluent? Shall such a practice of Christian virtues in worldly matters as rewards men with worldly substance, work their exclusion? A man ought not to be punished for being legitimately prosperous!

But our correspondent says: "Who are the men that have bid off the pews at a great premium, to the exclusion of 500 church-members and many others, who desired the benefits of the pastor's labors?"

We will tell him who they are. They are men who have souls to be saved or lost. They are men, who, if rich, need preaching all the more because they are rich. They are men who have families just as dear to them as if they were poor. They are men with little boys and girls, with sons and daughters, under temptation and needing guidance. They are men who are peculiarly liable to self-indulgence, to selfish luxury, to pride and hardness of heart, and who require all the aid of faithful preaching to incline them to humility, generosity, and benevolence! The poor need the Gospel for reasons peculiar to their condition, and the rich just as much for reasons peculiar to their estate.

But, in the particular case in hand, those who have bid off pews at high premiums, are men, many of them, who, when we took this pastorate were just beginning a business life, and have grown up to ripe manhood side by side with us. They are, many of them, those whom we married, whose children we baptized, or whose hearts we comforted in the hour in which, over small open graves, they strove to write in their hearts, "Thy will be done," but found that tears washed out the letters as fast as they were written. They are the very persons, in a great number of cases, who, under our teaching, have beheld a great light, and have learned to say, "Our Father," to God, with their whole heart!

It is very easy for men "who do not live in large cities to believe that it is right or Christian for one congregation to expend $25,000 for themselves, etc." If men that have money knew what to do with it half as well as those do, who give them advice without knowing anything about their affairs, what a thrifty world this would be! What a church spends annually is great or little, according to circumstances. There are many country churches where $2,500 a year would be more extravagant than in others would be

$25,000. But in this particular case the surplus funds are employed in paying off the debts and mortgages which lie upon the property, and we hope that it is not unchristian for a church to pay its honest debts!

And, in closing, we will only say, that, from the beginning, no church ever more conscientiously endeavored to give the Gospel to all classes, rich or poor, resident or strangers. For ten years the members of this society have cheerfully submitted to an inconvenience for the sake of the poor and of strangers, such as has rarely had a parallel. Gentlemen have paid hundreds of dollars for pews, which were, with the exception of a single Sabbath in the year, more or less filled with the poor. Hundreds of men have been very cheerfully excluded Sabbath after Sabbath from their pews, for the sake of accommodating strangers. Every Sabbath day, families who have paid hundreds of dollars for a pew, coming to church, find it preoccupied by the poor and the stranger, and it is the rare exception that, in such a case, there is any irritation. Generally, the owner distributes his family as best he can, takes a seat in the aisles, or stands up in the entry. And this is not an occasional thing. It is the regular experience of the congregation, year after year. And we submit to all who think as our friend above writes, whether the endeavor of a large Christian church to conduct themselves hospitably, kindly, charitably, to all ranks and conditions of men rich or poor, black or white, bond or free, and who pay large sums for the convenience of welcome strangers, and of their neighbors not less welcome, ought to be rewarded with representations which lead the public to think that Plymouth church is a bazaar of pews, bought and sold by selfish, speculating, rich men!

ORGAN-PLAYING.

The Organ, long expected, has arrived, been unpacked, set up, and gloried over. The great players of the region round about, or of distant celebrity, have had the grand organ exhibition; and this magnificent instrument has been put through all its paces, in a manner which has surprised every one, and, if it had had a conscious existence, must have surprised the organ itself most of all. It has piped, fluted, trumpeted, brayed, thundered; it has played so loud that everybody was deafened, and so soft that nobody could hear. The pedals played for thunder, the flutes languished and coquetted, and the swell died away in delicious suffocation, like one singing a sweet song under the bedclothes. Now it leads down a stupendous waltz with full bass, sounding very much as if, in summer, a thunder-storm should play above our heads, "Come, haste to the wedding," or "Money-Musk." Then come marches, gallops, and hornpipes. An organ playing hornpipes ought to have elephants for dancers.

At length a fugue is to show the whole scope and power of the instrument. The theme, like a cautious rat, peeps out to see if the coast is clear; and after a few hesitations, comes forth and begins to frisk a little, and run up and down to see what it can find. It finds just what it did not want, a purring tenor lying in ambush and waiting for a spring, and as the theme comes incautiously near, the savage cat of a tenor pitches at it, misses its hold, and then takes after it with terrible earnestness. But the tenor has miscalculated the agility of the theme. All that it could do, with the most desperate effort, was to keep the theme from running back into its hole again, and so they ran up and down, around and around, dodging, eluding, whipping in and out of every corner and nook, till the whole organ was aroused, and the bass began to take part, but unluckily slipped and rolled down stairs, and lay at the bottom raving and growling in the most awful manner, and nothing could appease it. Sometimes the theme was caught by one part, and dandled for a moment, when, with a snatch, another part took it and ran off exultant, until unawares the same trick was played on it, and finally, all the parts being greatly exercised in mind, began to chase each other promiscuously in and out, up and down, now separating and now rushing in full tilt together, until everything in the organ loses patience, and all the "stops" are drawn, and, in spite of all that the brave organist could do—who flew about and bobbed up and down, feet, hands, head, and all—the tune broke up into a real row, and every part was clubbing every other one, until at length, patience being no longer a virtue, the organist with two or three terrific crashes put an end to the riot, and brought the great organ back to silence!

Then came congratulations. The organist shook hands with the builder, and the builder shook hands with the organist, and both of them shook hands with the committee; and the young men who thought it their duty to know something about music looked wise, and the young ladies looked wise too, and the minister looked silly, and the parishioners generally looked stupid, and all agreed that there never was such an organ—no, never. And the builder assured the committee that he had done a little more than the contract stipulated; for he was very anxious to have a good organ in *that* church! And the wise men of the committee talked significantly of what a treasure they had got. The sexton gave a second look at the furnace, lest the church should take it into its head, now, of all times, to burn up; and he gave the key an extra twist in the lock, lest some thief should run off with the organ.

And now, who shall play the organ? is the question. And in the end, who has not played it? First perhaps, a lady who teaches music is exalted to the responsibility. Her taste is cultivated, her nerves are fine, her muscles feeble, her courage small, and her fear great. She touches the great organ as if she were a trembling worshipper, fearing to arouse some terrible deity. All the meek stops are used, but none of the terrible ones, and the great instrument is made to walk in velvet slippers every Sabbath, and after each stanza the organ humbly repeats the last strain in the tune. The instrument is quite subdued. It is the modern exemplification of Ariadne riding safely on a tamed leopard. But few women have strength for the mechanical labor. It ought not to be so. Women ought to have better health, more muscle, more power, and, one of these days, doubtless, will have.

Next, an amateur player is procured, who was said to have exquisite taste and finished execution. A few pieces for the organ he knew by heart, a pretty way of varying a theme, a sentimental feeling, and reasonable correctness in accompaniment.

Next came an Organist, who believed that all this small playing, this petty sweetness, was a disgrace to the powers of the instrument. He meant to lead forth the long pent-up force, and accordingly he took for his first theme, apparently, the Deluge, and the audience had it poured upon them in every conceivable form—wind, rain, floods, thunder, lightning, with all the promiscuous stops, which are put in all large organs to produce a screeching brilliancy, full drawn, to signify universal misery and to produce it. That man gave the church their full money's worth. He flooded the house. The voices of the choir were like birds chirping in a thunder-storm. He had heard that the singing of a congregation should be borne up upon the music of the organ and as it were floated, and he seemed to be aiming, for the most part, to provide a full Atlantic ocean for the slender choir to make its stormy voyages upon.

A fortunate quarrel disposed of him, and the Organ went back to the tender performer. But before long a wonderful man was called, whose fame, as he related it, was excessive. He could do anything—play anything. If one style did not suit, just give him a hint, and he would take on another. He could give you opera, ecclesiastical music, stately symphony of Beethoven, the brilliant fripperies of Verdi, the solemn and simple grandeur of Handel, or the last waltz, the most popular song (suitably converted for the purpose)—anything, in short. The church must surely be hard to please, if he could not suit them. He opened his organ as a peddler opens his tin boxes, and displaying all its wares, says, Now, what do you want? Here is a little of almost everything!

He took his turn. Then came a young man of a true and deep nature, to whom music was simply a symbol of something higher, a language which in itself is but little, but a glorious thing when laden with the sentiments and thoughts of a great heart. But he was not a Christian man, and the organ was not to him a Christian instrument, but simply a grand gothic instrument, to be studied, just as a Protestant would study a cathedral, in the mere spirit of architecture, and not at all in sympathy with its religious significance or uses. And before long he went abroad to perfect himself in his musical studies. But not till a most ludicrous event befell him. On a Christmas day a great performance was to be given. The church was full. All were musically expectant. It had been given out that something might be expected. And surely something was had a little more than was expected. For, when every stop was drawn, that the opening might be with a sublime choral effect, the down-pressing of his hands brought forth not only the full expected chord, but also a cat, that by some strange chance had got into the organ. She went up over the top as if gunpowder had helped her. Down she plunged into the choir, took the track around the front bulwark of the gallery, until opposite the pulpit, whence she dashed down one of the supporting columns, made for the broad aisle, where a little dog joined in the affray, and both went down toward the street door at an astonishing pace. Our organist, who, on the first appearance of this element in his piece, snatched back his hands, had forgotten to relax his muscles, and was to be seen following the cat with his eyes, with his head turned, while his astonished hands stood straight out before him, rigid as marble!

But in all these vicissitudes, and in all this long series of players, good playing has been the accident, while the thing meant and attempted has been, in the main, a perversion of music, a breaking of the Sabbath day, and a religious nuisance. The only alleviation in the case was, that the general ignorance of the proper function of church-music saved the Christian congregation from feeling what an outrage they had suffered. But, we must try this topic once more, before we can get it fairly finished.

HOW TO BECOME A CHRISTIAN.*

There cannot be too much effort made to bring before the minds of men the truths of Christ. But, when men are made attentive to them, it seems to me, that they should be made to feel the obligation to obey Christ, without so much urging, conversation, and persuasive labor. Among uneducated heathen, it would be different; but in a Christian country, where you have literally known almost nothing else than the truths of the Gospel, presented not alone in the didactic and logical form, but presented evermore in that most blessed form in which the true Gospel is preached, namely, in the example of a praying father, a praying mother, a praying brother or sister, a consistent friend, wife or child, nothing more ought to be required. How men that have been taught in the household and in the church, by example as well as by precept, should fall into the mistake of supposing that whenever they begin to be inquirers they need then to go through another and special course of training, I cannot understand. I do not think that there is an intelligent

* An Address delivered at a religious meeting in Burton's Old Theatre.

man in this congregation that is not abundantly qualified to-day, before the sun goes down, to become a true Christian in the spiritual and experimental sense of the term.

More than that. Unless there has been some kind of an official touch, a man's conversion is scarcely thought to be complete; unless some appointed class-leader, some elder, some deacon, above all, some minister, some eminent minister, has talked with him, explained it to him, upheld him in this hour, encouraged his hope and brought him clear out, he does not feel as though he were right. Whatever may be the hope he enjoys, there is still the impression that the work of grace requires the interposition of some official instruction.

I wish you to be rid of this. A man who knows enough to take care of his business, to live obediently to the laws of the land, to live in the affections of the family, knows enough to begin a Christian life. Religion and religious doctrines are very different things. We do not ask you to accept a theory of religious doctrine; nor any system of philosophy. We ask you simply to begin a religious life and to begin it now.

Are you willing to be a Christian? Are you willing from this hour to hold your disposition, your life-powers, and all your business, under the control of Christ? Will you go to school to Christ and become a scholar, for the sake of learning how to live aright? For, if you will, then you are a disciple of Christ. Disciple means scholar. A Christian is nothing but a sinful man who has put himself to school to Christ for the honest purpose of becoming better.

It is not needful that you should have a great deal of feeling. Willingness to obey the will of Christ as fast as it is made known to you is better than feeling. It is not necessary for you to go through such a period of conviction of sin, as some men have. If you see the evil of your sinful life enough to wish to forsake it, that is repentance enough to begin with. Repentance is good for nothing except to turn away a man from evil, and you need not wait for any more than will suffice for that. The less feeling there is required to effect a moral revolution the better.

I would not have you wait for ministers, or for Christians. You can be a Christian without help from either. They will gladly help you. But you ought not to lean on them. Go to your own work at once. It is a question between your soul and God. Will you acknowledge God as your Father? Will you, from this hour, make it your business to conduct your whole life in accordance with God's will revealed in the Gospel of Christ?

You may become a Christian now, and go home to your household, and be enabled to ask a blessing at your table to-day; you may stretch forth your hands, to the amazement of your wife and children, and, like a Christian man, ask a blessing upon your dinner, though it may be the first time in your life; you may go home to night and begin family prayers where the sound of your voice in prayer has never been heard. I urge you to take that course, and to take it at once.

The word of God requires us so love the Lord our God with all our heart, with all our soul, with all our mind, and our neighbor as ourself.

Will you deliberately undertake to begin your life over again, from this hour, under this law? Will you undertake to regard things as right or wrong, as they agree or disagree with that rule? Will you acknowledge yourself bound, henceforth, to act under that charter?

"Can I, then, do this by mere volition?" Can you any more go down to the Battery by volition? and yet you know that volition will produce that result. For a proper volition always implies, not alone a choice of a thing, but also all the steps needed to accomplish this end. To determine that you will be warm, implies kindling a fire, or putting on clothing, or better yet, active exercise. You cannot be rich by wishing, but by choosing you can; for choosing a thing always implies that you choose the appropriate means of obtaining it. And so every man may come into that state of love and benevolence required by Christ, if he will employ the word of God, prayer as the inspiration and daily practice in ordinary conduct, as the means.

"But can I suddenly, in a moment, reconstruct my character, change my conduct, alter my relations to things that are wrong, and be a thorough Christian in a moment?" No; you cannot be a perfect Christian in a moment, but you can begin to be an imperfect Christian in a moment. A man cannot make a journey in an instant, but he can begin instantly A man cannot cleanse his hands in a moment, but he can begin to wash. A man cannot reclaim a piece of land in an hour, but he can begin the work, with the determination to perform the whole. The prodigal son could not go back to his father at one step, but he could determine to perform the whole journey, and take the first step, and the next, and the next, perseveringly, and in right good earnest. Thus, to be a Christian is to enter upon a life which has its imperfect beginning, its rude development, its imperfections and mistakes, its successive states of growth, its gradual attainments, and its full final perfection only in another world.

"But, is it right to call myself a Christian, when I do not do everything that Christ commands?" If you mean to obey in everything, if you are pained when you fail, if you resist evil, and seek deliverance from it, Christ will prove to you the most lenient and gracious teacher that scholar ever had. A child is not expelled from school for one poor lesson, nor for much dullness, nor for heedlessness, nor for disobedience, if the teacher knows that, on the whole, the child means to be a good scholar, if he confesses his faults and strives to amend. God brings up those who become his children with a great deal more patience, a great deal more forbearance, and tenderness of love, than any mother exercises toward a difficult and fractious child. No faults lead her to give him up, so long as there is hope that at length he will do better, and do well. And God is greater in love than any mother.

And, if you will now accept this law of love, hold yourself bound by it, undertake to carry it out every day, not be discouraged by failures, persevere in spite of imperfections, you shall find in Christ such graciousness, such a forbearing and forgiving nature, as you will never find in any man.

The moment that you realize this goodness of Christ, his helpfulness to you, his lenient, forgiving, sympathizing spirit, then you know what faith in Christ means. If such a Saviour attracts you and you strive all the more ardently, from love toward him, and trust in him, then you are a Christian: not a religious man merely, but a Christian.

A man may worship through awe, or through a sense of duty, and I think there are hundreds of men in the churches who are only religious men, and not Christians. A man who feels toward God only awe or fear; who obeys merely from a sense of duty; who is under the dominion of conscience rather than of love, may be religious, but he is not a Christian. Such men live by conscience, they live by a bond, bound by fear. Their life is literally one of service; they are fatally servants of God, not in the sense in which the words are largely used in the Scriptures, meaning simply disciples of Christ, but they are most literally God's hired men, or worse—God's bondmen. Men must learn no longer merely to fear God, no longer to tremble as before the tyrannical master of a despotic government; but to come unto Him through Jesus Christ, and say, "Lord, I love thee, I trust thee, and I will serve thee because I love thee."

Any man who knows enough to love his children, his father, mother, brother or sister, has theological knowledge enough to know the Lord Jesus Christ.

Now the question is this: Do you choose to do it? If we were to put this question to any of you: Do you really choose to love the Lord Jesus Christ? I suppose every man of you would say, "I do." But stop, there is a great distinction between desiring a thing and choosing a thing; a man may desire without choosing. Do you suppose there is a man in the Tombs who does not desire to be an honest man? But he does not choose to be; there are other things which he desires more than that; he desires money more than he does honesty; he desires the means of debauchery and revelry more than he does honesty. Probably there is not a man given to his cups, in the city of New York, who, if you should ask him, "Do you not desire to become a reformed and temperate man?" would not say, Yes. He desires it, but he does not choose it; there are other things that he desires more, and he chooses the things which he desires most.

Ask a poor ragged vagabond, "Do you not desire riches?" Of course, he says he does. But he does not choose it, and you cannot make him choose it; he does desire to be rich, but he desires to be lazy much more than that—therefore he is a vagabond. A man desires to be a scholar, but he does not choose it, because he likes his leisure much better than application. You desire an article of merchandise which you see along the street; but when you inquire the price, you will not take it because you desire the money more. Almost every man desires something which he does not choose. We are full of desires, but we only choose those things for the possession of which we are willing to deny the solicitation of all antagonistic desires. That man who is willing to forego everything that stands in the way of the object which he desires, that man only can be said to have chosen it.

Now I put the question to you, Do you desire the love of Christ? Do you desire it more than you do your pleasures, more than ambition, more than selfish indulgences? Are you willing to say before God, I desire it more than all things in the world? If you do, I know not why you should not at once *begin* to be Christian. You are competent to choose your business; you do not need to ask any lawyers, doctors or ministers in order to do that. You are competent to choose your own course of life; you are competent to choose your own pleasures, and you never think of asking of others how to secure them. Why do you not stand upon your own power—or rather upon God's power, which works within yours—and become a Christian by your own volition, just as you become a lawyer, a physician, a merchant, a traveller, a scholar?

Why do you not take three minutes of this sovereign power of choice, to become a Christian? A man perhaps will say, "I desire to make that choice to-day." What he ought to say is this: "I make the choice. I make it now, and forever. I do in the presence of Almighty God, with all my soul determine, that I will, through the love of Christ, make his wish, the supreme law of my life within and without. Not only in my relation directly to God, but in all my conduct toward my fellow-men, I will be governed by the revealed wish and law of God. Trusting to his mercy for pardon in all things wherein I come short, and depending on him for strength, I will make my work his work, and try like Jesus to find my meat and drink in doing God's holy will." Who of you can solemnly promise this before God? Look at it all around and decide. Who can say, not that he will not be imperfect in carrying it out, but who can say, "that is to be my idea of life, that is to be my model, after which I am this hour and henceforth forever to strive?" Is there a man who can take that step? But, you say, "a man may take that step, and may become by mere choice a Christian in that way; but there is no love springs up —there is no grace in his heart or soul; and how is he to have that peace, that joy, that rest, that we hear Christians talking about? In other words, how is a man to have in his soul the sweet sense that his power is not in himself, but of Christ?" I answer, the Lord will send that—but in his own way and time. Leave it to him.

If feeling comes first, let it come. But do not wait for it. Move on. Follow your decision upon the path of duty, and you will by and by have all the feeling you need. Jesus Christ sits on the throne of the universe for the very purpose of giving sympathy and effectual help to every man who says, "Lord, I am needy; Lord, I am bestormed and out of my course, and I come to thee for sympathy and assistance." Upon that ground we are to look to Christ; we have the power to choose him, and, if we do, we shall feel that mighty love, that conscious sympathy and presence, that power of God upon the heart of every man, which shall give him peace and joy. If you doubt, come unto Christ and you shall know whether it does not make you blessed. This willingness on your part, this faith in Christ, is the element that shall bring you in the right direction, to a consciousness of peace in Jesus Christ. But the great trouble is, I think, that you do not wish to be Christians so much as you wish other things.

One of the most memorable things that took place last winter was the opening of a place as an eating-house, free to the hungry, in one of the streets of this city. The kind actor in this charity thought that he had no better way to use his money than to feed the hungry and the poor; so he opened a room and made this declaration: "If any are hungry, here is food for them; let them come and eat." Now, in the case of certain grades of men, there was no trouble about it. The man who was in the ditch, and so low that he knew that he was a miserable, degraded creature, would scramble up quickly when he heard of this place; run to it and betake himself to the food with almost indecent haste. And the man who had been dodging around from one expedient to another, till now he was nearly famished and did not know where to go to keep from starvation, hears that here there were great, bountiful rounds of beef and glorious loaves of bread, any quantity, indeed, of provision, and away he runs to see if it was really so; he would not talk much, or preach much, but he would practise a great deal; for, let me tell you that your hungry men care very little for the theory of eating or digestion. It is the practice which they dote upon.

But here comes a man who has been more respectable: he has lived in genteel society and given dinner parties in his prosperous days; the times have been rather hard upon him, but he expects that the spring will set him up all right again; he has been home with everybody who asked him to eat, has been to everybody's house but his own, for there was nothing to eat there; he has borrowed all the money he could, but now no one asks him to dine, and he can borrow no more. He has gone to bed hungry at night, and oh! what dreams he has had out of that gnawing stomach; he wakes up in the morning and says to himself, "I wonder where I can get any breakfast?" He thinks to be sure of that dining-saloon just opened, where there is plenty of food to be had for nothing; but he says, "I cannot go down there, I cannot humble myself so much; I, who have been able, and in the habit of giving charity, to go down there and get my food, and become a beggar? I can't do that!" So, he wanders about till noon, and though the hunger gnaws at his stomach, and he is faint and weary, he will not go in yet, so he wanders on till about sundown.

But at sun-down he says to himself—and hunger is an excellent logician—"After all, am I not acting foolishly? I am so weak I can hardly stand, and it does seem to me that I cannot sleep to-night for the gnawings of hunger. Oh, how I want this food; I think I will just go down the street." So away he goes, like a great many men who have come in here to-day, saying that they just came in to see what was going on, but who know that down deep in their own hearts there is something else beside curiosity which they cannot resist. Well, away he goes down the street, and looks in to see who is there; then he watches to see if anybody is looking at him, or if anybody knows him; he goes away and walks up the square, but he is reminded from within that he had better come back again. This time he walks right by the door, and looks in askance to see if anybody is in there; he hears the cheerful noise of the knives and forks, smells the wholesome food, hears the laughter of joyful men, hungry men doing work meet for hunger. Now, suppose that, as he stands there, he should see, among those going down, the butcher and baker loaded with great piles of meat and bread, and should stop them to say: "I am almost dead with hunger, I have been invited here to take something to eat, but before I go down I should like to know the precise process by which flour is made into bread!"—just as men come to me, wishing me to explain to them the doctrines of justification, sovereignty, atonement, and other things, when they are dying for want of Christ's loving help! So this man stops the baker to ask him how bread is made, but the butcher and the baker step in with their load.

He listens again to the cheerful music of the rattling dishes—and there is no such music to a hungry man's ear, and says, "I can't go in yet; I am not satisfied as to the way these things are made." So he walks away, but hunger gives him another turn, and back he goes and looks in again, and says, "If it wasn't for—, if it wasn't for—;" then he looks up the street to see if anybody is looking at him, and says, "I will just go down one step." He steps down, and the attraction is so great that he goes in; nobody seems to know him, nobody seems surprised; he reaches out his hand and takes hold of a dry crust, and the tears come into his eyes as he puts it into his mouth. Oh, how sweet it is! With that he sits right down and makes a feast, and as he rises up again, he says to himself, "Oh, what a fool I was, that I did not come long before and often." Are there not just such fools in this congregation? You go up and down, to and fro, before Christ's table, when there is bread that will cause that hunger to cease forever, and water drawn from the river that comes from God's throne; and yet you have gone back, thinking what your wife would say, what your father would say, what your partner would say, what your gay companions would say. But you feel the gnawings of hunger, and, as you look at the spread table, you say, "Oh, how we need this food, but we dare not come and take it." Oh! it is shame, pride, or fear, that keeps you thus back. Oh, if there was only hunger enough to bring you to the right point, then, having once tasted, you would rise up from that feast, with the blessed assurance that yet once again you should sit down at a still nobler table, at the marriage supper of the Lamb!

Now, if there are any in this congregation that have seen the bounty spread forth in the love of Christ, which they can have "without money and without price," as promised by Jesus Christ, do not let them wait for somebody to explain it any more. Try it yourselves to-day!

I am ashamed of myself, often, to be an object of more faith than my Saviour; yet I have persons coming to me every day of my life, with their wants and troubles, instead of going to Christ. How eagerly they believe every statement I make; how they hang upon my sympathy, and hope I will let them come again to-morrow. I say to myself, if you would only come to Christ with half the faith that brings you to me, you might be rejoicing in half an hour. Suppose now, that instead of a man sinful and erring like yourselves, you should put in my place the august form of the Lord Jesus Christ, full of benignity, glorious with goodness, and with a sweetness that is more than any mother ever knew for her darling child, waiting patiently, bending over you and saying, "Come unto me and take my yoke upon you;" "learn of me and ye shall find rest to your souls," "for he that cometh unto me I will in no wise cast out." Suppose you should hear Jesus Christ saying, "I have been out to seek and search for lost men, and I have found you, and I am persuading you to come to me; believe me that I love you, that I love you now." If there is a man that has one thought toward God, it is because the love of God is drawing him sympathetically to himself. It is a blessed thought that Jesus Christ is longing for you, and I would that you might turn still more earnestly to Jesus Christ and say, "Lord, I believe thee, I believe thou lovest me; I believe thou desirest to make me thine, and from this hour it shall be the object of my life to please thee, and the one firm object of my life to serve thee." Will you try the effect of that vow, some of you, to-day? Try it at once, even now, while I am speaking.

I always feel most for those who are furthest from grace, perhaps because I see in them some likeness to myself. But my Master also had a special regard for such. One of the most touching things in the life of Christ, is the way in which the wretched looked at him. The literary, the philosophical, the rich, the great political men of that day did not think much of Christ; but he had such a sweet way of carrying himself in all Jerusalem, that whenever he went into a house to sit down and rest, all the vagabonds and wretches came round about him, as though he was their patron. They felt "somebody cares for me; somebody, instead of thumping me with a truncheon, instead of putting my hands in manacles, loves and cares for me." They did not know what to make of the quiet, gentle effect of the character of Christ; and wherever he went all manner of wicked men poured round about him. Such was his sweetness that all the wretched and miserable came to see him; such was the impression he made upon the lowest class in Jerusalem. Why should we not all be like him?

Whenever I know of a man that nobody else prays for, it seems as if my heart would break for him. If I hear of a man that has broken away from all instruction, instead of saying, "he is a devil, I would much rather say he is my brother, and I must heartily pray for him." When I walk up Broadway, 'tis a pain to me to look up and down the street and see so many, with apparently nobody to care for their souls. Now, if there is in this house to-day any man who is wicked and degraded; if there is any man who sells rum—and that makes about as bad a man as can be in this world—I don't say this to hurt your feelings, but because, as a servant of Christ, I must talk plainly to every man;—if there is a man in this congregation that has gotten his living by stealing, from the most vulgar form of stealing up to the most respectable, genteel way in which so-called honest men steal, and call it financiering; if there are any who live in any way discreditably in the eye of the world or in the eye of God; any who make catering to lust or passion their means of livelihood; if there are any who have stood upon these boards, not to instruct, but simply to amuse or degrade their fellow-men; actors, managers, or any others—give me your hand, you are my brethren! It is the blood of Christ that makes you and me related, which is more precious than the blood of your father or my father. My soul goes out for you; and I long that you should know how Christ feels for you. Oh! wandering sheep, be not ye lost! Christ calls to you by my voice. He sends me here to say to some man who is on the point of decision, but who thinks it is of no use to try to be good any longer;—drink, perhaps, may be taking you down; or your passions are dragging you down, and you do not know how to resist the insidious pleasures which surround you; or your companions are taking you down, and nobody, as you think, cares for you—nobody prays for you or gives you instruction. Yes, there is one man who does—I care for you; not out of my own nature, but because the spirit of my Master makes me thus care for your soul. He sent me to tell you that He—glorious as he is—that He cares for you ten thousand times more than I do. He loves you—He longs for you; and there shall not be one man who makes one faint motion toward a better life whom He will not stand ready to receive. He shall send forth the angels, saying unto them, "Take care of that man, and bear him up lest at any time he dash his foot against a stone."

But, let me tell you, in this matter you must be in earnest; you must be thoroughly resolved. Prayers have this morning been asked in your hearing for a Christian woman who, at the peril of life, has fled from slavery. Now, I want to know if there is a man in this congregation who desires to get rid of his sins as much as this poor woman did to get rid of her slavery? She was willing to put her life in her hand, and, for days, without food, without drink, to seek for liberty as for her very life.

Is there a slave in this congregation? A slave to Satan or to his own passions? Is there any who wants to escape as much as this poor woman did? Who strikes for liberty in Jesus Christ? Who desires to say to-day, not about one habit, but of all bad habits, "I desire to reform—I will reform?" It is easier to reform all at once than it is to reform one thing at a time. If a man wishes to wash a spot, big as a penny, clean on a dirty hand, he will find it much easier to wash the whole hand than that one spot. This gradual repentance is like a man who wants to be taken out from a burning building, but who says to those about him, "Now, don't take me out too suddenly; take me down first to a room where it is not quite so hot as it is here; and then to another room, where there is still less heat, and so take me out gradually." Why, the man would be a cinder before you got him out! A man who wants to reform should reform perpendicularly! If you mean to quit drinking, quit it at once, and become a Christian? If you want to be an honest man, go to God! Begin there. It is easier to reform any vice by becoming a Christian at once, than to attempt it from a lower motive. Take upon you the highest bond of truth! A man who tries to reform without the help of God, is like the man who tries to breathe without air. Now, is there any man here who seeks for reform?—there is hope for you; there is prayer for you; and better than that, there is God for you—there is Christ for you! I hope and desire that in consequence of these remarks, some man who has been bound in sin may be converted. Who shall it be? Shall it be you? Some of you whose friends have been laboring for you, SHALL IT NOT BE YOU?

GOD'S WITNESS TO CHRISTIAN FIDELITY.

REPORTER'S PRELIMINARY STATEMENT.

[An occasion of unusual interest, and one which will be long memorable to those who witnessed it, was celebrated last Sunday morning in Plymouth Congregational Church, Brooklyn. The unusual religious feeling which has been apparent in this congregation for some months past, has of late been coming to harvest, and the fruits are now being gathered. The prayer-meetings have long been crowded, and the weekly lectures transferred from the lecture-room to the main building, in consequence of the thronged attendance. This church, during its comparatively brief history of less than eleven years, has experienced several revivals of great power and long continuance; but never one of greater extent or more gratifying character than the present. The first indications of unusual seriousness in the congregation were observed about the time of the beginning of the General Awakening, last fall; and the feeling has since been continually increasing, without any present token of decline. The great audiences attending the Sabbath services have given evidence of deep seriousness, and the successive occasions of public worship have steadily grown more and more solemn and impressive. For two months past, at the close of the evening sermons, the pastor has regularly invited the unconverted persons in the congregation who desired prayers in their behalf, to rise in their seats, and thus to make that public commitment of themselves which has so often been found to be the beginning act of conversion.

Since the communion in March (when a very large accession was made to the church) up to last Sabbath, which was the next following communion season, one hundred and ninety persons presented themselves for admission; of which number one hundred and sixty-five were to make a public profession of their faith in Christ, and twenty-five to be received by letters from other churches. How seldom is it the privilege of a single church to receive into its fellowship, at a regular communion occurring at an interval of only two months from a previous one, which was also signalized by a large ingathering, so great a number of those who have newly passed from death unto life, and become—publicly and before the world—disciples of the Lord and Saviour Jesus Christ!

An occasion of so much interest was appropriately celebrated with joyfulness and thanksgiving. In commemoration of the event, the pulpit was beautifully decorated with flowers—which, if there were still altars for sacrifice, would be the most beautiful and the most touching offerings that could ever be laid upon them; while behind the desk, and facing the company of converts, was hung in cloth the inscription, "For ye were as sheep gone astray, but are now returned unto the Shepherd and Bishop of your souls." The Rev. Dr. Lyman Beecher sat in the pulpit, a venerable witness of the scene, reminding one of Summerfield's picture of "Jacob leaning upon his staff." Five rows of pews, extending in semi-circular form around the pulpit, were occupied exclusively by the candidates. The edifice was crowded to its utmost capacity in every part, including aisles, passages, doorways, vestibule, and pulpit-steps, while hundreds of persons, notwithstanding the rain at the time of the beginning of the services, were unable to obtain admission within seeing or hearing distances.

After the usual opening invocation and singing, the pastor read the long list of names of persons propounded for membership; which brought tears to many eyes in the congregation, as relatives and friends were found to be upon it, including in some instances almost entire families, with many parents and children, brothers and sisters, born at the same time into the kingdom of God. It was almost like the reading of a page out of the "Lamb's book of life."

Two verses of Doddridge's hymn were then sung, beginning—

"O happy day, that fixed my choice."

The union of three thousand voices in a hymn of praise, to two hundred of whom, gathered around the pulpit, it was a "new song in their mouth," was so solemn and inspiring, that there could have been but few in the house not affected by it.

The usual brief ceremonial of admission was then performed, consisting in the reading of the "articles of faith," and the "covenant with the church," to the converts standing, and their bowing assent—in the baptism of such as had never before received the rite, of whom there were thirty females and twelve males—in the reading of the covenant to those received by letter—and in the welcome act of fellowship by the church, expressed by the members rising in their seats in token of admitting their new brethren into their number.

It should be mentioned that on Thursday evening previous to the communion, twenty-three of the candidates were baptized, at their own request, by immersion. The ceremony was performed by Mr. Beecher, in presence of a crowded assembly, in the Baptist church in Pierrepont street.

The opening exercises were concluded with singing the three remaining verses of the same hymn, which, thus divided, is admirably adapted to such an occasion—beginning with the third verse,

> " 'Tis done, the greatest transaction's done;
> I am the Lord's and He is mine."

A sermon was then preached, which, owing to the exercises that had already preceded, and to the communion which was to follow it, was unusually brief, and of which—from both the general interest of the occasion, and of the discourse itself—we give an unabridged and complete report as follows :]

"Till we all come in the unity of the faith, and of the knowledge of the Son of God, unto a perfect man, unto the measure of the stature of the fullness of Christ; that we henceforth be no more children, tossed to and fro, and carried about with every wind of doctrine, by the sleight of men, and cunning craftiness, whereby they lie in wait to deceive; but speaking the truth in love, may grow up

unto him in all things, which is the head, even Christ; from whom the whole body fitly joined together and compacted by that which every joint supplieth, according to the effectual working in the measure of every part, maketh increase of the body unto the edifying of itself in love."—EPH. iv. 13-16.

This is addressed to those who were but just entering upon a course of Christian discipleship; and it is peculiarly appropriate to an occasion like this. This morning God hath caused the gates of this temple to be thrown open, to receive as many as would constitute a new and large church! Such a day as this has never before dawned upon this Christian brotherhood.

This church is but eleven years old. It has been blessed with five seasons of peculiar religious growth. They have not been at the expense of intermediate seasons. Much has lately been said of revivals; and many have derided them as rare and occasional freshets of feeling, in churches that ordinarily have none. That this is sometimes the fact is indisputable. But it need not be. A revival of religion is not an abnormal state. It is based upon natural laws. Like all other true states, it will be sound and beneficial, or imperfect and mischievous, according to the knowledge and skill with which men employ the great and stated agencies of Truth.

Five revivals have been experienced in eleven years in this church. Not only has this not been the case because the intermediate periods were unspiritual and declining; but there has been a continual growth in the spirituality of the church, and each revival has lifted the church higher. And when the special social religious element has subsided, it has not left the church cold, hard, insensitive, and fruitless. For, if you except the communion season which follows the summer pastoral vacation (and at which we do not aim to receive members) there has been scarcely a communion season in this church for years, at which persons have not been received from the world. And there have been awakenings and conversions more or less frequent during every year, and during every month, from year to year. Eleven years ago this month, this church was formed with twenty-five members. To-day it stands up to praise God with the grateful hearts of 1,377; and of this great company, 673 have been received from the world, and upon good evidence of conversion.

You must not uncharitably regard this as boasting. I have no time for that; I have a higher end in view.

I wish it to be remembered that this church has had its whole life and development during a very critical period of American history. The Gospel of Christ, in every age, has a new work to perform, a new growth to develop, new applications to the ever-changing phases of society to be made. I need not tell you through what a memorable and eventful series of changes God has brought this nation.

In preaching the Gospel to you, I have taken it for granted that my duty was to preach a living Gospel, to living men, about living questions. I have not confined my attention to one subject. I have preached Christ as the fountain-head of all spiritual life, and the perfect exemplar. I have taught you that a deep, inward spiritual life, begun by God's Spirit, and daily nourished by God's personal presence, is the foundation of all true Christian morals. I have taught you that love to God and to man is the characteristic element of all true Christian reformatory labor. And you will bear me witness that I have anxiously, and ten times, yes, a hundred times more than anything else, taught, labored, and besought that you prepare yourselves for all external work by faith in Jesus Christ, by humility, by zeal tempered with discretion, by fervent sympathy with each other and with the whole brotherhood of mankind. And I have incessantly stimulated you to work in an atmosphere of love.

Thus prepared, I have sought to inspire you with higher ideals of life in every one of its elements; with a higher notion of personal character; with a nobler sense of true manhood; with a purer and deeper way of personal living; with a richer and higher idea of the family state; with more noble habits of secular life. I have searched the family, the store, the shop, the office, the street, the ship, the farm, with the lighted candle of the Gospel, and sought to develop in your mind the idea of a symmetrical Christian character, both contemplative and executive, both spiritual and philanthropic, both domestic and public. I have not forgotten things personal in things domestic, nor things secular in domestic truths, nor your public duties by any over-scrupulous ecclesiastic and church relationship. And in the fulfillment of this work you know very well that I have neither neglected public questions nor yet intruded them so often as to give them disproportionate importance. I have called you to believe the deep and fundamental truth of Christ's atonement, on the human side of it, namely, that men are unspeakably precious and valuable beyond all estimation before God! I have said that the meanest and lowest creature on the globe is of transcendent dignity, and has rights sacred as the throne of God. For, what shall measure the worth of a creature for whose salvation Christ would die? One drop of Christ's blood is worth a globe, though it were one orbicular diamond. Souls are the jewels of God, not metals or stones.

I have taken hearty and earnest part in the struggles of our day for the great Christian Doctrines of Human Liberty, and I have led no unwilling church into the conflict. In this matter (pardon me if I speak of myself) I have determined to have no interests, no reputation, and no position or influence, aside from these great truths. I have committed my soul to God's keeping, and have neither asked nor cared what men might think, or say, or do. Too thankful to live in such a day, and to work in such a field, I have only feared that my sight might grow dull, my heart grow feeble, and my hand become weak in this work so dear to the heart of Christ! As Christ has embraced the human soul in his own, so hath he taught me to call all men my brethren. And I have preached, lectured, written, and gone forth unhesitatingly and before the whole people, to bear witness to the great Gospel of Christ in the one preëminent and transcendent application of it to the great pulsating, living interest of this age and nation.

Now, why have I said all this? For two reasons.

First, Because God has raised up this church as seal and testimony. It stands before the nation as a church consecrated to Christ, not only in a general way, but as a church that bears an unfaltering witness to Christian Reform. It stands before the world for Temperance; for Liberty and against Slavery; for Humanity and against all oppression in trade, in commerce, or in civil relations. And what has been God's testimony?

Has this been a church split and divided by intestine quarrels? For eleven years your church meetings have been open to the freest speech. And I call you to witness that there has never been a difficulty so large as a man's hand, nay, so large as a finger, in this society or church! We have gone through all discussions of the most perilous and exciting questions, and all men have had unrestrained liberty, and yet love has not been quenched. And we stand this day a living brotherhood. You love me. I love you, most heartily. And you love each other, and dwell in more than peace—yea, in great joy and gladness together. And it is a thing that has become noticeable, and noticed, that there is in this congregation a spirit of general and undissembled love. This is God's blessing and God's witness to the righteousness of your cause!

Moreover, while you have been faithful, in some degree, to Christ's work among the poor, see how he has set the seal to it by the repeated revivals sent among and upon you! To those who ignorantly denounce you for not preaching the Gospel, we answer, within eleven years there have been five precious revivals of religion here, and many hundreds of conversions.

Is this the history of a church without a Gospel? I declare my solemn conviction, that God has spiritually blessed you because it was the very Gospel which we preached. Not a descant to the rich, not an essay to the refined, not a favoring of the prosperous, but a Gospel of pity, love, and salvation, temporal and eternal, to every tribe, race, and class of men

And I am willing to go before the impartial tribunal of coming times, and declare that by this fidelity to liberty, to good morals, to humanity, to the indispensable and integral elements of true spiritual religion, we have been prospered.

The other reason that led me to this history, was, that I might bear witness, not alone to the reality, but to the beneficence of Revivals of Religion.

They are not the mere alternative heats which follow worldly chills. Revivals are founded upon natural laws, just as are all other instrumental religious elements. They may be wisely dealt with. They may be ignorantly dealt with. But they do not exist because the church, having been low, seeks to equilibrate itself by being unduly excited. They belong to the social and religious nature of men, gathered together in churches or communities.

As it respects this church, I bear witness, that at each period this church has risen, in consequence of such visitations, to a higher level of Christian life, and kept it! The church by each season has risen to a higher conception of Christian life, to higher and purer views of Christ, to clearer conceptions of duty and usefulness, to greater desire for doing good, and expertness in carrying forth that desire.

This church has been a Christian church, believing in the great cardinal doctrines held by evangelical Christians in common; and because it was a Christian church it has been a temperance body, a church full of zeal for liberty, and incessantly laborious in all the great humanities of our age. And yet, it has been expectant of revivals, and the grateful recipient of them. For, as God gives a great seed-time, and a great and general harvest to every year, and yet fills up the months also, with incidental and perpetual blossoming and ripening of some sweet thing; so he gives to every true and intelligent church constant budding, constant blossoming. But, beside that, is grander profusion—greater harvests, in which the whole year opens its bosom and exhibits its vast richness! There may be a harvest of cockles and chess, but that does not argue against true wheat or corn! There may be an autumn for the crab-apple and the bitter sloe, but that does not take from the glory of the orchard, nor from the exquisite flavor of its superabundant fruits.

A true course of fidelity thus is seen to stand between the two extremes of an empty Christianity and a scoffing Infidelity. It rejects the dead sepulchre, amid which inhuman Christians stand praising the dust and bones of those men of the past whom their pharisaic fathers slew. And it utterly refuses to go down to the hard and stony road of Naturalism, where the strong men but just subsist, and where, when the weak ask for bread, they must give them stones, and for eggs, scorpion doubts. They have nothing better to give!

And now for the future! To what have these new-comers been called? Are they to-day received into your bosom, that they may, henceforth, subside and be sheltered from labor, from self-denial, from achievement, yea, if need be, from battle unto death!

Nay, verily! you have merely begun. Your journey is yet to be performed. You have taken your staff; but the travelling is all before you. You have entered school; you are scholars. You have much to learn, and everything to practise; you are just beginning. Your experience thus far is but leaven, that is to leaven the whole meal.

The centre of all your aims is to be, according to the Scripture which I have read—the construction of your own character. You are to build hereafter toward the ideal of perfect manhood. "Till we all come in the unity of the faith and of the knowledge of the Son of God, unto a perfect man; unto the measure of the stature of the fullness of Christ." Hereafter, your aim is to be the reconstruction of your inward and your outward life, so that you shall attain to a full manhood—to the pattern and ideal of the Lord Jesus Christ.

Joys are not, therefore, what you are seeking—though joys will be yours; nor sorrows—though you will have them. It is not eminent vision that you seek. It is not mere zeal, not mere self-denial, not mere cross-bearing. These and such other graces as are either instruments or the sequences of your true

Christian life—you will have. But your aim is to be, to build up a Christian manhood—a spiritually manly character. When men build, it is not bricks that they aim at, nor stone, nor timber, nor lime, nor paint, though they use them all; they aim at a house. "Now, we are no more strangers and foreigners, but fellow-citizens with the saints, and of the household of God; and are built up upon the foundation of the apostles and prophets, Jesus Christ himself being the chief corner-stone; in whom all the building fitly framed together groweth unto a holy temple in the Lord; in whom ye also are builded together for a habitation of God through the Spirit." Our text gives the same thought, only under a different figure —of the body. Men do not seek to develop themselves in the hand alone, nor in the foot, nor in any one member. They seek the life of the whole body. And so you are called, not to be happy, not to be peaceful; you are called, not to suffering, not to self-denial, not to cross-bearing. Though all these things come upon you, they are merely instruments with which you are to build up a Christian manhood, in all its symmetry and perfection.

That manhood, although it is to be based upon your natural faculties, is a great deal more than the mere unfolding of these faculties. There is to be unfolding, and then a training to a model—which is Christ. And this does not mean a training to any mystic and impossible identity with God, in the greatness of His peculiar spiritual being; but a training to those elements of feeling which Christ manifested—to those aims which he accepted—to those practical elements of life which he exhibited. Christ is your model and teacher. You are not, therefore, to go to the World to ask what is honest, or what is pure, or what is true; you are to go to Christ and ask him, and, with that knowledge, to go back and live by it—let the world and its customs be what they may. You are not to go to your own circle, nor to any mere church or teacher; you are to go to the Lord and Saviour. There is his life; there is his conduct; there are his words. There you are to resort. If you need help to interpret what they mean, ask help of those that are wise in these things; yet your model is not to be minister, nor church, nor family, nor community—but Christ!

In this work, you are to remember that piety is a practical thing. "That ye henceforth be no more children, tossed to and fro, and carried about with every wind of doctrine, by the will of men and cunning craftiness, whereby they lie in wait to deceive." Piety is not an explanation of all possible religious truths. It is not casuistry, nor ethical discussion. It is the rearing up of your daily life upon the pattern of Christ Jesus. To that you are called. Christians, like other men, may investigate; they may reason; they may study; they may construct philosophies; but this is no necessary part of their Christian life. That to which they are called is the finding out of truth for the sake of better living—not the finding out of truth for the sake of knowing how one fits into another. You are called into the church in an age of speculation. Everything is up for investigation. No book, no custom, no system, no institution

—though a thousand years have made it venerable, is or can be exempt from search and test. I do not wish to warn you against discussion, nor against thinking, nor against progress. But that which is to make you Christian men is not involved in research, nor in philosophy. It lies within the reach of the simplest soul—within reach of the most ignorant. It is written over and over again, almost in every possible form. "The righteousness which is of faith speaketh in this wise, Say not in thine heart, who shall ascend into heaven? that is, to bring Christ down from above; or who shall descend into the deep? that is, to bring up Christ again from the dead. But what saith it? The word is nigh thee, even in thy mouth, and in thy heart, that is, the word of faith which we preach." Your Christian character does not stand in your being able to solve all curious, knotty questions. It stands in your being able to solve the mischief of pride in your heart—in controlling your selfishness—in making sweet that which is bitter—in lifting up that which is low—in exalting that which is high still higher—in making your whole life redolent of Christian love. You are called to this. Let other men investigate doctrines and philosophies, and you yourselves may, but there is something, without these, that stands near enough to every one of you: the construction of your own private personal character and conduct upon the model of Christ. There be many men who will preach another Gospel to you; but the Gospel for you is—Christ in you the hope of glory. There are many men who will trouble you with the dust of the Bible, its foundation knocked from under it, and the superstructure all taken down; but what you need is not curious speculation, but rich and pure living—deep-hearted piety, to build you up higher and higher in a true manhood; to prepare you for sorrow and trouble; to prepare you for bereavements and afflictions; to prepare you for the grand passage of death; to prepare you to stand immortal in the kingdom of God and of our Lord and Saviour Jesus Christ. While, if you are perplexed and puzzled with various questions, you may investigate freely, see to it that no troubles in respect to external circumstances move you from that which is the marrow of the truth—Christ your model, and a character shaped and fashioned according to his example.

The element in which everything grows and ripens in this outward world is that conjoined element which the sun gives—light and heat. To-day is Nature's great communion day! Ten million times ten million new-born leaves are holding up their tender hands to greet the sun. What is that which evokes them all? What is that in which they all live, and are to live all summer long? What is that which is to ripen them till they all glow like gold in autumn? It is the warmth and light of the sun —the great atmosphere with which God bathes all nature! Now we are to live in one great atmosphere which is to be about us—the atmosphere of Christian love. When I speak of love, I do not mean the drops that trickle down when we strike the rocky heart with the prophet's wand, gushing for the day and then dried up; but love springing up and filling the whole heart, always, to overflowing. I mean, first, thou shalt love the Lord thy God, and then, out of that same fountain, thou shalt love thy neighbor as thyself. See how curiously this is here traced—like curious figures worked in gold: "That henceforth ye be no more children, tossed to and fro, and carried about with every wind of doctrine by sleight of men and cunning craftiness whereby they lie in wait to deceive; but, speaking the truth in love, may grow up unto him in all things, which is the head, even Christ."

One thing more. What a consummation is this to-day! We stand upon the dividing-point, and reach forth into the past and the future! Who were your fathers and mothers? Where the village in which your infancy nestled? What has been the course and history of your life? Look back from the point and privilege of to-day! How many prayers are now answered on your appearing here to-day! How many tears, shed like dew in the silence of the night, are now made radiant, like dews when the morning sun rises upon them! Mothers, that have prayed for you, and died praying, and have gone home to glory, behold you from heaven to-day! For though we may not know what is going on in heaven, heaven knows what is going on upon earth. And they that are redeemed behold you, and bless God with double joy for your joy to-day. What temptations have you escaped and left behind you forever and forever! What evils have you turned yourselves from! What a life have you abandoned, and what a glorious life have you entered upon!

Now turn and look the other way. What is to be your history? Some of you are to be poor; but you have that which is worth more than riches. Some of you are to be obscure; nay, he on whose head Christ hath put his hand, can never be other than illustrious! Some of you are to have a hard and burdensome way in life; but no burden is comparable to the cross, and he who has learned to carry the cross of Christ, can carry the globe itself after that! Some of you perhaps are to go forth upon the ocean, and to die, and be buried in its waves. Some of you are to go among strangers, to fall down in the forest where no man hath been, and where there will be none to wipe the death moisture from your forehead. But the Lord Jesus Christ hath said, "I will never leave you nor forsake you." Die where he please, die when he please, he dies unto life who dies with Christ ministering to him.

And now, my dear Christian brethren, I cannot tell you with what joy I receive you, one by one. Although I have been so busy that I could not sit down to take the luxury of joy with each one of you, one after another—for you came too fast for that—yet I propose to myself a better time with you in heaven than ever I shall have upon earth. But to-day let me pause in my work; let me sit down with you to-day in the bower of Christ's love; and let me be happy, and be ye happy, as you and I shall taste the bread and the wine for the first time in your lives, to-day. No such bread has ever grown as that which you shall taste to-day! No grape was ever crushed of such precious life-blood as that with which to-day we shall symbolize the blood of Christ Jesus, shed for the remission of your sins! O children of Christ, new-born! O disciples of Christ, new-learned! O heirs of glory, expectant of heaven!—I bid you GOD SPEED! And if ever in after times you are carried into temptations, if ever you are waylaid by secret enemies in your own heart, if ever you are driven hither and thither from your steadfastness—wherever you may be in the dark hour—I bid you remember this bright and radiant morning, and this joyful consecration which you this day have made; and if in that hour of darkness there is nothing in the present to sustain you, draw from the magazine of the past, and let memory nerve you to stand steadfast and faithful unto the end! And when we shall have passed what most men call the river, but what has become by faith the rill of death—scarcely wetting the palms of our feet, while we walk across singing triumphs all the way over;—if you go before I do, greet me; if I go before, I shall look back for you, and reach out joyful hands from among that multitude that shall stand to greet you when you come to your Father's kingdom. By and by we shall be with the ransomed of the Lord, and there, crowned with eternal joy, we shall lift up our voices forever and ever in praise of him who hath this day loved us, and given himself for us. Amen! Amen!

THE PROGRESS OF CHRISTIANITY.*

The ability of the missionary society to do good abroad, depends very much on the opinion entertained of it at home. Whenever a difficulty occurs there, it must be removed. And there is such a difficulty now. There are some individuals whose faith is so strong that they always give themselves up to their feelings without reasoning. There are others who follow their heads first, and only give liberty to their hearts afterward. First, it was necessary with them that the head should see clearly and reasonably what was to be done, before their hearts were permitted to get up much steam. These are, after all, the most useful men in this cause, as in any other. Now, is this work of evangelizing the world a divine work? If it is divine, how shall we explain the great hiatus in its progress? Eighteen hundred years ago it commenced, and made glorious strides toward completion; but then it seemed as if the great command had been suspended for ages, the command given by Christ before his ascension, "Go ye into all the world and preach the Gospel to every creature." Why had not the work gone on? When the apostles, with the fiery tongues of Pentecost yet

* An Address delivered at the Anniversary of the A. B. C. F. M. May, 1847.

burning on their heads, went forth, the nations fell before them like withered grass before the autumnal fires. But our progress is like that of snails. Theirs, like that of lions. Hath God forgotten? His arm then stretched forth with might, has it grown weary? Or was the success of the apostles' preaching and labors merely the result of human enthusiasm, which has its ebbing and flowing, its action and reaction, its periodic times? Has it died away through so many centuries, and have we at last raised it to a merely temporary resurrection? Are there any marks of divinity about the great scheme?

When the Gospel was first preached, the immensity of its work can scarcely be conceived by us at the present day. The apostles had not only to convert men, individual men, but to convert the world. The Gospel was to infuse its leaven into all that men had done in the world, into all their laws, their manners and customs, their social and domestic relations, their political institutions, and the whole framework of society. These, too, were all to be divinely baptized, just as much as the men themselves. We must not suffer ourselves to be deceived by low conceptions of the work which had to be done. Remember the words of Christ himself. The kingdom of heaven was to be like leaven which a woman took and hid—*hid* in three measures of meal. Now, when you take leaven, and put it into the meal, you do not see anything like a spontaneous fermentation. It is hidden—you cannot see it, nor can you see its operation until the fermentation is complete. In like manner Christ came. He put the leaven into three centuries, and there it was hid, working and working under the surface, invisible to the eye, until by and by there was a little breaking forth here, and a little there, and then, when the results began to appear, men, having lost the connection between cause and effect, said, "Whence is this?" They had lost sight of the leaven, it was placed there so long ago. We must remember that this meal was placed in a pretty large dish. It was the whole world. When Christ came, the world was four thousand years old, and its progress from the first had been steadily upward in all intellectual and manual branches; but this growth had taken place under the influence of depraved hearts—of selfishness, of pride and of cruelty. The Gospel was now to undo and overlay all that bad hearts and bad understandings had been doing in the world for these four thousand years. It had not only to convert the men in the world, but the world itself. Go to a corrupt village—some God-forsaken spot, where all is vice and iniquity, and convert one man; let everything around him continue depraved and degrading as it was before, and with this evil influence constantly working upon him, what will be the result? May be he will stand—yes, that's the word, *stand;* but he will not travel. Thus, suppose that, after a great portion of the Roman empire had been converted, the old Roman priestly government had been suffered to remain, with the old heathen worship, the old social customs, the old laws, and everything else as in its pagan state, why, these mounted batteries of theirs would have swept the flanks and rear of the Christian army perpetually.

There would have been no gradual melioration of the world. It would have stood, perhaps, but a converted man must not only stand, he must grow in grace. If it were God's plan to work by miracles, the conversion of the world had been as easy as the creation or the flood. But he intends his truth to work its way by the natural operation of those laws by which the mind of man is governed. Was this change, a change which was to be wrought in Religion and Politics, in the capitol and the forum, in literature and the laws, in marriage and manners, in the study and in the shop, was all this to be the work of time, or of a day? Go to some of the most polluted purlieus of this city, take thence a boy who was literally born in sin, the son of the vilest of parents, a youth who has been trained and graduated in iniquity; suppose that it is discovered that he is related to some one of your high families, let one who is a gentleman and a Christian take him from his filthy den, wash, literally wash, shave, and shear him, dress him, brings him into his family and adopt him for his own. Suppose, too, that it is with the boy's own consent, and he says: "I will be to you a son." Is he as yet really changed by all this? Only in external things. He has yet an imagination which must be gone through, all its vile and reeking passages explored and cleansed; and you must pour into his mind the riches of knowledge, of the laws, of morality and honesty, delicacy, purity and truth. His whole sphere has to be changed. You cannot take such a one, clean him and dress him, give him a long moral lecture at nine o'clock at night, and expect him to get up a thoroughly changed man in the morning—no, nor in a year. If, beginning at the age of sixteen, the work has been completed by the time he is twenty-one, the work has been done quickly. If, in this time, you have scoured out those sewers of his mind, and converted them into channels of God's pure and refreshing grace—I say again you have done the work quickly! Now, if it is such long labor with one boy, with all the influences of Christianity breathing around him—if, from the nature of the mind itself, under even the most favorable circumstances, the change must be so slow, what length of time will it take for a whole world? A world, too, where wickedness was organized and with its gigantic front, and black heart festering in corruption, said to the Gospel, "we will have none of you," —a world which was that darkness into which the Gospel was sent, and the darkness comprehended it not. The leaven must be hid within three measures of meal, and it will take its own time to work.

Sometimes the best way to reform is to destroy, as in the case of weeds. Sometimes defects could be cured by making additions or taking away obstructions or superfluities, by purifying and cleansing, without destroying the fabric itself. But when the edifice is old, and badly built in the first place, when every crack and cranny is overflowing with vermin, all scouring, and patching, and painting, is labor thrown away; you must pull it down, stone from stone, and then, when these stones have been thoroughly cleansed, you may, with fresh mortar, construct a new and noble dwelling. Now when the old heathen government presented its huge front to the first attack of the Gospel, with its doors barred, its ramparts mounted, its windows guarded, and all its avenues fortified, you might as well preach to the front of Astor's Hotel, and expect it to drop tears of penitence; you might have assaulted it in front and rear, and bombarded it from year to year, and all without securing a surrender. But did you ever see a stream meet a sturdy rock in its course, how it parts and flows, one channel on this side and another on that? So the stream of the Gospel ran around the fortress of paganism. But there was another work going on. For while the waters ran on, gurgling like music, they were gradually sapping the foundations of the mighty citadel; buttress after buttress gave way, tower after tower sank down to rise no more, until at last the whole structure fell in hopeless ruins. So has it been in Europe. Revolution after Revolution, change after change, wars after wars, constantly swaying backward and forward.

I once knew a student of Religion, who took up Mosheim's "Church History," and on finishing it, said: "Well, if this is your religion, I will have nothing to do with it; why, it is nothing but fighting, fighting, forever and always fighting!" But only go into a field of wheat and examine the grain. You are delighted with the long green leaves and the beautiful golden grain.—Suppose you see it by and by cut down, and after being soundly thrashed, stowed in bags, and taken to the mill. There, it is thrown into the hopper, it goes between the millstones, and on appearing below, you are astonished at the result. Where is now all the comeliness, and grace, and wondrous mechanism, and bending beauty of the original grain? All gone! This seems very hard, yet every housewife could tell you that you cannot make bread without it. Thus it was with the old society. It was full of rough stones and jagged rocks, savage customs, cruelties, superstitions, lusts, bad laws, vile manners and customs, and how could all this be molded for Christ? The voice of history said, by attrition, by wars, revolutions, and commotions of every kind. These did the grinding up, just as in the flowing of torrents and streams the rough stones are worn smooth. These wars and revolutions, he knew, were called civil and political, and not religious. But did not God know all about them? Did not his prophets foresee them, and does not his hand guide them for the fulfillment of his purposes? Then they were religious. Nor, if you regard the laws of the human mind, had this progress been slow. It led through war and bloodshed, but it must reach its consummation. Has any such consummation taken place? Draw the contrast between our day and the apostolic time.

One hundred years after the death of Christ, where were the arts, painting, poetry, sculpture, architecture? Where were learning, refinement, the civil law, the influence of the court, the money and commerce—the very warp and woof of society?—They were all on the side of heathenism. The symbol of Christianity was then the empty cross—empty because Christ, who had hung thereon, was ascended up to heaven. Now that 1800 years have passed, where is heathenism, with all her pomp and pride, her strength and royal robes? She is fallen into the last stage of muttering decrepitude. Whose fleets are those that whiten every sea? Whose arts, and arms, and wealth are those that astonish and rule the world? Whose are the schools and colleges, the learning, the wisdom, the treasure of the earth? All in the hands of Christians. It seemed, too, that the richest temporal blessings had always followed the nations that had the most spiritual life. This was the oft repeated promise of the Bible, and every finger-board of history points to the contrast. Christianity now stands triumphant in the world; her whole solid front is formed, and her face is set as though she would go up to Jerusalem. And what has been done to cause this? Why, all the questions have been raised that could be raised; question after question has been decided, and the decisions have been baptized in blood. This was necessary before the Gospel could get full swing at society. Hitherto, men suffered from intervening obstacles. They were brought up to hear with government ears or parental ears, or to look at things through this lens or that of prejudice; but by and by they were coming to listen with their own ears, and look without lenses—without any diverting or distorting medium, at truth. It was objected, that the churches were so divided and agitated, that new sects were starting up as thick as mosquitoes, that new societies and new-fangled notions of every kind were multiplying in a fearful ratio. What of it? While the Lord God omnipotent reigneth, the end of all this cannot be doubtful. But there was one thing to be noticed.—

Ostensibly, all these agitations and novelties had but one sole end in view, one object at bottom; the improvement of the human race. Not an infidel but is compelled to do this before he can obtain a hearing. When was ever the like of this seen in the world's history before? Why, this is the very foundation principle of the Bible itself! And is this what the old, selfish, proud world has come to? She that used so scornfully to smite the face of the preacher?—Is Saul among the prophets at last? God works on patterns of such vast size, that we cannot see them. And we should learn to look on all obstructions and trials, persecutions, sufferings, as only momentary sorrows. They cannot last long. Along the banks of the Mississippi, here and there, may be seen a backward eddy, but who would, therefore, think the whole huge river had ceased flowing onward? So, from the time of the apostles, though there had been backward eddies in the stream of the Church, yet in every period of hundreds of years, might be marked a distinct flowing onward of the main tide, until now it can never be stopped so long as God lives! The question is no longer, whether the consummation will come, but when? As things are now, we lend not only the Bible, but we lend the influence of our churches, our schools, town institutions, laws, hospitals, commerce, stores and shops, the whole spirit of our society to the evangelization of the world—for everything is more or less an instrument of Christianity. By this incalculable influence are we backed. When we strike with puny arm, the blow is accompanied by a rebounding stroke from all Christendom. We have gained momentum and rapidity, and can now go through a revolution, changing public sentiment from selfishness to benevolence, in twenty-five or thirty years. In fine: those laboring in the field must have a faith above the necessity of seeing the consummation. We know that the influence of Calvary can never die. I may die in the wilderness, and you may die on the sea; but the road to heaven is as short from India as it is from Indiana, and when once in heaven we shall see a much better sight than Moses saw from the top of Pisgah, and every one may gaze on it who has done one jot or one tittle to advance the work. Whisper it then into the ears of your children, that "the field is the world!" Ye who are bringing up your own flesh and blood to delight in dress, in worldly aggrandizement, in wealth, in ambition, in honor, have you not seen what the Lord is doing? Have you not seen that his service is becoming the path to honor? that working for the world, is the shortest road to promotion in our day? Teach your children to give up their soul and body and strength to their master's service. Thus shall they be nearer to God and God to them. Say unto him—"Lo! here are our children!" Bring them up to believe that they must not live for themselves, but for others. May God breathe the richness and fullness of this spirit over his universal Church.

DUTIES OF RELIGIOUS PUBLISHING SOCIETIES.*

It is not possible for Christians to have come to these anniversaries this year, without a solemn sense of the presence of God moving in the affairs of the world, with a majesty and revealed power transcending the ordinary measure of the Divine Providence. He is now speaking, as only God can speak, by the voice of fear, by the pangs of terror, by the shakings of revolutions, by wars, and by rumors of war. Every man who is accustomed to read the word of God with his eye upon the times, as its best interpretation, and who reads the times in which he lives by the illumination of God's Word, must be aware that we stand upon the eve of great things, either for good or for mischief, and if for mischief, only for greater good by and by; for, when God sows trouble, it is the seed out of which he means to reap righteousness in the end.

There is no more any quiet in all the earth; there is no longer anywhere apathy; there are almost no places on the globe where men are torpid, except in Tract Societies; and every land, every continent, every race, every nation, is stirring as forests shake when winds are moving upon them. All men are

* An Address delivered in Dr. Cheever's church, New York, before the (Boston) American Tract Society, May 12th, 1859.

looking out to know what things are about to befall the earth. In our own way, we, too, in this happy land, are agitated. We are not stirred up by war, nor alarmed by rumors of war. We are not shaken by revolution, nor shattered by intestine dissensions; although many hearts among us are hot. Passions are wild here, as in other lands; great interests are at stake; mighty conflicts are waged; and yet, the laws are unbroken, the peace of the State abides sure, the household is serene, secular affairs flow in their ordinary channels, deep and strong as the flow of rivers.

What is the reason that those causes which in other lands break out into wars, with us produce only discussions? How is it that we settle by our breath, and by ink, those interests which abroad are settled by the sword, and by the crash of wasting artillery? Why do not those wild and tumultuous elements which in other lands rend communities as earthquakes crack the earth, bring revolutions to us?

Because God has taught us upon this side of the ocean that liberty, which cures evils, also prevents them. Discussions in schools and in popular assemblies is better than all diplomacy and crafty statesmanship for the interests of peace; for where the tongue is tied, the sword is free. America binds up the sword by giving the tongue liberty. It is our faith that liberty does not belong alone to the hand and to the foot, but to the thoughts, to the conscience, and to the tongue to give forth what conscience and the understanding prompt. Therefore it is, while emperors, and kings, and little kings, and priests, and little priests, are being tossed up and down as ships or chips are tossed on the broad ocean of storms, we, agitating deeper questions, are preserved in quiet.

I know that there are some men who fear the results of discussion among us, and predict national rupture and disunion. Men there are whose keel is fear, and all whose ribs are cowardice, and whose whole life is but a quaking voyage of apprehension. They are always about to sink. The function of their life is gone if there be no ill-omened auguries darkening the future. Some men there are who sleep on this matter of disunion. They wake on it. It is their food at morning; it is their noonday meal; they sup upon it. It is their Sunday devotion, and their week-day horror. Disunion! You might just as well fear that the continent would break in two because running rivers cleanse their waters on its back, and the restless ocean laps its sides, as that this Union will break in two because men wage wars of opinion, and in free discussion bring all interests to the arbitration of reason.

Indeed, I fear that this people is too selfish ever to break asunder. Our danger is not in disunion. The devil has too large investments in this land to admit of disunion. There is nothing that Satan would gain by it—much that Christ might. Why, then, are we not in danger? Simply because we have learned to trust the people, and to make them trustworthy by intelligence, by moral education, and by the unrestrained, yet regulated use of their rights as free men. Other lands make the individual weak, to make the State strong; but we teach and believe that the strength of the State is in the strength of its individual members. We put trust, not alone in collective man, but in the individual man. And that we may not be deceived, by the whole force of our educational institutions and our political arrangements, we seek to make the individual man, the land over, trustworthy.

Our nation, by its organic political institutions, is but a continental debating society. Our newspapers, and winged books, daily bear before every individual of the land every question that affects the welfare of the State. Our people are invited, and provoked, to the most searching scrutiny, to the formation of their own independent opinions, to the fullest expression of their convictions, and to the utmost liberty of waging moral battle for that which they deem right and just. And when, out of this universal activity, out of the conflict of interests and judgments and experiences of a whole people, final results are obtained, they take the form of laws, and walk among us supreme, not simply by the enactment of legislators, but supreme by the convictions of an intelligent people.

I would that this lesson of the freedom of discussion and its benefits had been learned as perfectly by all as it has been by some; or, rather, as perfectly by some among us, as it has been by all the rest of the community. But it would seem as if some men gained education only by the loss of common sense. There are thousands in whom prosperity and intelligence have wrought a conceit which makes them distrustful of the common people. They are arrogant, contemptuous of those beneath them in social position, and stand together in classes, with mutual flatteries and a common conceit. They are bound together in a common emptiness, as the staves of a barrel are bound together around the vacuity of an unfilled centre. Nor have I ever before seen a more remarkable instance of the contempt with which conceited men look upon free discussion, than that which was exhibited upon the platform of the Tract Society, at its recent anniversary, on the boards of the Opera House in New York. Whatever prejudices have hitherto existed against the morals of an opera house, must, since that platform held such actors, receive double force; and I am sure that no ordinary play, and no opera, bad even as Don Giovanni itself, can have a more mischievous effect upon the popular mind, than the shameless exhibition which took place on that occasion, and by the reverend and legal actors. There it was that one of the most distinguished civilians of New York was pleased to inform the audience, in a speech preliminary to the gagging of that audience, that a deliberative body was not a safe place for the discussion of grave questions. The Reverend Daniel Lord it was—for so I read his title in the report of the *Tribune*, though when he took orders I am not informed—the Reverend Daniel Lord declared that the excited feelings of deliberative bodies and popular assemblies were not favorable to investigations of truth. The mouths of the lions among whom ancient Daniel fell were not shut half so tight as the mouths of those among whom the modern Daniel fell.

When I looked around, and saw that almost every other man in that assembly was a grey-haired man; that hundreds of them were pastors inured to debate all their lives—men who had given their thoughts both to books and to the discussions of living men—an assembly, the average age of whose members could not fall short of fifty years, and then heard this eminent legal gentleman, himself a grey-haired man, to whom impetuosity and fire seemed anything but congenial, descanting upon the danger of being consumed by the wild-fire of deliberative assemblies, I could not but think that there was just about as much need of sending fire-engines to graveyards to put out tombstones, as of repressive measures in such an assembly to extinguish the conflagrations kindled by free discussion.

That the Tract Society should ever have needed that any should remind them of their duty to the poorest among the poor, and the most ignorant among the ignorant—four million American slaves—is itself enough disgrace. That when the voice of a Christian people, sounding louder and louder every year and coming up from twenty States, like the sound of many waters and mighty thunderings, demanding that the Society, which professed to express in its publications the full truths of the Christian religion, should give utterance to some religious truth bearing upon this most serious and most grievous evil of our times and nation, they should stop their ears, and taking counsel of sinister interests, refuse to bear their testimony; that every year dumbness should be defended by them as a

Christian virtue, and moral cowardice pleaded as a duty, was enough to bring up again into our ears that solemn denunciation which eighteen hundred years ago made Jerusalem tremble—"Woe unto you scribes, pharisees and lawyers!"

And now, upon this day, in compact of evil, stood again, in this extemporized temple, priest and lawyer, determined to justify their own recreancy, and to forbid other people the rights of that free speech which they had guiltily refused to employ. And this anniversary meeting of the Tract Society had for its primary object, this one thing—to gag men, and to prevent free discussion. They dreaded honest men's tongues. They knew that if those that were there gathered together, had had the right to pass in review their conduct, in the light of God's law, in the light of God's providence, in the light of sober Christian reason, they could no more stand up, tough as they are, broadspread and rooted in prosperity, than the mightiest oaks can stand when God sends thunderbolts from heaven upon them.

And so they called not this year, as last, the special pleaders of the clergy, but the tricksters of the law, prepared with every mean device of caucus and political manœuvre, to anticipate and ward off free speech, and shield themselves behind this enforced silence. Not one word was allowed to be said at that meeting upon those questions which the Almighty God has sent upon this nation; which, in spite of wrath, and leagued resistance of men of might, and wealth, and worldly wisdom, he has, for twenty-five years, sunk deeper and deeper in the hearts of men;

with which he hath already wrought a revolutions of opinion, and by which yet he will change the face of affairs in this whole land. None of those things which you think, which I think, which all men are thinking, which they themselves, per force, think, were allowed to be spoken, but only pettifogging things, technical things, managing, wire-pulling, caucusing things. Their object was to keep men from talking who had something earnest to say, and let those men talk who desired to say nothing. It was, therefore, a plea against fullness, richness and substance of moral conviction, in favor of emptiness and pretence. And it became very evident that the time had come when this [Boston] American Tract Society, which had priority in the field over the other that held there its disgraceful Anniversary, should again resume its independence, and, in appropriate methods, express the Christian sentiment of the Church in our day.

The Boston Tract Society has been, like some old gentleman retiring from business, leaving to his sons the conduct of his affairs; and yet, always, he keeps a sharp eye upon their management. When, at length, he perceives that their prosperity is turning their heads, and that they are running the concern into imminent perils, he assumes again into his own hands the lapsed management. And so it is time that this Society should come forward again, and say to these young men in the Opera House, "You are scarcely competent to conduct the religious literature of the Church."

But, before I speak further, allow me to call your attention to some of the views uttered upon the occasion of the late Anniversary, by the chief speaker, and the most specious one, Daniel Lord. The following are his words: "As to the donors"—speaking of the contributors of the Tract Society, he says—"As to the donors, they give their property to the charity; it is an entire gift, parting with their right as proprietors. After a thing is given, every man, woman, and child knows, that the giver can no longer control or direct it. If, therefore, all those who have contributed to make up this fund from the beginning of this Society, even if the venerated dead could be raised to be present, they could have no right to interfere with or change the administration of the fund. They gave it away. But for what purpose, on what plan did they give it? Ascertain this, and you ascertain the character of the property and the plan of its management. Learn on what plan it was solicited and received, and then the property is to be protected and devoted to this plan. And every consideration not only of law, but of justice and morality, of honor, religion, and gratitude, secure its management in the very way and to the precise object intended. It is thus eminently a *trust* property. The Society does not own it for itself. If all of its members could be collected together, and should agree to apply it to their own use, such an attempt would shock, and such an act be idle. Nor can they deviate in its use or management from the plan on which it is given, for the same reason."

Here let me say that with all the apparent fairness of this statement, it is thoroughly deceitful, for it mentions the object or purpose for which these funds were contributed, and the plan of management, as if they were one, and the same thing, and the words *purpose* and *plan* are used as convertible terms, bearing equivalent meanings; whereas, no distinction can be more important, no distinction can touch the very marrow of things more really than that which exists between the object for which funds are contributed, and the plan of administration by which they shall be used for that object. Mr. Lord, however, speaking of the objects and purposes for which they were given, goes on to discuss, not what those objects are, which is the very question at issue between him and us—between him and the indignant community—but, by a dexterous and quiet change, proceeds to discuss the questions of society management. He proceeds thus:

"The plan of this charity is contained in its written constitution; and, first, let us consider who are its beneficiaries. They are the ignorant, the unenlightened, the needy, over the whole country. And how are they to receive the benefits? By the circulation of religious tracts. Circulation may fairly be used as a name to represent the beneficiaries. The object of the charity is not to declare the principles of its managers or members; not to discuss or settle controversies; not to declare for or against slavery; but to enlighten its beneficiaries by the circulation of tracts. This is the limit of its action, on the plainest reading of the paper."

Let the public, then, ponder this declaration made by this eminent attorney, in the presence of the managers of the American Tract Society, at its Anniversary meeting, in the Opera House. Let every man in the United States ponder this received, and, by the management, uncontradicted, declaration that the object for which the funds of the American Tract Society were solicited was not the discussion or settlement of controversies; was not the declarations of the principles of its managers or members; was not to declare for or against slavery; but that it was simply the mechanical business of circulating tracts without regard to what those tracts contain. If this specious plea of Mr. Lord means anything, it means that tracts are to be circulated by the Society without regard to the character of their contents, after they shall once have become tracts. But where are tracts born? What is the origin of a tract? Who makes them? Who generates them? Who is their father? Do they grow on trees? Are they dug out of catacombs and pyramids? Are they, like gold and silver, like diamonds and pearls, things created from the foundation of the world? And is the American Tract Society but a vast catapult, built to fire these foreordained and prepared missives and missiles into the midst of the community? Is the American Tract Society, according to Mr. Lord, analogous to the United States Mail service, receiving into its leathern pouches already-written letters, with which the government has no right to meddle, and in whose contents it does not concern itself, and whose sole business it is to circulate them, and deposit them at the points to which they are directed? Is the American Tract Society, then, a vast religious Express Company, which is to receive packages of tracts and books, and circulate them? And is this the business of the Tract Society, not to make tracts, not to express great religious truths, not to develop great principles in their relations to the actual human want in the times in which we live? Is it the object of the American Tract Society merely to circulate something? This, certainly, is the position that Mr. Lord seems to take.

Nor have we heard one indignant protest from any member of the Executive Committee, or of the management, of the Tract Society. If such things are right before a jury; if it be deemed right to gain a temporary victory for one's clients, at the expense of fact, and from any Courts of Justice, it certainly will not be deemed right by the reflecting and religious community, for a man to stand upon the religious platform of a prominent benevolent society, and to declare so deceptive and so false a thing as that the funds of this Society were solicited, and were originally given, for the purpose simply of circulating tracts without any regard to the contents which they contained. On the other hand, nothing was more universally well understood than that the American Tract Society was organized for the purpose of *preparing* tracts as well as *circulating* them, which should apply the great principles of Divine truth revealed in the sacred Scriptures, to the actual wants, to the errors, to the sins, to the experiences of mankind. That the management were to judge what was expedient, may be true; but that the management, in the very nature of the trust committed to them, were forbidden to discuss principles, and to declare their own views of moral truth, is an assertion so monstrous, so infidel to all faith in Scripture, and to religion itself, that I marvel that so many men, that knew better, did not stop their ill-advised advocate on the spot, and correct a misrepresentation which, in the end, cannot fail to be most damaging to the interests of these special pleaders and pettifogging managers.

According to this doctrine, then, if smuggling should become a practice along our whole northern coast, and maritime churches should have smuggling deacons, and smuggling ministers, and smuggling members, the management of the American Tract Society would have no right to declare their views in respect to the moral character of this act; and unless they could have tracts already grown, on this subject, hanging on the bushes, or wrapped up in the cerements of the past, they would have no right to declare or discuss the Christian principles which govern this subject! When the American Tract Society issued the most searching and fearless tracts, discussing the evils of intemperance, they transcended their power, and abused their trust, according to their own attorney! They had no business "to declare the principles of its managers or members" on this subject.

When any great evil in the growing light of Christianity is lifted up by the providence of God, and made the mark at which the Church should address its moral power, the Tract Society cannot, except by an abuse of their trust, if this doctrine be true that we have heard, discuss the nature of the evil, or the duties of Christian men respecting it, nor in any wise touch it. "Their business," says Mr. Lord, "is not to discuss, but to circulate." And so, instead of a body of intelligent Christian men gathered together to give universality to the truths of the Gospel, we have but a vast charitable corporation, collected together for the mere mechanical purpose of circulation. The Society is to know no more what passes through it than a fanning machine, that knows neither the grain which it saves nor the chaff which it drives away. But we quote again:

"However proper, then, a treatise might be, however suitable, if it could be circulated to do good, yet it cannot be circulated, it cannot be printed at the expense of the fund, without a breach of trust. What would be said of printing a tract in a language which those to whom it was to be sent did not understand? And yet how does that differ from printing tracts, which those to whom they are addressed will not receive. Tracts on slavery might be able in their teaching; tracts against polygamy the like; but how idle to attempt to send the latter to the Mormons, or the former to other parts of the country, where they would be excluded. And this circumstance, of whether they could or could not be circulated, must be determined as a preliminary question of fact by the managers of the Society."

Let every honest Christian man in these United States consider this abominable doctrine that the duty of a Christian Tract Society, in circulating the truth, is to be judged and limited by the wishes of corrupt and wicked men. If wicked men are willing to receive light upon their wickedness, the Tract

Society is permitted to send them knowledge; but if wicked men do not desire that light should shine into their darkness, Mr. Lord declares, that without a perversion of their trust, the Tract Society cannot send them unwished-for and unwelcome Christian truth. He declares, most explicitly, that the preliminary business of the Tract Society is to ascertain whether men are willing to receive the truth of Christ, and that if they are not, they are in duty bound, as administrators of a solemn trust, to withhold that truth!

Was this, then, the doctrine of that Christ who came, not to bring peace, but the sword? Was this the example of that teaching Saviour who confronted the whole priestly rabble, and lawyer crew, that then, as now again in our day, held the holiest places, that they might pervert them only to the basest uses? Was this the example of those apostolic heroes, who went abroad, followed by mobs of infuriated men; by enraged mechanics, whose business was interfered with by their high morality; pursued and thrust at by wandering mountebanks, whose gains they destroyed by restoring their victims to health and sanity? Was this the spirit that breathed through those men, who in every age, have been found worthy of the name of Christ—teachers, confessors, martyrs, saintly pastors, and unsubdued preachers, who have borne solemn testimony against all wickedness, and brought upon themselves endless mischiefs, because they would not forbear, and because they would cast upon the unwilling face of darkness, the whole effulgence of the light of God? And yet,

Mr. Lord dared to say—and there was not one priest upon the platform that chose to contradict the declaration—that tracts on slavery, and tracts against polygamy, and the like, must not be sent to those that were guilty of either sin, unless it was known beforehand that these sinners were willing to receive them!

And this is what the Tract Society, with all their high-sounding pretences, with all their paraded piety, and all their ostentatious conscientiousness, have at last led the Church to! That truth of Christ which was revealed to be, not the suppliant and the slave of men's caprices and appetites, but the master of their conscience, the lord of their faith, the supreme arbiter of their lives—that truth which is God's only vicegerent upon earth, open-browed, clear-eyed, and with a tongue that speaks in every language the same things, and with divine authority, is, by this last declaration of the American Tract Society, through their attorney, to ask permission of the intemperate before it declares the sins of intemperance; to ask the consent of the incontinent before it rebukes, by the blaze of Gospel chastity, the foul corruptions of licentiousness; to ask the hard hand before it preaches the duty of lenity and mercy to the weak; to ask the Sabbath-breaker's permission before it issues tracts on the sanctity of God's day; to ask the gambling and the racing crew whether they may print tracts against the special immoralities to which they are liable; to ask the thief whether they may circulate tracts upon dishonesty; the robber, whether they may set forth the claims of justice; for, says

Mr. Lord, "Tracts on Slavery might be very able in their teaching, tracts against polygamy the like, but how idle to attempt to send the latter to the Mormons, or the former to other parts of the country where they would be excluded."

But this is not all. Let us, for a moment, argue the question upon Mr. Lord's own ground. We demand to know by what right it is said that tracts will not be read in the South on the duties of master and slaves? How has it been ascertained that they will not be welcome? Have these men taken counsel of political firebrands? Have they taken counsel of their cowardice? Have they taken counsel of those men who, long committed against the agitation of slavery, are now ashamed to yield, and to own, by yielding, that their whole past career has been mistaken? The proper method of ascertaining whether tracts would be read, is to make them, to offer them; and when judiciously constructed tracts have been tried, with all kindness and perseverance, and are turned back upon the depository of the Society, then it will be time to declare that they have been rejected. But to stand upon the precipice of their cowardice; to grow dizzy by the mere looking over into the abyss below; to refuse any attempt whatever, practically to test the question—this belongs to those peculiar notions of Christian enterprise which are characteristic of the American Tract Society.

On the other hand, I declare that there are hundreds and thousands, and hundreds of thousands of men, throughout all the slave States, who will assuredly receive, with gratitude, suitable tracts upon this subject, and read them with conscientious earnestness for the truth. I declare my conviction that men living in the slave States, by ten thousands, hate slavery vastly more than do the managers of the American Tract Society; are less apologists for it; are less indifferent to its wastes and its woes; are more in sympathy with that spirit of liberty in the New Testament, which has consumed so much evil in the world, and is destined to consume every vestige of slavery and of oppression. There are thousands of ministers that will circulate tracts written in a spirit of Christian love, bearing witness against the selfishness and the wrong of those that defraud the laborer of his wages. Nay, there are thousands of men who believe that slavery is a divine institution, who yet desire to have the duties of the master more thoroughly explored and taught; who earnestly desire to carry themselves toward their slaves with some degree of conscientiousness and Christian fidelity. There is not in these United States, there is not upon this continent, there is not on the broad field of the world, a province of labor more inviting, more urgent, that promises a more abundant remuneration, than the slave States of America. Nowhere else has the conscience lain so long fallow; nowhere else are men more open to honest truths, spoken in a manly way; nowhere else are men more frank in recanting when they are wrong; nowhere else more fearless in doing that which they see to be right. And I believe, in my soul, that if instead of our northern doughfaces, the management of this American Tract Society could be put into the hands of any of thousands of men who might be selected from the slaveholders of the South, we should have a better expression from them of Christian truth on the subject of human rights, than now we are able to obtain from these men, whose highest conception of duty seems to be, to do right by the permission of evil, to scatter light under the direction of darkness, and to establish righteousness by the consent of iniquity. I will myself stand pledged—if any word of mine may be a guaranty—that if the American Tract Society will print appropriate tracts upon this subject, in a Christian temper, and with Christian fidelity expressing the truth of God, I will circulate twenty million pages in one year. If the Society will take the offer, I will take the job.

Mr. Lord then goes on to describe the duties of the managers of this property. The life members of this Society, together with the life directors, at an annual meeting, elect the President, the Vice-President, the Secretaries and the Directors. Then these directors, together with the life directors, elect the Executive Committee. This Executive Committee then assumes all the authority and functions of the Society. The whole force of the Society dies when they have put the Executive Committee into their chairs. In respect to this, Mr. Lord says:

"How idle, then, to instruct this Committee? What right have the members, who have exerted their power of management by the election, to interfere with this veto power? But the attempt to instruct the Committee assumes to take away not the veto of one, but the discretion of all. The plan of the charity has not in it such an inconsistency. And how impracticable to execute such a construction of it. The publication and circulation of tracts must depend on occasions, on emergencies, to be acted upon as they rise. It has been wisely committed to a select, an elected body, on the American idea of a representative system; not on the rash, reckless and often arbitrary models of a mere democracy, casually collected and swayed by impulse."

True, technically there may be no right in the Society to instruct; but the American Tract Society every year brings its cause into all the churches of the land, and professes to act in sympathy with their wishes. When, then, at the annual meeting, the Church, by its pastors and eminent laymen, come into their assemblies, and express their ideas of Christian duty and Christian fidelity, shall their mouths be stopped by the technical plea that such free speech is an unwarrantable attempt to instruct? Are we to add to all the other powers of this Executive Committee the ascription of sufficient wisdom in their own selves? Are they also to be supposed to be infallible in judgment? Has Mr. Lord found out, likewise, among the other memorable things which he has discovered, that the Executive Committee are not to be approached, in deliberative popular assemblies, by advice, by suggestion, by persuasion, by reasoning, by deliberative wisdom? When, since the days that our colonies sprang up on these shores, has it ever before been known that a great religious society, dependent upon the churches for its support, should sit without rebuke to hear the practice of discussion and deliberation in popular bodies decried? And yet, the Managers of the American Tract Society permitted Mr. Lord to characterize our American religious assemblies in language such as this:

"A popular meeting, swayed by passionate eloquence, sympathizing in local feelings, would be a most unsafe depository of the functions in question. It is also likely to be composed most extensively of those who reside nearest to the place of meeting, and the course of the charity would thus be made dependent, in a degree, on the place of meeting; and might vary as that should be New York, or Boston, or Syracuse, or Rochester."

And afterward, speaking of the superiority of the judgment of this Executive Committee over the judgment of the Society that was assembled in the Academy of Music, he says:

"This trust has been wisely committed to a select, an elected body, on the American idea of a representative system; not on the rash, reckless and often arbitrary models of mere democracy, casually collected and swayed by impulse."

And yet—and no man knows it better than Mr. Lord—such is the power of the popular will, when that will is based upon information, upon intelligence, and upon experience, that there is not a court of justice in the United States, that can long maintain an opinion adverse to that which has been formed by the great court of the million outside of itself. The majesty of the decisions of the people, in all questions which are within the reach of their discretion, overawes all bodies known to our community. The United States Senate would not presume to pursue, for a year, unless under the merest party influences, a course of legislation against which the intelligent people in every State should rise up in their popular assemblies and protest. There is not a State Legislature in all this Confederacy that would choose or dare to pursue a course which was known to be against the deliberate judgment of the great majority of their constituents. There is not a body known to our political system that is not compelled to hold, and that practically does not hold, in the utmost respect, the known judgment and wishes of the masses of men in this community. It is reserved for the American Tract Society to stand up in the midst of churches, and of a Christian community that in immense majorities condemn their conduct, and declare themselves superior to such considerations—an elected body, by being representative, made superior to the rash democracy of popular deliberate assemblies, as Mr. Lord is pleased to style them!

And before whom were these disparaging words uttered? In whose presence did this Executive Committee permit Mr. Lord to arrogate their superiority? Venerable men there were, that were venerable when some of the Committee were born. Men were there in scores, whose reading and habits of wise reflection have made them as able in statesmanship as they have been learned in theology. There is no better school on earth in which to accumulate wisdom than the pastor's office; and from out of discussions; from studies where they had elaborated thought in the calm seclusion of studious leisure, from the field where, among men of every temperament and of every habit of thought, they had held argument; from actual contact with living, glowing, sympathetic life, they had come up hither, to hear Mr. Lord declare, that the Executive Committee was a body so superior that they were not to be instructed by the debates and the discussions of such an assembly as that!

It would seem bad enough for the American Tract Society to refuse to proclaim a Gospel of liberty, or a Gospel of rights to four million of men on this continent; but to attempt to justify their guilty silence by decrying and gagging a Christian deliberative assembly, by undermining the foundations of free speech, by destroying faith in the wisdom of popular deliberative bodies, was to act as oppressors always act; for usurpation never fails to go on to injustice. Men whose rights have been taken away from them, are always forbidden to complain. The Sceptre and the Gag go together, the world over. The American Tract Society, after contemptuously refusing to exercise free speech in behalf of the oppressed, next, and characteristically, muzzled free speech and free discussion of their own conduct. Every man knows that there was never a more ruthless thing done in a Christian assembly than that which took place yesterday. It is bad enough to see the gross and wanton injustice of arrogant men that manage the wires of political affairs; but to see a body of Christian ministers and laymen bringing into their service the supple bands of lawyers, springing every parliamentary trick and device in the face of free speech, dodging issues, and hiding their own moral delinquencies, by robbing men of the right of exposing them—this is one of the worst things that has ever happened in the long annals of degradation and crime brought upon us by slavery. In a religious body, among clergymen from all parts of the United States; in a popular assembly, and by men reeking with devotion, and fuming with prayers, it is odious and disgusting beyond all reach of language.

And, now, let the common people of these United States understand how this thing stands. According to this new construction, the people are to give the money; the Executive Committee are to spend it as they please; and the people are not at liberty to advise them, nor utter a word of protest, except out of doors. You, who give the funds, if you give as much as twenty dollars a year, and think to take out a certificate of life membership; or, giving fifty dollars a year, if you think to take out a certificate of life-directorship, are permitted to go into the Court of the Gentiles once a year, not to influence the direction of your funds, but simply, under whip and rein, under preconcerted political managements with the previous question, and the laying of the question on the table, cutting off all debate and explanation, are to be permitted to vote for directors and secretaries. If you be only a twenty-dollar life member, that ends your function. Like an insect that has laid its egg, when your vote is dropped, you drop, too, and are dead. Then the directors are permitted one additional step in life. They vote for the Executive Committee, and after that they die, too, and are to be heard of no more, until the time comes for butterflies to fly again the next year, when, breaking out of their chrysalis state, once more they may shake the wings of ballot, and but once, to drop again into the annual slumber. When once the Executive Committee are elected, you are at their mercy. You are not to say a single word. You are not to advise them. You are not recognized as being in existence.

I should delight to be an agent collecting money for this Society for a short period. I would address the farmers with the usual eloquence of those who solicit charity, describing, first, the unspeakable wants of the ignorant population of our land; and next, the unspeakable piety of the members of the Executive Committee of the American Tract Society; and next, of that mysterious power which God has given to gold and silver to bring together the much-needed piety of the one extreme to the much-needed ignorance of the other. "This is your duty," I should say to the farmers, who, with hard toil and laborious economy, have been endeavoring, penny by penny, to put their sons through the academy or college, that they may make ministers or missionaries of them, or that they may become honorable civilians, or intelligent laborers of any grade—"It is your duty to help in this glorious cause of tract distribution." "But," says the farmer in his stupidity, "what will become of my money if I shall give it—what will be done with it?" "Why, it is going into the Treasury of the Lord." "But what treasurer is that who holds the Lord's bag?" "Why, it is held by these devout and sainted men who pray all day, and almost all night, and then deny free discussion on a platform for the purposes of the Lord." "But what is to be done with our money? What do they mean to print? What do they mean to circulate?" My friends, I should be obliged to say, "You are meddling with matters which do not concern you. It is your business to give the money: it is our business to spend it. If you wish to know how it is spent, in due time, after it is all gone, you shall find the tracks of it here in our annual report."

Gentlemen, this American Tract Society is a multiform and gigantic mill. It has its run of stones. Some are appointed for wheat, some for corn, but more for cobs; and they do not profess to consult the will of those that approach their door with bags of grain: they simply say to them, "This is what we grind in this mill; if you choose to put your wheat into that hopper we will grind wheat; your corn into that hopper we will grind corn; your cobs into yonder hopper, and we will give you cob-meal; but we do not profess to be directed any further by the will of our customers than we choose. Here are our arrangements; take them if you please. If you do not like them, go somewhere else. We shall grind just as we have arranged to grind. We will put in no new stones, and make no alterations in our mill to suit the notions of the people that live hereabouts."

And so, the American Tract Society say, "Gentlemen, pour your pocket-grists into our mill. We have arranged how this shall be spent. We shall make no changes. We are not to be instructed. We are not to be influenced by the wild democracy of popular deliberative bodies of old men. It is our business to use these sacred funds; yours only to give us a chance to use them."

And so I imagine that country gentlemen who had, with very great pains and self-denial, been able to give twenty and fifty dollars, that they might become life-members and life-directors of the American Tract Society, approached this great city at its recent anniversary, and were present in the Academy of Music. They have come, as they fondly supposed, to take some part in the administration of affairs. When they go to the door of the Academy, he of the red ticket is put on one side of the house; and he of the white ticket on the other side; while he of the green ticket is mounted up to the place of privilege upon the operatic stage. The business proceeds. Something seems continually to be going on behind the scenes. There is whispering, and buzzing, and consultation. A fore-arranged result is to be dragged through the assembly. One thing there certainly is not to be; no discussion is to be allowed; no free speech is to take any part in this meeting. At length, when the hour has passed, our country member and director go out, and, meeting in the passage-way, a little puzzled as to what they have done, one looks the other in the face, and says—"What did you do on your side of the house?" And the other replies, "And what did you do on your side?" and both join in saying, "What have they done on their side?"

I will defy anybody on earth to tell what has been done, except that two men have been duped, and a third has got the money. And all this misconduct takes place under the sweetest names of religion and devotion. These men propose no mischief without a holy sigh; they violate no right without a pious groan; they never decry free discussion without lifting up their eyes to heaven; they wrest from us no privileges, except with the clasping and holding up devout hands in the act of prayer. These are all good men, who read their Bibles, I think, until some places in them must have become worn out, and their contents forgotten. Surely, men must be very pious who can endure conduct that would put to shame a democratic political caucus.

I was yesterday urged vehemently to mingle in this scene and to speak. But I loathed and scorned the offer. Is it for a man like me to play in such a scene as that, and watch the sudden opportunity to jump upon the stage, there to be shoved or put down, as might suit the convenience of the reverend lawyers, tricksters, or what-not? I believe in free speech, not for myself alone, but never half so sacredly as for him against whom I have exercised my speech. Free speech does not mean my right to say what I please, but your right to speak back again. If there is anything in this world as sacred as religion itself, it is the right which religion gives to speak of religion, to speak of its principles, to apply them to every phase of the human welfare; and if this land and age shall stand by and behold the destruction of these most sacred rights on the very platform of religious benevolence, and in the very professed service of religion by religious men, then we have reached a crisis indeed—a crisis, not of external force, but of decay of internal and fundamental principles and rights.

But these men have mistaken the temper of the times, and spirit of the common people. There is a public sentiment that will drown out even the Tract Society. There is a public sentiment which, if it be slow, is slow only that it may be certain and effectual. Confidence will not be revoked hastily. It will not be too eagerly concluded that men once trusted have become arrogant in office and corrupted by power and seduced by the blandishments of flattery and success. But when once that confidence is withdrawn, it will never return. If, then, there is any seeming delay, it is only such delay as belongs to the steps of majesty. When God is throned in clouds, and armed with lightning, and approaches to judgment and to justice, so sure in his heart is the day of retribution, that he needs not to make haste. There is no being so certain as God, and none so slow; for, since the days of Moses and the prophets, there has never been an age when men, feeling the bitter wants of the world, have not been compelled, their own patience worn out, to cry, "How long, O Lord, how long!" To-day martyrs cry, to-day oppressed and suffering patriots from out of dungeon vaults do cry; to-day with million voices not suppressed, suffering slaves cry out, "O Lord, how long!" And yet He dwells in eternity and in silence, and takes to himself the infinite leisure of eternity. But though he seems to delay, he never fails to come, and at length it shall be said, "Our God shall come and shall not keep silence." And I believe that God will yet mark with the most condign punishment, those men who, under the name of religion, and for the sake of screening themselves from responsibilities toward the poor and the oppressed, have violated our liberties and our rights. I do not say that these men are not Christians. Peter, I suppose, was a Christian when he denied his Lord. I hope these men are Christians. But if that is Christianity which they practise, they have another New Testament than mine.

I turn now to another branch of the subject. For the last hundred years, God has been developing in this world some of the later and more wonderful results of Christianity. First, Christianity acts as a power upon the individual; next, upon men in their social relations—setting up the family, establishing neighborhoods, promoting refinement in our households and in communities. Next, it takes hold upon laws and institutions, then, upon customs, and, finally, upon the organic forms of society itself. And in the mighty conflicts which result from this strife of good with bad, of right with wrong, of love with selfishness, the very frame of life is often shaken, and society itself, broken up, passes away, or assumes new forms. Beyond even this there is a work which Christianity is developing. Touched by its divine spirit, every quality springs up, in each age with new branches, and pushes forth blossoms, and hangs redolent and glowing with surprising fruits. The higher developments of the nobler feelings begin to embody themselves, and give to life not only new ideas, but a before unimagined and, to the natural man, inconceivable grandeur and moral glory, both in things esthetic and in things ethic.

Since the world began, it has been the doctrine of proud and haughty men, that the weak were made to serve the strong;—and as, among lions and brute beasts, the fierce and the strong destroy the weak, and the race is propagated only from the more stalwart individuals, so this belluine morality has been adopted and practised by societies of men.

The weak have been despised, have been crushed, have been pushed down to the bottom, have been made to grind in dark places, to work for that which they reaped not, to sow in tears, in sorrow, in hopeless despondency, that the indolent and the wicked above them might reap that which they requited not. Nor has this spirit been suffered to take the spontaneous form which pride would give it. It has come under the organizing power of Philosophy, and it has received organic forms, until, now, selfishness has become legal and regular national and organic wickedness, based upon wrong; and so framed into a law and into systems of law, that round about this interior Satanic element of cruel selfishness has been gathered whatever there was venerable in authority, whatever there was impressive in symbol, whatever there was beautiful in Art, whatever there was attractive to the eye, to the ear, and to every sense. And men, weak and ignorant men! have been taught to clasp with tendrils of affection and veneration systems whose very marrow and life were the destruction of the poor for the sake of the rich, the oppression of the weak for the pleasure of the strong.

But now, at length, the world has so far grown, in

God's Providence and grace, that, emerging from infinite confusions and turmoils of pride and selfishness, this question is seeking at length for a new adjudication at the bar of Christ's heart. For more than a hundred years past that which has underlayed all movements, that which has been the rudder of all progress, that which has been the animating principle of all reform, has been, not, what are the rights of the strong, of the wise, of the rich, of the powerful in station and rank; but, what are the rights of the poor and the weak, and what are the duties of those that are strong to the weak! By that same power which causes the sun to send summer into the soil, and wakes from their rude dirt all things sweet and beautiful, wholesome things from noxious, clean things from fetid, fair and beautiful things from waste and homeliness, literature has been taught to bring forth new fruits, and in our age, instead of that derisive spirit which characterized the literature of England in the days of Pope and of Sterne, of Swift and of Dryden, there is breathed into it and throughout it the most humane and yearning spirit of benevolence! Even kings, not knowing what they do (as ships that are sidewise swept over an unknown current do not know that they are drifting) have been obliged to declare humane sentiments and to conform, in their policy, to this divine world-current. Every nation of the globe, to-day, is moving in directions given by this gulf stream of God! Never before on so broad a scale was Christian power active in this world. Great as are the fruits of preaching, noble as are the tasks and accomplishments of self-denying missionaries among the heathen, sweet and beautiful as are the aspects of Christian life in pure and heavenly families, yet, not in any, or all of these, is Christ so manifestly at work as in these great world-heavings, in these unrecognized, but universally felt movements, for the reconstruction of society, of commerce, of civil polity, of human life itself, upon the basis of humanity and benevolence.

What shall the strong do with the weak? This is to-day the question which God makes Asia to answer. With this he questions Africa. With this he catechizes every fractious nation of Europe. With this question he is shaking America. Nor is there yet found one nation on the earth, though their Christianity has dwelt with them so long that their cathedrals are hoary with age and their altars burnt out with perpetual fires, that has yet learned to answer this sublime interrogatory of ages!

The duty of the strong to the weak? Great Britain says that the duty of the strong to the weak is to compel them to perform remunerating industries! Europe declares that the duty of the strong is to make the iron hand of power yet stronger, and to hold in more absolute subjection the now pinched and cramped masses of the people. Africa, low, brutal, animal, hears the question, but knows not enough even to comprehend its meaning; and God speaks to that benighted continent, as a child might speak to the ocean—calling out for its father, its mother, or its companions; and only the ceaseless beating of the surf upon the shore, wave thundering after wave, is its answer!

All the world over, the power of Christianity has made the more intelligent stronger and continually stronger; but as yet, it has left the others relatively weaker than before. The top of society has gone up, but the bottom has not followed it in any due proportion.

And now, hath God answered this question? Hath he declared his own mind? or anywhere recorded those letters which are never to be effaced, those letters declarative of his will? When God gave the law to antiquity, he wrote it upon tables of stone, amid the august terrors of Sinai's top. When he gave to the world his later law, he wrote upon the living heart of Christ in the silent majesty of Calvary! And in his EXAMPLE we learn our duty.

Was it, then, to build himself up, that the Infinite descended to our finite condition? Wandering among ignorant and wicked men, was it for his own glory that Christ groped? Was it that which he sought in buffetings and mockery of a trial, in the fatal hour of condemnation, in the slow cross-burdened walk to Calvary, in the hours of unutterable anguish, which not even the sun itself could behold? Was it in the silence of the rock sepulchre, garden-loved, that he sought the elements of his own aggrandizement? Or, was it rather to teach us by the whole power and majesty of his example that he that would be *chief must be servant of all?* Was it not to teach us that, *though rich, for our sakes he became poor, that we, through his poverty, might become rich?* And, henceforth, is not the world's doctrine this Gospel, that Power, Refinement, Intelligence, Wealth, Station, must hold themselves subject, under the law of love, to the uses of all that are unfortunate, of all that are weak, of all that are trodden down? The sun hangs in glory over the earth, not with its rays to beat down, but, by all the power of its attraction, to draw forth from out of the homely soil and dirt growth of infinite things of beauty. And God hangs above all things to draw all up out of weakness and wickedness toward him. And every man of mankind is to take his superiority as a level, an engine by which he must draw all lesser men up to or toward his condition. There is but one Father Universal; there is but one Family; there is but one Brotherhood; and throughout all the boundless races and infinite numbers of men, there is not a stranger, an alien, a foreigner! Ye be all brethren and members one of another!

Is not this one of the many mysteries that are disclosing themselves from the sublime act of Christ's incarnation and atonement? If on earth there be one thing memorable, which, wanting no monument, shall lift up its undiminished head through eternal ages, itself its own monument, is it not that act by which the God of glory bowed down his Almighty head, and slept beneath all life and in the bosom of Death, that he might destroy the one and give eternal power to the other? No angelic head radiant with reflected glory was that which pillowed itself upon the rock! The moral and the marvel of this sacrifice required that men should know that the Absolute, the Everlasting, the Universal Father, lived and moved by a law of love, which made him willing minister and servant of the weakest. And by the voice of his own life, by the voice of Calvary, by the death, and by the resurrection of his son, by the ever-living care and fostering love of Christ advanced to be a Prince and Saviour in Heaven, God is now teaching mankind, unwilling scholars as they are, that the duty of the strong toward the weak is to love them, to take care of them, to educate them, to strengthen them, to lift them up with the might of their strength to the very height of their own privileges! And so, men shall be helped, and you, helping them, shall be thrice blessed yourselves; for, *it is more blessed to give than to receive!* and, power gone out of you for others returns to you again from their hearts increased a thousand fold!

Interpreted from this sublime example, what is the morality of the British Empire, whose sway in India has been almost purely commercial, and which has looked at men almost only in their relation to the opium-gardens and the indigo-fields? Judged in the light of Christ's precious example, what monarchy in Europe, for five hundred years, is not condemned, and what regnant policy, or statecraft, what blood-enriched territory, is not blackened and made odious by the serene teaching of Love?

And we, of America, with suffering heart and vailed faces, can any abhorrence be greater, to any Christian, than that which we feel when we behold the latest born of Time, most blessed, best taught, richest in the heritage of all great things that martyrs, and confessors, and dying patriots have bequeathed to the world, have been most recreant, most cruel, most haughty to the poor, most despotic to the weak? It is in America that old Roman slavery flourishes as it never flourished in its own native soil. The Imperial sceptre was milder than the Democratic oppression! But God has not left himself without a witness, nor us without a testimony that he means to save us! Beginning far back in years, he has pressed unwelcome truths upon this nation with growing urgency! At first, this truth of Christian humanity was born among us with infant face, and with the weakness of a babe. It seemed easy to overwhelm it. And strong men rushed upon it. Herods there were, in every church, in every sect, in every State, in every legislature, in every neighborhood, up and out, seeking this child Jesus to destroy it! But all of these, again, slew without slaying; and he grew in stature, until, now, Christ, represented in his poor and despised ones, is stronger than all politics, than all churches, than all commerce, than all civil affairs, "and the government shall be upon his shoulders!"

Near fifty years have passed since this sublime movement. In that time ten thousand men, repenting that sooner they did not see the light that dawned over where the young child lay, have borne noble testimony; and the living words of God's truth have been spoken in ten thousand pulpits; books have begun to march in long procession; newspapers, in turn, have given their power to this cause, until, at length, popular enthusiasm inflamed, the whole community has risen up, and is bearing earnest and solemn testimony to the rights of the enslaved, and the duties of Christian men and patriots! In this long conflict, that Society, which was originated by holy men, for just such solemn work as this; which was erected to be a platform from which the artillery of the Gospel might sweep every evil; which was organized that, by the power of organization, those tougher iniquities which defied individual labor might find, in its organic power, more than a match; this great, this mighty association, has stood to be traitorous to its own great trust, to admire itself, to laud its own fruitless piety, and, surveying its presses, its loaded, groaning shelves, and its pious officers, to cry out, is not this Great Babylon which I have built! If there be on earth, at this day, one sight more melancholy or more shameful than another, it is the sight of an American Christian Association, established for no other end than the propagation of Gospel moralities, that, for half a century, has refused to bear a testimony in behalf of four million men, overrun, and infested with every immorality which oppression can breed, weighed down with every evil which it is the intent of the Gospel to alleviate, destroyed by every malignant mischief from which the Gospel was meant to be a salvation. To withhold bread from starving cities, medicine from dying hospitals, rescue from wolf-imperilled children, would be nothing compared with that stately and inhuman phariseeism which, for twice a score of years, has beheld without one pulsation of pity, without one outreaching of the hands, without one utterance of the voice, this greatest error and wickedness known in our land and generation. If the crime itself be hideous, the excuse is yet more nefarious. The Tract Management have refused their supreme duty under the plea of preaching the Gospel! Thus telling the world that there is a Gospel that can be preached devoid of pity for the poor, empty of all sympathy for the oppressed, deaf to the groans of slaves, and dumb to all the petitions of the degraded and neglected! It were bad enough to despise God's poor, but to excuse it by a plea which maligns the very heart of Christ, and slanders the spirit of his Gospel, is a crime yet more unpardonable!

It is a pain and piercing to my heart that the Church of Christ has not been found, with banner advanced, far beyond all other bodies, leading on the world to a victory. I can never forget that my father and my mother were members of Christ's Church upon earth. And, even if Christ himself had not sanctified the Church, this would have been enough for me, that my father's and mother's hearts had made it sacred!

But when both Father in heaven and father on earth have left their memories in the bosom of the Church, she must receive from me all that the yearning heart, the deepest sensibility, and the most earnest love and enthusiasm can bestow. If she might only be true to her trust, what matters it what becomes of you or me? If the name of Christ and his Church might glow with the renown of heroic humanities and difficult duties faithfully done, let us be cast aside, as old and shattered armor, or as the rind of golden fruit, peeled off that some longing lip might suck the pulp! Willingly would I lie down by the wayside; willingly would I have my hand paralyzed and my tongue silenced; willingly would I submit to that most grievous and bitter calamity to an active man, to stand uselessly aside and see the world go past in all its movements of enterprise and adventure, if only by such sacrifice of myself I might behold achievement, courage, enterprise, and heroic endeavor, in the revered Church of Christ! How long shall her ear be drowsy? How long shall she sleep in the garden where Christ, in anguish, sweats drops of blood? When will she wake, if not to save her Master, at least to go with him to trial and to disgrace, out of which shall come victory and glory?

What, for more than thirty years, has been the agitation of this land? What has been that deep undertone sounding up through all the clash of business, and over-sounding all the voices of politics, and all the voices of the pulpit? It has not been the swell of the ocean, driven of storms upon our coast; it has not been the sighing of the wind through our western forests—this deep thunder-toned diapason, rolling through the land, has been the sighing of the slave; and four million voices have lifted up before God prayers and pleadings which have shaken the very throne of mercy. Throughout all this time the Church heard that voice, but would not know that it was the voice of God, speaking through the afflictions of his despised ones. But he hath rolled it more and more audibly upon the ear, and at length all the land has consented to listen, and to understand its meaning, and to yield to its petition.

A great revolution has taken place in the opinions and feelings of this whole nation. In my own day a mighty conflict has risen, passed on, and ended victoriously for the right. I remember the days of early mobs. I remember when anti-slavery sentiments were spoken but in whispers, as guilty things. I remember when to be known as an Abolitionist was to be disowned. I stood to see Birney's printing press broken to pieces at Cincinnati, and dragged into the Ohio River, and patrolled the streets armed, under public requisition, to defend the dwellings of the poor colored population against the ruthless threatenings of the mob. I remember when the pioneer lecturers in the antislavery cause were driven by unvitalized eggs from place to place throughout the West. I remember well the day when storehouses were sacked, and dwellings pillaged, in this city of New York. I remember when a venerable man and minister escaped with his life from his own house because he was an advocate of the enslaved.

Within twenty years those parties which were the most tyrannic have been ground out of existence. Those churches that were the most intolerant of free discussion on the question of human rights, have been overrun by this providence of God, in favor of freedom, and subdued to the truth. Synods, which acted as dykes, have been overwhelmed and submerged by the rising flood. General Assemblies, like ships leaking on the sea, with all their pumps and every device of caulking, have but just kept themselves dry, and have been driven hither and thither by this omnipotent flood. Those opinions which twenty years ago would have shut up every avenue of political honor in the North, are now found indispensable to the first step of advancement in political life. The wheel has turned around. The top is the bottom, and the bottom has gone up to the top. A moral revolution has taken place upon half a continent, and a decree has gone forth judging the wickedness of slavery, and establishing the righteousness of liberty.

During this whole struggle, the American Tract Society, which was organized to speak God's truth to man, has stood and beheld the whole conflict without opening its lips, or uttering one single word. Churches that were unfaithful have been brought into line; States that were recreant have become faithful; neighborhoods that were false to liberty have been converted to the truth; institutions that scowled, and repulsed her claims, have long since embraced the cause; but the American Tract Society, with fatal consistency, from the beginning to the end, has stood dumb. Its silence has testified that in its judgment there was nothing in the Gospel which it was its duty to speak in behalf of the oppressed. In all the Word of God there was no lesson of liberty of sufficient importance for it to publish. In that work which Christ was doing in our own age, it would have no part nor lot. Going back to the sepulchre, it buried itself in the past, and refused to follow the Saviour in all his new works of love which he was performing in our midst. The Gospel which it has preached has been a historic Gospel. But the living work of God, and the mightiest work of our time, it has ignored, despised, rejected; and I charge upon this Society the guilt of rejecting Christ. It has refused to bear his Cross, to suffer with him, to be pierced with his thorns, or to tread in his footsteps. If in the day of judgment it shall be counted a sin to have spoken for the enslaved, with any potency of voice, no condemnation against the Tract Society will be issued, whatever may befall you or me. They have never thus sinned.

Had this Society been established for the publication of some special class of works, and had they then refused to publish works that did not belong to their specialty, they had been right. In England there is a Shaksperian Society, whose business it is to publish only of Shakspeare. There is a Camden Society, with their historic specialty. There is a Hansard Knollis Society, with their select list. And if the American Tract Society had been a denominational, doctrinal society, or an ecclesiological society, or any departmental publishing association, we should not have blamed her that she refused any extrinsic work; but she was organized by Christian men, to declare the whole counsel of God on the subject of public morals, to this nation. She was organized to give a Christian literature, based upon Christian morals and Christian truth, to this nation and to our times.

Under such circumstances, a deliberate and continual refusal to utter the truth of the Bible upon the subject of human rights, when millions were clamoring for knowledge upon this subject, and when God, by his providence, was turning all good men's thoughts to these things, can be interpreted in no other way than as a mighty infidelity to the truth committed to their hands.

And this mighty neglect has been made more remarkable and shameful by the particularity with which it has reprehended and hunted petty misdemeanors and minute transgressions. Upon ordinary stealing, it has never feared to declare the whole counsel of God; but the stealing of men, women and children, has never yet been counted by it a crime worthy of reprehension. To steal a *thing* has roused their holy anger, but to steal a *person* leaves them quite complacent. The violation of religious days; the disregard of conventional religious usage; random irreverence or profanity,—these have afforded them targets for all their artillery; but the violation of the most sacred rights, social, civil, religious and domestic, of four millions of men, has called forth from them not one single word. This great overgrown Society, with a hundred presses, goes out to seek the man that chews tobacco, and runs him down, with all its authority, for the wickedness of this indulgence; but the polygamy of the slave plantation; the customary adulteries of slave relations; the breaking of hearts in the separation of families; the unbounded concubinage of master and female slaves; the separations of children; the ruthless sales of human beings, coupled and catalogued with brute animals,—upon all these things it has looked; and though urged, and besought, and pleaded with, to this hour it has steadily refused to open its mouth or to say one word. And yet, it pretends to be a Society for the publication of Christian truth and Christian doctrine!

Do young men and maidens, after the long day's toils, see fit to gather together, and dance out the hours of night? The American Tract Society instantly arrays against them the moral influence of the Gospel. Does some slave-trader, within sound of the national Capitol, gather together a band of hundreds of slave men, and slave women, and slave children, and begin that infernal coffle-dance between the slave-pen and the burning plantation? Against this not one word can it find it its duty to speak from out of God's truth. If ever, in our day, there was a case which called again for Christ to speak and denounce the miserable hypocrisy of men that tithed mint, anise and cumin, but neglected the weightier matters of the law—judgment, justice and mercy—this is the one.

And what is that Gospel which they have preached? Suppose that all our Bibles were destroyed, and we were again to reconstruct the teachings of God's Word from the publications of the American Tract Society, what Gospel could we rear out of them? It would be a Gospel from which would be left out that sublime enunciating sermon of Christ—"The Spirit of the Lord is upon me, because he hath anointed me to preach the Gospel to the poor; he hath sent me to heal the broken-hearted, to preach deliverance to the captives, and recovering of sight to the blind, to set at liberty them that are bruised, to preach the acceptable year of the Lord." We could find in it no humanity for the oppressed; no sympathy for yearning, sorrowing slave-mothers; no Golden Rule for slave masters; no doctrine upon national justice. Through the Bible which the American Tract Society have given this world, despotism might drive its chariot without a block or hindrance. Along that Gospel road which the American Tract Society have thrown up, the most foul and flagrant sins that are ever committed by oppression might walk unchallenged by any sentinel, unarrested by any officer. In so far as that Gospel is concerned, which the American Tract Society has spread before this nation, John Newton might again open the slave trade, unrebuked, upon the coast of Africa. Fleets might land uncounted armies of slaves, and vast auctions, sundering every natural tie, disperse them all over the continent, and lecherous power and rank brutality might domineer over the weak and helpless, and all forms of dishonesty rising from the petty proportion of civil stealing into tyrannic robberies, and despotic usurpations of every human right and liberty, and yet without one word of warning, one word of rebuke, one word of judgment, from that Gospel which the American Tract Society has given to this nation!

And all this vast and wanton neglect is justified by the plea that they are ordained not to meddle in controversies, and to take sides with parties, but to preach the Gospel. Is this Gospel a thing that can be preached while every human interest is neglected or disowned? Is that Christ's Gospel that does not meddle with living interests? Is the Gospel a bundle of abstract truths, a bouquet of sentimentalities, an airy realm of sweet imaginations and heavenly visions? Is there a Gospel of Christ that can be preached consistently with the neglect of every want in life? Is there, then, in this world, a Gospel of Christ which is nothing for four million imbruted slaves that cry day and night before God? It were bad enough to maintain such wanton neglect and inhumanity toward the poor; but to justify it by a plea which destroys the charter of our religion, and belies the very genius of the Gospel, is a wickedness which combines in it all the most malignant traits of infidelity. And whatever may be true of the private lives and dispositions of the individuals who compose the Management of this Tract Society, there can be no doubt that they have made the Tract Society an engine of infidelity. They have denied Christ; they have crucified him again in his poor; they have shut up their hearts against those things which were dearest to the soul of the Saviour; they have propagated the letter, and sacrificed the spirit of Christianity. And no defection of doctrine, and no mistaken theories of piety, and no enthusiasms of moral sentiment, and no malignancies of fanaticism, can, in the end, be worse than that fatal dogma which the American Tract Society practically teach—that there is a Gospel of doctrine which may be separated from duty; that there is a piety without morality; that there is a religious sentimentality disconnected from religious ethics; that devotion may be separated from humanity; and that God will accept prayers, and readings, and preachings, and singings, and self-denials, in place of mercy, and charity, and helpfulness to the poor, and release to those in bondage.

If I were called upon to state who most promote infidelity, do you think that I should say it was such as Theodore Parker? He is open and above-board. We know his whole theory and philosophy. Mistaken as he is, he is not the most dangerous man. Do you think, then, that it is Garrison and Phillips—him of the iron tongue, and him of the golden lips? No, not them. Earnest, unswerving, faithful to their convictions, they represent the fanaticism of that part of the Gospel which the Tract Society has abandoned and rejected. Then it must be those infamous peddlers of infidel books, that are dangerous. I should just as soon think of calling men dangerous who peddle cockroaches, and rats and vermin. The men who seek such books are spoiled already. I will tell you who are the dangerous infidels. Now, as in the days of Christ, the men who hide worldly hearts behind spiritual sentiments; the men that substitute devotion for humanity; the men who insist upon sacrifices in place of mercy and justice; the men who have a text for every sin of omission and commission, and holy precedents for every devout neglect; who make long prayers while devouring widows' houses; who lift up holy eyes whenever they are about to do a wicked thing; who pursue a smooth selfishness; and who build themselves places of power, and fortify their influence by all the words and phrases of duty and devotedness; these are the infidel men who take the garments of Christ to do the work of the devil in. These men who profess to do the work of righteousness while they impede the work of true religion by their shams, stand, in our day, where the Scribes and Pharisees stood in Christ's day.

Jerusalem lives its life over again in New York. The Temple stands again in Nassau street, and the priests and the lawyers may be found there at the same arts which priest and lawyer practised in the Temple of old. Laws and institutions grow old and perish, but the human heart, never; and the hypocrisies of inhuman religious men in the days of Christ, which brought down his divinest indignation, reappear again in every age. As spiders spin their cobwebs in kings' palaces, so, in the holiest places, hypocrisy weaves its web, and lurks for its victims.

The heresies which Christ feared were not of the head, but of the heart—the heresy of selfishness; the heresy of religious pride; the haughty indifference of those that were in prosperity to those that were in trouble and adversity; the neglect of the poor, the ignorant, the vicious, the criminal. It was not in the Temple that his steps were most found, nor his voice oftenest heard. The religious class he made his enemies, because it was against the religious class that he levelled his most terrible denunciations. There may be such a thing as religious aristocracy, and contemptuous religious refinement. Devotion has its selfishness, worship may become a luxury. And in the day of Christ, the arrogance of the priest, the subtle cunning of the lawyer, and the conceited spirituality of the devout, brought down the most terrible denunciations from the divine lips. And Christ taught then a lesson just as much needed now, that all religion is void and worthless which leaves the ignorant untaught, the wronged unredressed, the poor unsuccored, the imprisoned unvisited, and the captive unreleased. And in the days of Christ, by Christ's own hands, the whole weight of the Gospel was pivoted upon humanity in man to man.

One cannot look upon this ostentatious particularity about minor morals in the Tract Society, and this persistent neglect of great humanities, without repugnance. Imagine an army upon our frontiers, charged with the defence of the people. All around the rude huts of the pioneers primeval forests stand unbroken. In their shadows and twilights lurk countless bands of savage enemies. Their flocks and their herds are imperilled by wolves and bears. Venomous serpents yet infest the region. Upon some alarm, the settlers crowd the fort, beseeching protection. The savage foe are upon them. Their houses are burned; their crops are destroyed; wolves suck the blood of their herds with impunity; but no soldier can be had. Armed with combs, and searching the heads of children, they reply, "We cannot leave these important matters to look after Indians."

Four millions of men cry out that the foot of the oppressor is upon them. Four millions of men say, "We do not own our wives, nor our little ones. We are living in adultery. We cannot go where we will. Our bodies are not our own; our time is not our own.

Every right is snatched from us. Brethren, come forth and help us." But the Tract Society, lifting its devout head from its domesticity, plies its fine-tooth-comb philanthropy upon quids of tobacco; upon sins of dancing; upon the transient peccadilloes of morality.

Had the Executive Committee of the American Tract Society stood in the place of the twelve Apostles in the primitive days of the Church, the world would have never had a Gospel. Not one man of them would have dared to preach in Jerusalem; not one man of them would have taken the buffet of an angry world. Some lawyer would have been found easily satisfying them that to preach a thing which men did not want to hear was throwing away their labor. Some Daniel Lord would have risen up in their midst, and declared that they had as well speak in a foreign tongue as preach things which the people did not wish to hear. No Peter would have brought on Pentecost in Jerusalem. No Paul would have risen up, and traversed the globe with a fidelity which arrayed against him the wealth, the refinement, the religion, and the learning of the selfish world.

Think you that the holy Apostles asked leave of men to speak? Did these sons of thunder go to their mission chiefly careful how to save their own reputations? But had it been these gentlemen of the Tract Society, we should have had a new rendering of the campaign. The Executive Committee would never have preached Christianity in old raging Jerusalem. Christ would never have lost his life if he had pursued the prudent policy of this influence-loving Tract Society. The apostles would have grown grey in Jerusalem if they could have been permitted to preach only what men wished to hear. They were persecuted for outspoken fidelity. Christ's last and worst offence, and that which was the proximate cause of his death, was his unsparing and terrible rebuke of that religion which made *Devotion* a substitute for *Humanity.* The Pharisees were so anxious for the Church and its institutions, that they sacrificed the very qualities for which a church is instituted. And the Tract Society are now on the very moral ground occupied by the old Pharisees. It is for the sake of saving an institution formed only for the spread of Truth they are sacrificing that very Truth. For the sake of keeping unharmed an Institution of Benevolence, they are refusing the most sacred duties of Benevolence. Moral qualities have become less valued than the machinery by which these qualities were to be propagated! Under the plea of preaching Christ, they are refusing the very deeds which led Christ to his victorious death. For the sake of sending the Gospel all over the land, they have emptied themselves of that very courage—of that divine fidelity—of that tender consideration for the helpless, which made the Gospel what it is. In the Apostles' hands there was a Gospel of Courage. In the Tract Society's hands it is a Gospel of Cowardice. The Tract Society means to save its life, and so loses it. The Apostles were willing to lose their lives daily, and so saved them. It is not what influence men keep that makes them strong, but what they give up for Christ's sake. From the Cross and the Sepulchre Christ began to reign. Before, he was a man of sorrow—afterward, a Prince and Saviour! The Apostles gloried in persecution. Suffering was a badge of Fidelity. They carried the Gospel into the world as a torch is carried into a cave, bringing down around them every creature that could not bear the light. That Gospel is now a dark lantern, and the Tract Society carry it into the vast cavern of slavery with such care not to open it, that every bird of darkness sleeps on, undisturbed. Their Gospel is a torch reversed! Had these tract men been the Apostles, we should now be Gentiles, and the whole earth heathens.

THE END.

THE

WORKS OF CHARLES LAMB,

Comprising his Letters, Poems, Essays of Elia, Essays upon Shakspeare, Hogarth, etc., and a Sketch of his life, with the final Memorials. By T. Noon Talfourd. With a Portrait. 5 vols., 12mo.

Price in Cloth,	. . . .	**$6 25**
"	**Sheep, library style,**	**7 50**
"	**Half Calf, extra,**	**11 25**
"	**Half Calf, antique,**	**11 25**

"His curious reading and research, the shrewd observation, fancies, and conceptions of his whole life, were poured into these monthly essays (Elia) with many scenes drawn from his past career—its mirthful and mournful experiences. In some of the essays, topics of humble and domestic life are set off with lively illustrations, fine satire, or graceful description; others are devoted to criticism, and remarks are thrown out at once original and profound. Perhaps nothing so suggestive or striking in this department of literature had appeared since the days of Steele and Addison."—*Encyclopædia Britannica.*

"All these essays (Elia) are carefully elaborated, yet never were works written in a higher defiance to the conventional pomp of style. A sly hit, a happy pun, a humorous combination lets the lights into the intricacies of the subject, and supplies the place of ponderous sentences. Seeking his material for the most part in the common paths of life—often in the humblest—he gives an importance to everything, and sheds a grace over all."—*Sergeant Talfourd.*

"As an essayist, he is entitled to a place beside Rabelais, Montaigne, Sir Thomas Browne, Steele and Addison. * * * * He has refined wit, exquisite humor, a genuine and cordial vein of pleasantry, and heart-touching pathos."—*Cleveland's English Literature.*

***** The above will be sent by mail, post-paid, on receipt of price.**

W. H. Tinson, Printer and Stereotyper, 43 & 45 Centre St., N. Y.

THE

STANDARD ANCIENT CLASSICS.

*** The following Historical Works are printed in uniform octavo volumes, on fine paper, good type, and bound in a substantial manner. In ordering any of these works, to insure "the genuine edition," it will be well to designate the *octavo* edition.

The Hon. Daniel Webster, in his "Discourses before the New York Historical Society," speaking of the authors of these histories, says:

"Our great teachers and examples in the historical art are, doubtless, the eminent historians of the Greek and Roman ages. In their several ways, they are the masters to whom all succeeding times have looked for instruction and improvement. They are the models which have stood the test of time, and, like the glorious creations in marble of Grecian genius, have been always admired and never surpassed."

MURPHY'S TACITUS. New Edition, with Author's last Corrections. Portrait. 8vo.

Price in Cloth, $2 00; *Sheep, library style*, $2 50; *Half calf, antique*, $3 50.

BELOE'S HERODOTUS, with his Life by SCHMITZ. 8vo.

Price in Cloth, $2 00; *Sheep, library style*, $2 50; *Half calf, antique*, $3 50.

COOPER'S XENOPHON, the whole Works in one volume. 8vo.

Price in Cloth, $2 00; *Sheep, library style*, $2 50, *Half calf, antique*, $3 50.

SMITH'S THUCYDIDES. 8vo.

Price in Cloth, $2 00; *Sheep, library style*, $2 50; *Half calf, antique*, $3 50.

BAKER'S LIVY. 2 vols., 8vo.

Price in Cloth, $4 00; *Sheep, library style*, $5 00; *Half calf, antique*, $7 00.

DUNCAN'S CÆSAR AND ROSE'S SALLUST. 2 vols. in one.

Price in Cloth, $2 00; *Sheep, library style*; $2 50; *Half calf, antique*, $3 50.

***** The above will be sent by mail, post-paid, on receipt of price**

W. H. TINSON, Printer and Stereotyper, 43 & 45 Centre St., N. Y.

THE

WORKS OF WILLIAM HAZLITT,

Comprising his "Table Talk," "Lectures on Literature," "Essays," and "Spirit of the Age." 5 vols., 12mo.

Price in Cloth,	. . . .	**$6 25**
"	**Sheep, library style,**	**7 50**
"	**Half Calf, extra,**	**11 25**
"	**Half Calf, antique,**	**11 25**

"As a descriptive writer, in his best passages he ranks with Burke and Rousseau in delineation of sentiment, and in a rich rhetorical vein he has whole pages worthy of Taylor or Lord Bacon. There is nothing in Macaulay for profound gorgeous declamation superior to the character of Coleridge, or of Milton, or of Burke, or of a score of men of genius whose portraits he has painted with lore and with power. In pure criticism, who has done so much for the novelists, the essayists, writers of comedy, for the old dramatists and elder poets? Lamb's fine notes are merely notes, Coleridge's improvised criticisms are merely fragmentary, while, if Hazlitt has borrowed their opinions in some cases, he has made much more of them than they could have done themselves. Many of his papers are prose satires, while in others there are to be found exquisite *jeux d'esprit*, delicate banter, and the purest intellectual refinements upon works of wit and humor. In all, however, the critical quality predominates, be the form that of essay, criticism, sketch, biography, or even travels."—*From an article in the Democratic Review, by Wm. A. Jones.*

"One of the most remarkable of the miscellaneous writers of modern times is William Hazlitt, whose bold and vigorous tone of thinking, and acute criticism, found many admirers. His style is pungent, sparkling, and picturesque in expression."—*Cyclopædia of English Literature.*

***** The above will be sent by mail, post-paid, on receipt of price.**

W. H. Tinson, Printer and Stereotyper, 43 & 45 Centre St., N. Y.

www.ingramcontent.com/pod-product-compliance
Lightning Source LLC
LaVergne TN
LVHW020105110826
845151LV00001B/68

* 9 7 8 1 4 2 5 5 4 3 8 2 2 *